W9-BHP-251

Published by: Partners In Publishing, LLC, Natick, MA 01720

Editorial Directors: Mona Dolgov, Bob Warden, and Christian Stella
Editors: Christian Stella, Cali Rich, Lynn Clark, Elise Stella, Terresa Sullivan, and Cyndi Clark
Book Design: Leslie Anne Feagley
Food Photography: Christian Stella and Elise Stella
Lifestyle Photography: Quentin Bacon
Lifestyle Photography shot at Leicht Boston at Divine Design + Build/www.divinedesignbuild.com
Lifestyle Creative Director: Anne Sommers Welch
Recipe Development: Christian Stella, Bob Warden, Mona Dolgov, and Rachel Dolgov
Recipe Testing: Christian Stella, Andrea Schwob, and Stephen Delaney
Nutritional Advisors: Paulette Thompson, RD and Mona Dolgov

Library of Congress Cataloging-in-Publication Data has been applied for.
ISBN 978-1-4951-7921-1

First Edition
Printed in China

ACKNOWLEDGEMENTS:

To create this *first-of-its kind* cookbook, we assembled a very unique team. Developing delicious recipes, where every one is divisible by 100 to make it easy for you to eat the perfect portion, was a challenging, yet extremely rewarding task. We created a top notch team of talented chefs, recipe writers, testers, plus nutritionists to work with the chefs to check calorie math plus verify portion size, and to guide us in creating tasty, healthier recipes. Together, our team used easy and fun culinary tips and tricks to make each recipe. We also needed each page to be simple to use, as we really view this book not only as a cookbook, but as a go-to eating guide. We wanted to make sure that all 100 calorie portions, whether measured by cup, piece, or slice, were instantly understood.

This book was developed with dedication and passion, as our talented, food-loving team embraced the concept of *The Perfect Portion Cookbook,* and proudly contributed to its final content.

We give many thanks to: Christian Stella, who helped us develop and test every recipe, and Andrea Schwob and Stephen Delaney for recipe testing. More thanks to Christian and Elise Stella for beautiful recipe photography. Mega kudos to Leslie Anne Feagley for her creative book design, Quentin Bacon for recipe story photography, Anne Sommers Welch for creative story direction, Kendall Walker for website design, Lynn Clark, Cali Rich, Elise Stella, and Terresa Sullivan for their tireless editing, and Paulette Thompson, RD for her nutritional guidance and development of meal plans and reference charts. And a special call out to David Venable at QVC for his advice and taste buds.

Bob Warden: My mom was my best friend, and I believe, the best cook in the world. My contribution to this book is dedicated to mom and, of course, my wife Frances, whose constant support gives me the time to have all this fun, and finally to my children and grandchildren, who think Grandpa is a good cook.

Mona Dolgov: To my parents who continue to be my source of love and strength, my wonderful children, Rachel and Scotty, who motivated me to write a cookbook, and continue to inspire me and make me proud, and to my husband Doug, my best friend, whose unconditional love and support has allowed me to follow my dreams to make this world a better and healthier place to live. Together we have shared the best times, laughs, and best food around the kitchen table with our loving friends and family.

Anson Williams: I want to thank Bob Warden and Mona Dolgov. Without their talent and support, this book would not have been possible. An idea is meaningless without taking action. Bob and Mona not only bullet trained *The Perfect Portion Cookbook* ahead, but also had the patience to be my mentors, educating me on the importance of healthy eating and great recipes. I will be forever grateful to my amazing business partner, JoAnna Connell, who was instrumental in making my idea better and moving it forward.

Our plan is to continue our mission to make it easier to have the best of both worlds...to eat responsibly and enjoy doing it! Our journey has just begun. We have lots more to come!

TABLE OF CONTENTS

Breakfast 1

Soups, Salads & Sandwiches 2

Casseroles & One-Pot Meals 3

Everyday Meals 4

Sides **5**

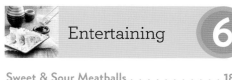 Entertaining **6**

 Holiday Favorites **7**

 Dressings, Sauces & Jams **8**

 Satisfying Snacks **9**

 Desserts **10**

THE **PERFECT** **P⦿RTION** COOKBOOK

Using the 100 Calorie Counting System

'm going to say it. No, I'm going to scream it. "I LOVE FOOD!"

And I especially love comfort food, from the recipes that nourish our soul with childhood memories of kneading biscuits beside a patient, flour-dusted grandmother to the smell of a fresh-baked pie coming out of the oven.

Yet as we happily revisit these classic recipes time and again, it's hard to ignore that most aren't light on the good stuff. Butter, cheese, and cream...what's not to love? I spent my early adulthood in front of the unforgiving camera, so I was motivated to balance my more decadent favorites with moderate portions, but now that I'm on the other side of the lens, it's easier for me to overindulge. I'm definitely not willing to give up my favorite meals to shed pounds, rather I simply want to maintain a healthy weight by making informed choices of what I'm eating. Yet the main challenge is

that I'm never sure if I'm eating a reasonable portion. All of the calorie-counting systems are complicated, hard to understand. Surely there's a way that I can enjoy eating without constantly questioning my serving size.

And Then It Happened!

I was shopping at my local market when I noticed 100 calorie portion snack packs, and lightning struck! What about creating a simple calorie-counting system for all recipes based on 100; recipes that divide into even 100 calorie portions. How easy a calorie count is that! Don't worry; I'm not suggesting that an entire meal would be 100 calories, but rather that each component of the meal would be in 100 calorie portions or a multiple of 100. This easy counting system would allow me to eat my favorite foods and KNOW I wasn't overeating. All I would have to do is decide what I wanted

ANSON'S FAVORITE SNACK:
10 "Hot Cocoa" Pretzels =
100 calories

to eat and choose how to allocate my 100 calorie portions for the day.

For example, when I directed *Star Trek* the chef made a stellar Loaded Baked Potato Soup, (page 50). It was so good in fact, I often found myself polishing off a couple of bowls without thinking about how much I was eating. What if the chef's recipe could be reworked to yield exactly 12 cups of delicious soup, with each ½-cup ladle measuring in at 100 calories? I might have 1½ cups of soup for lunch and know that I was consuming exactly 300 calories!

Mona's featured Meatballs Marinara with Tuscan Tomato Sauce was a big hit with Anson and Bob.

Now the obvious challenge of portioning decadent comfort food into 100 calorie increments is that the serving may look and feel skimpy. It was clear that some recipes would need a healthful makeover to ensure that the 100 calorie portion wasn't laughably small. In fact, what if I could re-create my favorite recipes into bigger, more filling portions that tasted just as good as the originals? It was a tall order, and I knew that I couldn't do it alone. I may be a great eater, but I'm hardly a chef or nutritionist. Lucky for me, I'm a friend of Bob Warden, a famous cookbook author and publisher. I own his best-selling pressure cooker book *Great Food Fast,* which is loaded with excellent comfort food.

After just one phone call, Bob was immediately hooked on the idea of comfort food recipes that are easily divisible into 100 calorie "perfect portions," with a healthful spin. His partner at Partners in Publishing, Mona Dolgov, was a natural addition to the team, as Mona is a nutritionist with over 25 years of experience in recipe and product development. Bob and Mona have already created many bestselling cookbooks together, so I knew if anyone could

bring this cookbook to life, it would be them.

I presented Bob, Mona, and their team of recipe developers with a huge challenge:

- Create phenomenal tasting recipes for 150 of America's favorite comfort foods that are easily divisible into 100 calorie portions.
- Pay close attention to the look of the 100 calorie portion, making sure to not skimp on size, but rather enhance with healthful changes.

Now, after over two years of nutritional research, recipe development, and calorie counting, we have created this revolutionary cookbook. (Well, I mostly did the tasting!) We give you 150 of America's and my favorite comfort foods, including everything from French Toast to Lasagna and Apple Turnovers, all with easy, perfect portion control, using our SIMPLE *100 Calorie Counting System.*

Now, without worry or guilt, we can all eat perfect portions of the foods we love and never overeat! Bon apétit!

—*Anson Williams*

CREATING THE **PERFECT PORTION** RECIPES...

The Development Process with YOU in Mind!

Our primary goal in writing this book was to highlight the importance of something that few other cookbooks are putting enough focus on...portion size. While the *100 Calorie Counting System* is clearly about "counting calories" in name, it is also a teaching tool to help you better understand realistic portion sizes and the calories within them.

All right, portioning aside, how does the food taste? You should know that though our recipes do have a healthy twist, they taste absolutely fantastic! All of the ingredients are the yummy ingredients you normally use to create great flavor, with just a few small swaps to make these meals better for you. There are plenty of cookbooks full of bland diet food, which is loaded with artificial ingredients that you don't actually want to eat. On the contrary, in this cookbook you'll find page after page of the inviting comfort food you know and love. We want you to be excited about cooking these recipes!

We have made sure that EVERY* recipe in this book has a calorie count that is evenly divisible by 100. How did we do that? First, we considered size. What is visually an acceptable small portion of each recipe: ⅓ cup or ½ cup, a 1½-inch bar or a 2-inch bar, and so on. This became the target 100 calorie portion. We then increased the scale of the recipe and slightly adjusted the ingredients and cooking methods with healthful tweaks, yet never compromised on deliciousness!

Keep in mind that this 100 calorie portion is only the starting point, a building block if you will. *100 Calorie Counting System* is NOT about eating only 100 calories at a time or depriving yourself of satisfying and filling meals, it is simply a way to visualize and measure your meals in 100 calorie portions that will cumulatively make up the serving that is right for you. You'll find that a single 100 calorie portion will satisfy you as a snack, while you may need four, five, or even six 100 calorie

portions of protein, veggie, and sides for your ideal dinner serving.

Speaking of food, you'll notice a bunch of recipes throughout the book that we're especially crazy about. These recipes have long been our family favorites so we had great motivation for scaling them into 100 calorie portions. We'll walk you through our interesting and often humorous development process and show you step-by-step photos of how the magic happened in the kitchen. We hope that you'll be inspired to make your own treasured recipes! You won't be sorry!

Another personal goal that we want to share is passing on easy and simple tips for healthy living. Our secret ingredient swaps, snacking advice, ingredient-calorie index, exercise tips, and healthy meal plans are all excellent tools for you to use.

There is no doubt that great comfort food is the heart for many of the wonderful memories of our lives. The comfort comes from the love and memories we share with our family and friends. And so we are thrilled to share our fantastic recipes with you and your family, with the hope that they become your own favorites. Sharing what we love...that's what life is all about, isn't it?

— *Bob and Mona*

* Except for chicken parts and recommendations for add-ins and dippers, where calorie counts were provided.

HOW TO USE THIS BOOK

Measuring 100 Calorie Portions

Each recipe in this book has an icon in the upper right corner that denotes the measurement used for a 100 calorie portion.

You will also see a "suggested" serving size and the number of suggested servings the recipe will make. This suggestion is based on the average serving size that you would expect to eat. This information will help you plan meals you may be creating for your family or friends, but in the end, you can always eat less or more than the suggested serving, based on your caloric needs.

Measuring out your perfect portion may seem new at first, but in time you'll be able to visualize portion sizes without measuring. We do recommend that you start by physically measuring out the portions until you become

MAC
& CHEESE
⅔ **CUP =
200
CALORIES**

MEATLOAF
**2 SLICES =
200
CALORIES**

GREEN
BEANS
**½ CUP =
100
CALORIES**

accustomed to the amount of food that fits on your serving utensils. Have fun with different utensils at home to use as a guide. You may find that your soup ladle or ice cream scoop is exactly ½ cup!

Whether you are looking to plan every aspect of your meals or are just looking to better understand portion sizes and the calories contained within them, the *100 Calorie Counting System* was developed to truly adapt to you, your needs, and your goals. In this digital age, there are plenty of ways to track the calories you've *already* had. Now you have the perfect way to plan and portion those calories out *before* you eat them. To help you define your daily calorie goals, refer to the Calorie Goal-Planning Guide on page 308.

500 CALORIE DINNER
Use our Classic Meatloaf (page 111), Stovetop Mac & Cheese
(page 79), and Green Beans Almondine (page 156).
Add an extra veggie if you have a 600 calorie goal.
See Cooked Veggie 100 Calorie Chart (page 327).

MAKING A MEAL PLAN

By developing recipes that are easily split into 100 calorie portions you can quickly mix and match snacks, sides, entrées, and even desserts to create a daily meal plan according to your target total calories for the day. This book truly lets you eat what you love, while making quick work out of tracking what you eat. It simply could not get any easier.

In general, a healthy meal plan is a balance of vegetables, fruits, lean protein, and whole grains, but to make a meal plan that is truly tailored to your personal needs and goals, we highly suggest consulting a nutritionist. If you are in poor health or have any detrimental health issues, you should consult a doctor before dramatically changing the way you eat.

To create your personal meal plan, simply split your day into meals and snacks. Ideally, you would disperse your calories somewhat evenly throughout the day. The quality and balance you create with each meal and snack with protein, good fats and healthy carbohydrates is key. Think of eating like adding logs to the fire. You want to keep the fire (energy) all day long.

We know every person's caloric needs are different, but let's say your daily target is 1,800 calories, and you enjoy eating 3 good-sized meals with a few snacks. First block out your meal calories and use the remainder for a snack. A breakfast of 400 calories, a lunch of 500 calories, and a dinner of 600 calories equals 1,500 calories, leaving you with 300 calories for 3-100 calories snacks or a perfectly portioned desserts.

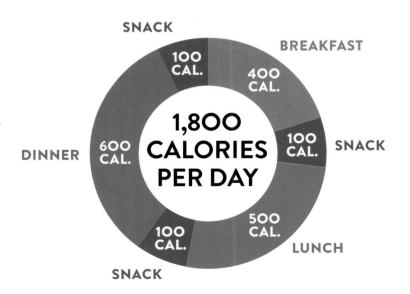

GLAZED
CARROTS

½ CUP =
100
CALORIES

CHICKEN
CORDON BLEU

½ BREAST =
200
CALORIES

BAKED
BABY
POTATOES

1 CUP = 200
CALORIES

500 CALORIE DINNER
Use our Chicken Cordon Bleu (page 121),
Crispy Baked Baby Potatoes (page 170),
and Glazed Carrots (page 164) recipes.

You don't need to count calories and keep track of them throughout the day. All you have to remember is 4, 5, and 6 with the allowance for several snacks or other indulgences.

And take each day at a time. Though you want to adhere to your total calorie count, your preference for calorie distribution may change from one day to the next. You may want to exchange your usual larger dinner serving for a larger lunch instead. Simply swap your lunch allotment to 600 calories and 500 for dinner. Or you can skip dessert and have 600 calories for both lunch and dinner. See how easy it is to plan an actual meal using our *100 Calorie Counting System*. Consider the 500 calorie dinner in the photograph above.

Larger or smaller daily calorie needs can be easily adapted to this plan by adding or subtracting calories from any meal or snack. If 2,100 calories is your target, simply add 300 calories wherever you'd like to enjoy them. You can add 100 calories to each of the 3 snacks, or add 100 calories to breakfast and 200 calories to dinner—when it comes to making a meal plan, you are ALWAYS in control.

1 BREAKFAST

PREP TIME: 10 MINUTES • BAKE TIME: 35 MINUTES

QUICHE LORRAINE

MAKES 6 BREAKFAST PORTIONS

Quiche Lorraine, the clear-cut king (or should we say "queen?") of quiches, shines for its simple combination of bacon and Swiss cheese in a savory custard filling. This version ditches the crust to allow for a much larger portion of the filling, because when it comes to cheese and bacon, isn't that all that really counts?

100 CALORIE COUNT=
$\frac{1}{12}$ QUICHE

Recommended Serving:
BREAKFAST – 200 Calories = 2 slices

Ingredients:

Nonstick cooking spray

5 thick-cut slices bacon

4 large eggs

4 large egg whites

1 cup 2% milk

½ teaspoon salt

¼ teaspoon pepper

⅛ teaspoon ground nutmeg

1 cup shredded Swiss cheese

1½ tablespoons chopped chives

Directions:

1. Preheat the oven to 375°F. Spray a 9-inch deep-dish pie plate with nonstick cooking spray.

2. Cook the bacon in a skillet over medium-high heat until crispy. Transfer to paper towels to cool. Crumble the cooled bacon, and set aside.

3. In a large mixing bowl, whisk together the eggs, egg whites, milk, salt, pepper, and nutmeg. Pour into the prepared pie plate.

4. Sprinkle the crumbled bacon, shredded Swiss cheese, and chopped chives over the egg mixture in the pie plate. Press down to gently submerge the ingredients into the eggs.

5. Bake for 35 minutes, or until the top of the quiche begins to brown and the center is springy to the touch. Let cool for at least 5 minutes before slicing.

HELPFUL TIP:

The better the cheese, the better your quiche will turn out. Look for imported Gruyère (a type of Swiss cheese that melts nicely) for the traditional cheese used to prepare Quiche Lorraine.

PREP TIME: 5 MINUTES • COOK TIME: 5 MINUTES

THE PERFECT OMELET

MAKES 1 BREAKFAST PORTION

Tender eggs filled with melted cheese and hearty meat and vegetables...so simple but so satisfying. We cook our omelet over moderate heat to prevent overbrowning and then fold the finished omelet twice for a simple and impressive presentation. Mix and match the ingredients below to build your favorite omelet.

100 **CALORIE COUNT =**

½ **OMELET**

Recommended Serving:
BREAKFAST – 200 Calories = 1 Omelet*

*See Fillings list for calorie additions.

Ingredients:

2 large eggs

1 tablespoon 2% milk

⅛ teaspoon salt

⅛ teaspoon pepper

1½ teaspoons butter

Fillings:

3 tablespoons shredded cheese (85 calories)

3 tablespoons shredded 2% milk cheese (60 calories)

3 tablespoons diced lean ham (50 calories)

2 slices cooked bacon (90 calories)

2 slices cooked turkey bacon (50 calories)

3 tablespoons diced onions (10 calories)

3 tablespoons diced bell pepper (10 calories)

2 mushrooms, diced (10 calories)

1 tablespoon chopped chives (1 calorie)

Directions:

1. In a mixing bowl, beat the eggs, milk, salt, and pepper until well blended.

2. Heat the butter in an 8-inch nonstick skillet over medium heat, tilting the pan to fully coat the bottom with melted butter.

3. Pour the egg mixture into the pan, and let sit until the edges begin to cook.

4. Use a rubber spatula to gently push the cooked edges of the eggs toward the center of the pan, and tilt the pan to allow uncooked egg to reach the edges. Continue doing this until the bottom of the omelet has set.

5. Cover the pan for 30 seconds, or until the top of the omelet is no longer runny.

6. Remove from the heat, and place the fillings down the center third of the omelet. Fold one side over the fillings, then fold the other side of the omelet over the top of the first side to overlap.

7. Cover for an additional 15 seconds to heat the fillings before transferring to a serving plate, seam-side down.

HELPFUL TIP:

You can also make a "Perfect Egg White Omelet" by substituting 3 large egg whites in place of the 2 large eggs and omitting the tablespoon of milk. This will lower the calories of the full omelet (without fillings) from 200 down to an even 100 calories.

PREP TIME: 15 MINUTES • COOK TIME: 15 MINUTES

SOUTHWESTERN SKILLET SCRAMBLE

MAKES 3 BREAKFAST PORTIONS

This protein-packed breakfast combines scrambled eggs and plenty of turkey sausage, onions, and peppers in one skillet. A pinch of cumin whisked into the eggs and a topping of melted Pepper Jack cheese adds just the right amount of spice, while a garnish of chopped fresh tomatoes and cilantro cools things off.

100 CALORIE COUNT=

$\frac{1}{6}$ **SKILLET**

Recommended Serving:
BREAKFAST – 200 calories = 2 slices

Ingredients:

Nonstick cooking spray

4 turkey breakfast sausage links (such as Jennie-O® brand)

⅓ cup diced red onion

⅓ cup diced green bell pepper

4 large eggs

2 large egg whites

¼ teaspoon salt

¼ teaspoon pepper

⅛ teaspoon ground cumin

¼ cup shredded Pepper Jack cheese

1 small tomato, diced

1 tablespoon chopped fresh cilantro

Directions:

1. Spray a large nonstick skillet with nonstick cooking spray, and place over medium-high heat.

2. Add the turkey sausage links to the skillet, and brown well, crumbling the links with a spatula as they cook.

3. Add the onion and bell pepper, and sauté for 3 minutes, or until bell peppers are crisp-tender.

4. In a mixing bowl, whisk together the eggs, egg whites, salt, pepper, and cumin. Add to the skillet, and cook, stirring occasionally, until the eggs are firm and scrambled.

5. Top the scramble with the Pepper Jack cheese, cover, and remove from heat. Let rest for 45 seconds to melt cheese.

6. Sprinkle the tomato and cilantro over the top of the scramble before serving.

HELPFUL TIP:

Fully cooked turkey sausage links (sold in the freezer section) can be cooked according to the package directions, chopped, and used in place of the fresh turkey sausage links in this recipe.

PREP TIME: 20 MINUTES • COOK TIME: 15 MINUTES

EGG WHITE & BROCCOLI FRITTATA

MAKES 2 BREAKFAST PORTIONS

Traditional omelets require a juggle of filling, rolling, and flipping, but fuss-free frittatas cook up as one large egg pancake. The combination of broccoli, onion, and bell pepper lends outstanding fresh flavor. And as a secret chef's trick, we whisk a little baking powder into the egg whites to ensure an evenly puffed frittata out of the oven. Hearty and absolutely heart healthy! What's not to love?

100 CALORIE COUNT =

$\frac{1}{4}$ **FRITTATA**

Recommended Serving:
BREAKFAST – 200 Calories = 2 Slices

Ingredients:

1 tablespoon olive oil

1½ cups chopped broccoli florets

¼ cup diced yellow onion

1 tablespoon water

¼ cup diced red bell pepper

½ teaspoon minced garlic

8 large egg whites

⅛ teaspoon baking powder

⅛ teaspoon salt

⅛ teaspoon pepper

3 tablespoons shredded Parmesan cheese

Directions:

1. Place the oven rack in the second-highest position and set the broiler to low heat.

2. Heat the oil in a large ovenproof skillet over medium-high heat. Add the broccoli and onion, and sauté for 2 minutes, or until onions begin to sweat.

3. Add a tablespoon of water to the skillet, cover, and let cook for an additional 2 minutes, just until broccoli is almost tender.

4. Add the bell pepper and garlic, and sauté, uncovered, for 1 minute. Reduce heat to medium.

5. In a mixing bowl, whisk together the egg whites, baking powder, salt, and pepper, and pour over the vegetables in the skillet. Cook, without stirring, until the bottom of the eggs are firm and the edges of the frittata are pulling away from the pan, 4–5 minutes.

6. Sprinkle the Parmesan cheese over the frittata, and transfer to the oven. Broil for just 2 minutes, or until the frittata has puffed up and the cheese is beginning to turn golden brown. Slice into 4 equal slices to serve.

HELPFUL TIP:

Frozen broccoli florets can also be used in this recipe, though it is best to chop them into smaller pieces than they are typically provided right out of the bag.

PREP TIME: 10 MINUTES • BAKE TIME: 15 MINUTES

BAKED HAM & EGG CUPS

MAKES 2 BREAKFAST PORTIONS

These baked egg cups taste like a ham, egg, and cheese breakfast take-out sandwich, only without the bread. Baked in muffin cups, they make an easy grab-and-go breakfast that you can prepare in advance and warm in the microwave before serving—though they are best fresh from the oven with slightly runny yolks.

1 EGG CUP

Recommended Serving:
BREAKFAST – 200 Calories = 2 Egg Cups

Ingredients:

Nonstick cooking spray

⅛ pound (2 ounces) thinly sliced lean deli ham

2 tablespoons sliced green onions

4 large eggs

Salt and pepper

2 tablespoons shredded sharp Cheddar cheese

Directions:

1. Preheat the oven to 375°F, and spray 4 muffin cups with nonstick cooking spray.

2. Place a thin slice of ham into each prepared muffin cup, and press the ham against the sides of the cups to follow the natural shape of the pan.

3. Sprinkle ½ tablespoon of green onions into each lined cup, and then crack a fresh egg over the top of the ham and onions in each.

4. Lightly season each egg with salt and pepper, and then bake for 10 minutes.

5. Top each egg with a light sprinkling of Cheddar cheese, and return to the oven to bake for an additional 5 minutes, or until whites are firm and cheese has melted. Serve garnished with additional sliced green onions, if desired.

HELPFUL TIP:

Thinly sliced ham is essential, as thicker ham will not form to the shape of the muffin cups. For larger ovals of sliced deli ham, you may need to cut each slice into four pieces and overlap the pieces to fit into the muffin cups.

PREP TIME: 10 MINUTES • COOK TIME: 6 MINUTES PER BATCH

FRENCH TOAST

MAKES 4 BREAKFAST PORTIONS

100 CALORIE COUNT =

1 SLICE

Recommended Serving:
BREAKFAST – 200 Calories = 2 Slices

Mona's Family Favorites: The winner of all French Toasts! The secret? Better Butter Batter! Mix melted butter right into the batter to make sure that each bite has big butter flavor. The combination of maple syrup, vanilla, and cinnamon makes this French Toast naturally sweet. Pair with fresh berries for a great breakfast.

Featured Recipe Story: See next page.

Ingredients:

2 large eggs

1 large egg white

½ cup 2% milk

1 tablespoon butter, melted

1 tablespoon sugar

2 teaspoons honey

½ teaspoon ground cinnamon

¼ teaspoon vanilla extract

¼ teaspoon salt

Nonstick cooking spray

8 slices "light" bread (see tip)

Directions:

1. In a wide mixing bowl, whisk together the eggs, egg white, milk, butter, sugar, honey, cinnamon, vanilla extract, and salt.

2. Spray a large griddle or nonstick skillet with nonstick cooking spray, and place over medium heat.

3. Working in batches of as many pieces of French Toast as you can fit on the griddle, dip each bread slice into the egg mixture to coat both sides before placing on the hot griddle.

4. Cook each piece until golden brown, about 3 minutes on each side.

5. Serve garnished with fresh berries (about 25 calories per ¼ cup) or topped with pure maple syrup (50 calories per tablespoon).

HELPFUL TIP:

Light bread is sold in loaves in the normal bread aisle. It usually contains only 45 calories per slice and far more fiber than ordinary white bread.

FRENCH TOAST
The Better Butter Batter — 100 Calorie Slice!

I THINK FRENCH TOAST IS THE PERFECT BREAKFAST for a lazy weekend. I love sitting in my robe and slippers and tucking into a couple of slices on a snowy winter morning. But, French Toast gets fattening quickly when you add lots of butter to the batter and the pan (which adds calories and fat, of course!) and lots of syrup on top (sugar!). So we came up with a cool way to get the rich flavor and sweetness without the calories. We created the BETTER BUTTER BATTER! (can you say that 3x fast!) What's the Better Butter Batter? You're about to find out!

Better Butter Batter! Adding just 1 tablespoon of melted butter to the batter provides great buttery taste. No need to add more butter to the pan to cook it.

See ya, Syrup! The sweet and spiced combo of sugar, honey, vanilla, and cinnamon in the batter will make you forget all about maple syrup. (But if you really can't live without it, just add 1 tablespoon of maple syrup or ½ cup fresh berries for only 50 calories.)

Lighten Up! Use light wheat bread, only 45 calories per slice, to cut calories in half. You can now have 2 slices of French toast for only 200 calories! This adds fiber, too (and you don't even taste it)!

A hearty, filling French Toast breakfast with half the calories has me counting the hours to the weekend! Better butter batter? Butter batter better? Batter better butter? Any way you say it, it says YUM!

1 Whisk 1 tablespoon of melted butter into the egg batter with sugar, honey, cinnamon, vanilla and salt.

4 Once the French Toast is cooked, place on a platter and add your favorite fresh fruit. We love fresh berries, but be creative, and add your favorite fruits of the season.

2 Make sure the additions to the egg batter are evenly distributed, so that coating the bread will get all of those great flavors.

3 Coat both sides of the bread to ensure the egg batter has been soaked in.

5 The French Toast is lightly sweetened from the honey in the batter and the fruit. If you want to add syrup. One tablespoon equals 50 calories.

6 This is the epitome of great comfort food without compromise. It's amazing how each slice is 100 calories. The whole crew loved it, and so will you!

PREP TIME: 25 MINUTES • COOK TIME: 10 MINUTES

SHREDDED HASH BROWNS

MAKES 5 SIDE DISH PORTIONS

It's hard to not love diner-style hash browns. Made by shredding potatoes, pressing them into a cake, and then frying, they are a simple and satisfying breakfast side that you can prepare using only a few pantry staples. But what about the downside? Many recipes use as much as ¼ cup of vegetable oil to fry the hash browns! By using a hot pre-heated skillet and quickly tossing the potatoes, we were able to use less than half of the oil and still get a crisp, golden hash brown with plenty of rich flavor.

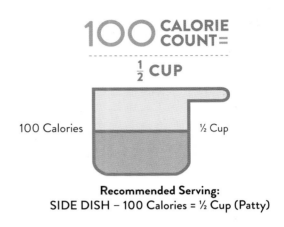

100 **CALORIE COUNT =**

½ **CUP**

100 Calories   ½ Cup

Recommended Serving:
SIDE DISH – 100 Calories = ½ Cup (Patty)

Ingredients:

1 pound russet potatoes, scrubbed

¼ teaspoon onion powder

¼ teaspoon salt

¼ teaspoon pepper

1 tablespoon canola oil

2 teaspoons butter

Directions:

1. Use the large holes of a box (cheese) grater to shred the potatoes, transferring them to a large bowl of water as you work (to prevent browning).

2. Drain and rinse the shredded potatoes to remove excess starch. Use your hands to squeeze any excess water from the potatoes, and then transfer to a dry bowl.

3. Add the onion powder, salt, and pepper to the shredded potatoes, and toss to combine. Spoon hash brown mixture into five ½ cup portions. Transfer to cutting board and flatten into 5 rounds.

4. Heat the oil and butter in a large skillet over medium-high heat, until the butter has melted and the pan is hot.

5. Add the shredded potatoes to the skillet, and quickly toss them to coat with oil and butter.

6. Flatten the potatoes against the bottom of the skillet, and let cook until crispy and golden brown, 4–5 minutes. Flip, and cook for an additional 4–5 minutes, or until potatoes are browned on both sides. Serve immediately.

HELPFUL TIP:

Peeling the potatoes before shredding them will give them the clean look of diner-style hash browns, but this is not necessary and will remove some of the natural fiber and nutrients found in potato skins.

PREP TIME: 20 MINUTES • COOK TIME: 15 MINUTES

SWEET POTATO HASH

MAKES 4 SIDE DISH PORTIONS

This loaded hash is a stunner, starring tender-on-the-inside and caramelized-on-the-outside sweet potatoes. We often think of serving hash with eggs, but this sweet and slightly spicy version is an excellent side dish for chicken, pork, and especially fish as well.

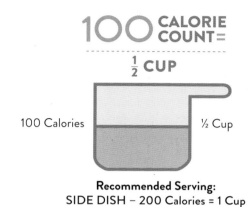

100 **CALORIE COUNT =**

½ **CUP**

100 Calories   ½ Cup

Recommended Serving:
SIDE DISH – 200 Calories = 1 Cup

Ingredients:

2½ cups cubed sweet potatoes, skin on

2 tablespoons olive oil

1 cup diced red bell pepper

⅔ cup diced red onion

1 teaspoon minced garlic

¼ teaspoon ground allspice

¼ teaspoon chili powder

¼ teaspoon salt

¼ teaspoon pepper

1 tablespoon chopped fresh sage

Directions:

1. Place the sweet potatoes in a large pot of boiling water, and boil until tender, about 5 minutes. Drain well.

2. Heat the oil in a large skillet over medium-high heat, and add the drained potatoes, red bell pepper, onion, and garlic. Sauté for 6 minutes, stirring occasionally, or until the potatoes begin to brown.

3. Sprinkle with the allspice, chili powder, salt, and pepper, and sauté for an additional 2–4 minutes, or until potatoes are crispy on the outside.

4. Remove from heat, and stir in the chopped sage before serving.

HELPFUL TIP:

If the potatoes are sticking to the skillet, they are simply not ready to be stirred. Let them cook until they have browned and they will easily lift away from the pan.

PREP TIME: 30 MINUTES • BAKE TIME: 17 MINUTES

THE 100 CALORIE BISCUIT

MAKES 6 BREAKFAST PORTIONS OR 12 BISCUITS

Some biscuit recipes replace butter with sour cream, but we found an even better solution. Tangy nonfat Greek yogurt produces a great tasting biscuit with a moist and fluffy crumb with even fewer calories. No skimping on size here, this winner measures in at a whopping 3 inches! Enjoy plenty of what you love!

Recommended Serving:
BREAKFAST – 200 Calories = 2 Biscuits

Ingredients:

2 cups all-purpose flour

1 tablespoon baking powder

1 teaspoon salt

⅔ cup low-fat buttermilk

½ cup plain nonfat Greek yogurt

2 tablespoons sugar

Directions:

1. Preheat the oven to 425°F, and line a sheet pan with parchment paper.

2. In a large mixing bowl, combine the flour, baking powder, and salt.

3. In a separate mixing bowl, combine all remaining ingredients.

4. Fold the wet ingredients into the dry ingredients, mixing until a dough has formed. Transfer to a floured countertop.

5. With your hands, lightly floured, gently fold dough over itself 4–5 times and then flatten out to 1-inch thick. Use a floured biscuit or cookie cutter to cut into 12 (3-inch) rounds, and transfer to the prepared sheet pan, crowding them around each other so that their edges are touching.

6. Bake for 15–17 minutes, or until golden brown. Serve immediately.

HELPFUL TIP:

You can also use the rim of a small drinking glass to cut the dough into the biscuit rounds; just be sure to lightly flour the glass first!

PREP TIME: 20 MINUTES • BAKE TIME: 25 MINUTES

BLUEBERRY MUFFINS

MAKES 12 MUFFINS OR 12 BREAKFAST PORTIONS

Forget about dense and cake-y, we wanted a delicate muffin that is all about the fruit. Reduced-fat milk lightens the crumb but still provides enough support for a whopping two cups of sweet blueberries. Our muffins are literally bursting with berries. This is the perfect recipe for berry season (June and July), when blueberries often go on sale for half price. Alternatively, an equal amount of frozen berries may be used, but thaw, rinse, and dry them before using.

100 **CALORIE COUNT =**

½ **MUFFIN**

Recommended Serving:
BREAKFAST – 200 Calories = 1 Muffin

Ingredients:

Nonstick cooking spray

2 cups all-purpose flour

1 cup sugar

2 teaspoons baking powder

¼ teaspoon salt

2 large eggs

⅔ cup 2% milk

¼ cup butter, melted

1½ teaspoons vanilla extract

2 cups fresh blueberries

Directions:

1. Preheat the oven to 375°F, and spray a 12-cup muffin tin with nonstick cooking spray (or line with paper liners).

2. In a large mixing bowl, combine the flour, sugar, baking powder, and salt.

3. In a separate mixing bowl, whisk together the eggs, milk, melted butter, and vanilla extract.

4. Fold the wet ingredients into the dry ingredients, mixing just until a batter has formed.

5. Gently fold the blueberries into the muffin batter, and spoon evenly into the prepared muffin cups.

6. Bake for 23–25 minutes, or until golden brown and springy to the touch. Let cool for 5 minutes before serving.

HELPFUL TIP:

When mixing the batter, there is no need to overdo it. Muffin batters should be a little lumpy. Overmixing will make the final muffins slightly denser.

PREP TIME: 5 MINUTES • COOK TIME: 10 MINUTES

BUTTERMILK PANCAKES

MAKES 7 PANCAKES

Bob's Farm to Table: On our farm in Iowa, we cultured our own buttermilk only one day a month, and I knew my favorite buttermilk pancakes would be on the table that morning. We've all had our share of heavy pancakes that sink like a brick. We found that this combination of tangy buttermilk and whole egg yielded a perfectly light and fluffy flapjack that didn't send us back to bed. These 100 calorie golden gems are a winning start to any day.

ONE 6-INCH PANCAKE

Recommended Serving:
SHORT STACK– 200 Calories = 2 Pancakes
TALL STACK– 300 Calories = 3 Pancakes

Ingredients:

1 cup all-purpose flour

1½ tablespoons sugar

¾ teaspoon baking powder

½ teaspoon baking soda

¼ teaspoon salt

1 cup buttermilk

1 large egg

Nonstick cooking spray

Directions:

1. In a large mixing bowl, combine the flour, sugar, baking powder, baking soda, and salt.

2. In a separate bowl, whisk together the buttermilk and egg, and then add to the dry ingredients, whisking until a smooth batter is formed.

3. Spray a large griddle or skillet with nonstick cooking spray, and place over medium heat.

4. Working in batches of as many pancakes as you can fit, pour ¼ cup of the batter onto the griddle for each 6-inch pancake.

5. Cook until bubbles form on the top of each pancake before flipping and cooking for 45 seconds on the opposite side, or until golden brown. Repeat this process until all the batter has been used.

HELPFUL TIP:

As a topping, there are about 100 calories in 2 tablespoons of pure maple syrup. Imitation maple syrup has a similar calorie count, but those calories come with a lot of corn syrup and artificial ingredients.

PREP TIME: 20 MINUTES • BAKE TIME: 1 HOUR

BANANA BREAD

MAKES 12 BREAKFAST PORTIONS

We produced a perfectly moist loaf with intense banana flavor by trading greasy oil for an equal combination of rich butter and lightly sweetened applesauce. Prepare a loaf Sunday night, and refrigerate, wrapped, for up to five days to cover your work day breakfasts. Microwave for ten seconds to rewarm. You'll definitely look forward to your work week.

Recommended Serving:
BREAKFAST – 200 Calories = 1 Slice

Ingredients:

Nonstick cooking spray

1 ½ cups all-purpose flour

1 teaspoon baking soda

½ teaspoon baking powder

¼ teaspoon salt

1 cup sugar

¼ cup butter, softened

¼ cup applesauce

3 large ripe bananas

2 large eggs, beaten

½ teaspoon vanilla extract

Directions:

1. Preheat the oven to 350°F, and spray a 9 x 5-inch loaf pan with nonstick cooking spray.

2. In a large mixing bowl, stir together the flour, baking soda, baking powder, and salt.

3. In a separate mixing bowl, cream together the sugar, butter, and applesauce.

4. Using a potato masher or food processor, mash the bananas into a thick paste.

5. Stir the mashed bananas, eggs, and vanilla extract into the sugar mixture.

6. Add the wet ingredients into the dry ingredients, mixing together just until combined into a batter.

7. Spread the batter into the prepared baking dish, and smooth out the top.

8. Bake for 1 hour, or until the center is springy to the touch. Let cool 30 minutes before slicing. Slice into 12 (¾-inch-thick) slices to make 200 calorie portions. Slice each slice in half vertically to make 100 calorie (half slice) portions.

HELPFUL TIP:

For the easiest release of the cooked bread, lightly flour the loaf pan after spraying with the nonstick cooking spray.

PREP TIME: 3 HOURS • BAKE TIME: 30 MINUTES

CINNAMON ROLLS

MAKES 16 BREAKFAST PORTIONS

Anson's American Treasures: My friend, Hope, makes the most amazing cinnamon rolls. The smell of them, coming out of the oven, stops me in my tracks. Amazingly, Bob and Mona were able to re-create her decadent delight with only 200 calories. Swapping applesauce for butter created a moist texture with a burst of sweet cinnamon flavor. OMG! You are going to love them.

100 CALORIE COUNT =

½ CINNAMON ROLL

100 Calories = ½ Cinnamon Roll

Recommended Serving:
BREAKFAST – 200 Calories = 1 Cinnamon Roll

Ingredients:

1 (0.25-ounce) packet active dry yeast

¼ cup sugar, divided

¼ cup warm water

¾ cup 2% milk, warmed

1 large egg, beaten

3 tablespoons butter, melted

¾ teaspoon salt

½ teaspoon vanilla extract

4 cups all-purpose flour

Nonstick cooking spray

Filling:

½ cup light brown sugar

⅓ cup applesauce

2 tablespoon ground cinnamon

Glaze:

¾ cup confectioners' sugar

1½ tablespoons milk

¾ teaspoon vanilla extract

Directions:

1. In a small bowl, stir the yeast and 2 teaspoons of the sugar into the warm water, and let stand 15 minutes.

2. In a large mixing bowl or stand mixer with the dough hook attached, combine the milk, egg, melted butter, salt, vanilla extract, and the remainder of the ¼ cup of sugar. Add the yeast and water mixture to the mixing bowl, and then slowly mix the flour into the wet ingredients until a dough has formed.

3. Spray a large mixing bowl with nonstick cooking spray. Form the dough into a large ball, and place into the prepared bowl. Cover loosely, and place in a warm spot to rise until it has doubled in size, at least 1 hour.

4. Spray a 13 x 9-inch baking dish with nonstick cooking spray. On a floured surface, roll the dough out into a large ¼-inch-thick rectangle.

5. Combine all the filling ingredients, and spread over the entire surface of the rectangle of dough.

6. Starting on the shortest end, roll the dough into a pinwheel, and then slice into 16 equal slices that are about ¾ inch thick. Arrange slices so that they are crowded together in the prepared baking dish. Cover, and let rise for 2 additional hours.

7. Preheat the oven to 350°F. Lightly spray the tops of the risen cinnamon rolls with nonstick cooking spray. Bake for 30 minutes, or until golden brown.

8. Prepare the glaze by using a fork to whisk together all the glaze ingredients. Let the cinnamon rolls cool for 5 minutes before drizzling with the glaze and serving.

PREP TIME: 5 MINUTES • COOK TIME: 30 MINUTES

STEEL-CUT OATMEAL

MAKES 1 BREAKFAST PORTION

Bob's Farm to Table: I've always preferred the heartier, nuttier flavor of steel-cut oatmeal over the more popular rolled oats. Less processed than "instant" oats, steel-cut oats are a whole grain that is rich in soluble fiber, leaving you feeling full longer. This recipe for simple, perfectly cooked oatmeal allows you to pick and choose what you would like to mix in or top your porridge with.

100 **CALORIE COUNT =**

$\frac{3}{4}$ **CUP**

100 Calories   ¾ Cup

Recommended Serving:
BREAKFAST – 200 Calories = 1½ Cups

Ingredients:

1½ cups water

⅓ cup steel-cut oats

⅛ teaspoon salt

For Oatmeal Toppings & Mix-Ins:

(see page 40)

Directions:

1 Bring the water to a boil in a small sauce pot over high heat.

2 Stir the oats and salt into the water, and bring back to a boil.

3 Reduce heat to low, and let simmer for 30 minutes. Do not stir. Serve immediately.

HELPFUL TIP:

Steel-cut oats can be prepared ahead and refrigerated for breakfasts all week. They will thicken in the fridge, but can be thinned back out with a little water or milk.

OATMEAL TOPPINGS & MIX-INS

½ cup blueberries
(40 calories)

½ cup sliced strawberries
(30 calories)

½ cup raspberries
(30 calories)

½ cup diced apple
(35 calories)

3 tablespoons raisins
(80 calories)

1 small banana, sliced
(90 calories)

3 tablespoons chopped almonds
(100 calories)

2 tablespoons chopped walnuts
(100 calories)

1 tablespoon pure maple syrup
(50 calories)

1 tablespoon honey
(65 calories)

1 tablespoon dark brown sugar
(50 calories)

¼ teaspoon ground cinnamon
(1 calorie)

½ teaspoon vanilla extract
(5 calories)

2 tablespoons half-and-half
(40 calories)

BLUE-
BERRIES
½ CUP =
40
CALORIES

ALMONDS
3 TABLESPOONS
= 100
CALORIES

STRAW-
BERRIES
½ CUP =
30
CALORIES

RASP-
BERRIES
½ CUP =
30
CALORIES

MAPLE
SYRUP

1 TABLESPOON
= 50
CALORIES

HALF
& HALF

2 TABLESPOONS
= 40
CALORIES

DICED
APPLE

½ CUP
= 35
CALORIES

HONEY

1 TABLESPOON
= 65
CALORIES

BROWN
SUGAR

1 TABLESPOON
= 50
CALORIES

RAISINS

3 TABLESPOONS
= 80
CALORIES

WALNUTS

2 TABLESPOONS
= 100
CALORIES

CINNAMON

¼ TEASPOON =
1 CALORIE

VANILLA
EXTRACT

½ TEASPOON =
5
CALORIES

BANANA

1 SMALL =
90
CALORIES

2 SOUPS, SALADS & SANDWICHES

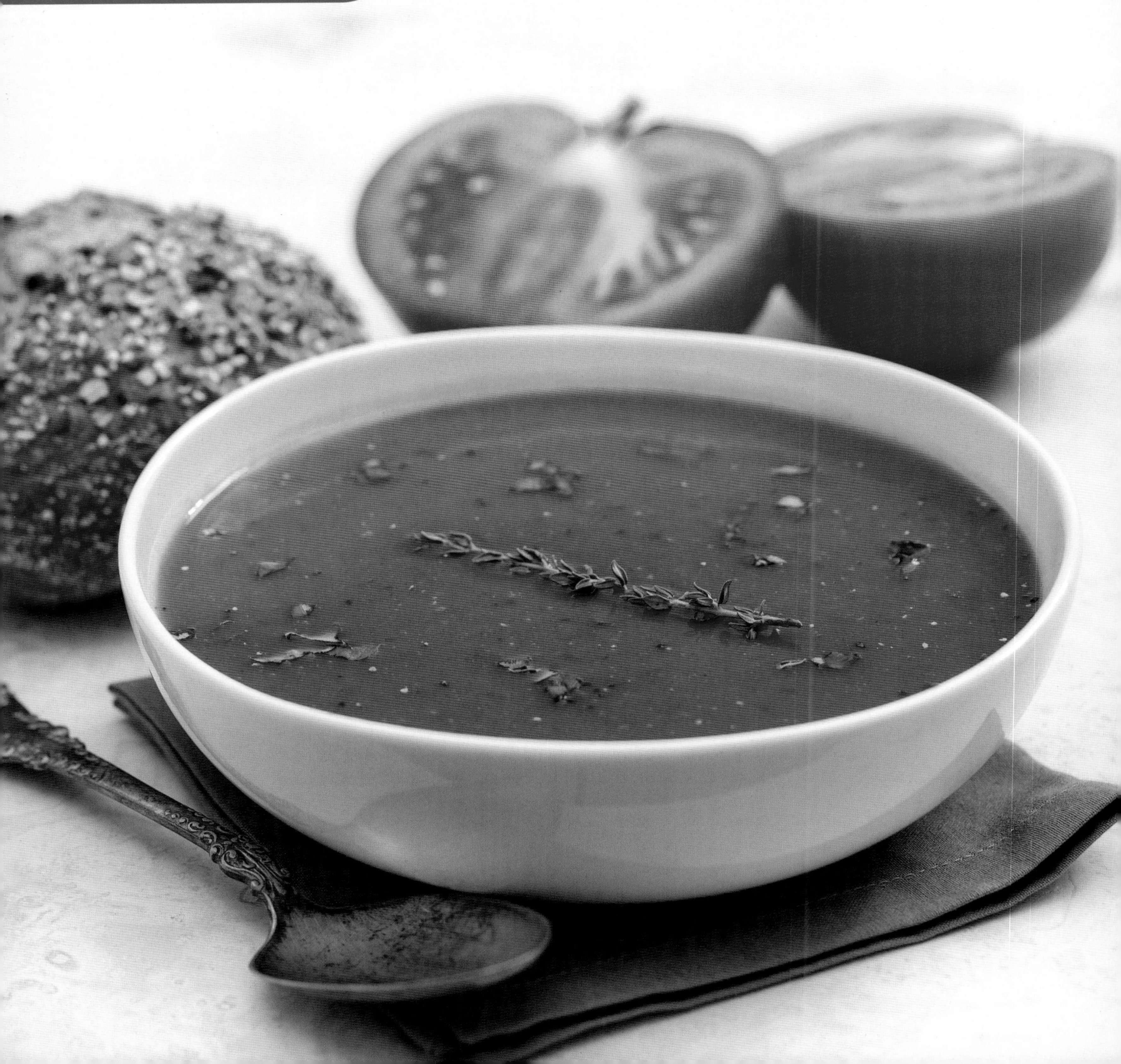

PREP TIME: 20 MINUTES • COOK TIME: 40 MINUTES

CLASSIC TOMATO SOUP

MAKES 4 LUNCH PORTIONS

A steamy bowl of tomato soup is about as comforting as comfort food can get! We use a little flour for thickening, yielding a soup that's so rich and creamy you'd swear there is cream in it. Serve with crusty bread, or go for that most classic combination and serve alongside our gooey Lillian's Grilled Cheese (see page 63) for dipping.

100 CALORIE COUNT =

½ **CUP**

100 Calories   ¾ Cup

Recommended Serving:
LUNCH – 200 Calories = 1½ Cups

Ingredients:

2 tablespoons butter

1 tablespoon olive oil

1 cup chopped yellow onion

2 teaspoons minced garlic

2 tablespoons all-purpose flour

1 (28-ounce) can stewed tomatoes, with liquid

3 cups chicken broth

1 tablespoon chopped fresh basil

1 teaspoon sugar

½ teaspoon dried thyme

½ teaspoon salt

¼ teaspoon pepper

Directions:

1. Heat the butter and oil in a stockpot over medium-high heat, until butter has melted.

2. Add the onions and garlic to the pot, and cook until the onions have softened, about 5 minutes.

3. Add the flour, and stir until the onions are evenly coated.

4. Add all the remaining ingredients, stir to combine, and bring to a simmer. Reduce heat to low, cover, and simmer for 35 minutes, stirring occasionally.

5. Remove from heat, and use an immersion (hand) blender to purée the soup, until smooth. You can also do this in a traditional blender or food processor, but it may take 2–3 batches. Serve garnished with additional chopped basil, if desired.

HELPFUL TIP:

It is safest to let the soup cool for at least 15 minutes before blending. After blending, return to the pot and warm before serving.

PREP TIME: 30 MINUTES • COOK TIME: 30 MINUTES

CHICKEN NOODLE SOUP

MAKES 6 LUNCH PORTIONS

This comfort food classic is chock-full of white meat chicken, vegetables, and tender egg noodles. It makes the perfect soup and salad combo lunch. There's no need for you to simmer this recipe all day, as it develops a surprising depth of flavor in only 30 minutes. That said, like most soups, you may find that the leftovers taste even better the next day!

100 **CALORIE COUNT =**

¾ **CUP**

100 Calories   ¾ Cup

Recommended Serving:
LUNCH – 300 Calories = 2 ¼ Cups

Ingredients:

1 tablespoon butter

1 pound boneless, skinless chicken breasts

1 ½ cups sliced carrots

1 cup diced yellow onion

¾ cup sliced celery

1 teaspoon minced garlic

¾ teaspoon dried thyme

12 cups chicken broth (see tip)

1 tablespoon lemon juice

1 bay leaf

½ teaspoon pepper

8 ounces egg noodles

¼ cup chopped fresh parsley

Salt

Directions:

1. Melt the butter in a stockpot over medium-high heat.

2. Add the chicken breasts to the pot, and cook until golden brown, about 4 minutes on each side. Transfer to a plate, and set aside.

3. Add the carrots, onion, celery, garlic, and thyme to the pot, and sauté for 3 minutes, just until onions are translucent.

4. Transfer the browned chicken back to the pot, and then add the chicken broth, lemon juice, bay leaf, and pepper.

5. Bring the soup to a boil, reduce heat to medium-low, cover, and let simmer for 10 minutes.

6. Add the egg noodles and raise the heat to medium. Bring back to a simmer and let cook for 5 minutes, or until noodles are tender. Turn off heat.

7. Transfer the chicken breasts to a clean plate, and use 2 forks to shred the meat. Return the shredded chicken to the pot.

8. Stir in chopped parsley, and season with salt to taste before serving.

HELPFUL TIP:

Chicken base mixed with water (according to the package directions to make 12 cups) can be used in place of the chicken broth in this recipe. You can find chicken base in small jars near the cartons of broth in the grocery store.

PREP TIME: 15 MINUTES • COOK TIME: 35 MINUTES

HEARTY LENTIL SOUP

MAKES 4 LUNCH PORTIONS

Bob's Farm to Table: Lentils are a fantastic source of fiber and protein that literally soak up the flavors in this hearty vegetarian soup. This is the perfect meal to warm up with on a cold winter day, but it's so nutritious and delicious that we're sure it'll become a year-round favorite. I make this soup every week and keep it on hand for a filling 100 calorie pick-me-up any time of day.

100 **CALORIE COUNT=**

$\frac{2}{3}$ **CUP**

100 Calories   ⅔ Cup

Recommended Serving:
LUNCH – 200 Calories = 1⅓ Cups

Ingredients:

1 tablespoon olive oil

1 yellow onion, diced

1 cup diced carrots

½ cup diced celery

1 tablespoon minced garlic

4 cups vegetable broth

1 cup green or brown lentils

1 (15-ounce) can diced tomatoes, with liquid

2 bay leaves

¾ teaspoon dried thyme

½ teaspoon pepper

¼ teaspoon ground cumin

2 cups chopped kale, stems removed

1 teaspoon lemon juice

¾ teaspoon salt

Directions:

1. Heat the olive oil in a stockpot over medium-high heat.

2. Add the onion, carrots, celery, and garlic to the pot, and sauté for 5 minutes.

3. Raise the heat to high, and add the vegetable broth, lentils, diced tomatoes, bay leaves, thyme, pepper, and cumin.

4. Bring the soup to a boil. Reduce heat to low, cover, and cook for 20 minutes, or until lentils are tender. If soup is too thick, add water, ¼ cup at a time, until your desired consistency is reached.

5. Add the kale, lemon juice, and salt to the pot, cover, and let simmer for an additional 10 minutes before serving.

HELPFUL TIP:

When cooking with lentils, it is recommended that you first sift through them to discard any irregular-looking lentils, as they may actually be a small stone.

PREP TIME: 20 MINUTES • COOK TIME: 30 MINUTES

LOADED BAKED POTATO SOUP

MAKES 8 LUNCH PORTIONS

Anson's American Treasures: While directing *Star Trek*, I remember eating rich and creamy potato soup for lunch. My all-time favorite! Bob and Mona created this unbelievable recipe that tastes even better. They swapped the heavy cream and sour cream with 2% milk and plain Greek yogurt, which still makes it comfort-food rich. And honestly, you won't know the difference!

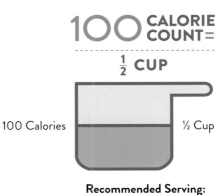

100 **CALORIE COUNT =**

½ **CUP**

100 Calories ½ Cup

Recommended Serving:
LUNCH – 300 Calories = 1½ Cups

Ingredients:

4 thick slices bacon

2 tablespoons butter

1 cup diced yellow onion

¼ cup all-purpose flour

2 cups chicken broth

4 cups 2% milk

2 ½ pounds russet potatoes, cubed

¾ teaspoon salt

½ teaspoon pepper

¼ teaspoon garlic powder

¼ teaspoon onion powder

6 ounces plain nonfat Greek yogurt

¼ cup chopped chives

½ cup shredded sharp Cheddar cheese

Directions:

1. Heat bacon in a stockpot over medium-high heat, and cook until crispy, about 5 minutes. Remove bacon from pot, finely crumble, and set aside.

2. Add the butter and diced onion to the bacon grease in the stockpot, and sauté for 2 minutes, just until onions are translucent.

3. Stir the flour into the pot to create a thick paste, and let cook for 1 minute.

4. Slowly whisk the chicken broth into the flour mixture until smooth.

5. Add the milk, potatoes, salt, pepper, garlic powder, and onion powder to the pot and stir to combine. Bring to a simmer, and reduce heat to medium low.

6. Cover the pot, and let simmer for 15 minutes, stirring occasionally, until potatoes are fork-tender.

7. Remove from heat, and stir in the Greek yogurt and chopped chives. Serve topped with the reserved bacon crumbles and shredded Cheddar cheese.

HELPFUL TIP:

To make the potatoes easier to cut into cubes, you can lightly soften them by microwaving (all potatoes at once) for 7 minutes. Let cool before chopping.

PREP TIME: 20 MINUTES • COOK TIME: 15 MINUTES

BROCCOLI CHEDDAR SOUP

MAKES 3 LUNCH PORTIONS

Many recipes combine the broccoli with just tons of cream and lots of cheese, but we thought outside the box. Sautéed carrots add a subtle sweetness that lends fantastic flavor and bulks up the nutrients, while the extra sharp Cheddar lends big flavor for less volume. Using 2% milk lightens it up without compromise. This soup is a hit any way you stir the pot.

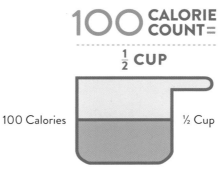

100 **CALORIE COUNT=**

½ **CUP**

100 Calories   ½ Cup

Recommended Serving:
LUNCH – 300 Calories = 1½ Cups

Ingredients:

1 pound broccoli florets, fresh or frozen

1 tablespoon butter

¾ cup shredded carrots

¾ cup diced yellow onion

1 teaspoon minced garlic

2 ½ cups chicken broth

½ teaspoon salt

¼ teaspoon pepper

3 tablespoons all-purpose flour

½ cup 2% milk

1 cup shredded extra sharp Cheddar cheese

Directions:

1 If using fresh broccoli, cook the florets in a pot of boiling water until tender, about 5 minutes. Drain and rinse the florets under cold water. If using frozen broccoli, thaw or defrost. Finely chop the cooked or defrosted broccoli florets before continuing.

2 Heat the butter in a stockpot over medium-high heat, and add the carrots, yellow onion, and minced garlic. Sauté for 3 minutes, just until the onions are translucent.

3 Add the chopped broccoli, chicken broth, salt, and pepper to the pot, and bring up to a boil. Reduce heat to medium-low, just enough heat to maintain a simmer.

4 In a small mixing bowl, whisk the flour into the milk before whisking into the simmering soup. Let the soup simmer for an additional 3 minutes, stirring constantly.

5 Remove from heat, and stir in Cheddar cheese before serving.

HELPFUL TIP:

You can also use this recipe to make a delicious cream of broccoli soup by omitting the shredded carrots and Cheddar cheese and using an immersion (hand blender) to blend the broccoli florets into the thickened broth before serving. This variation has only 60 calories per ½ cup!

PREP TIME: 20 MINUTES • COOK TIME: 20 MINUTES

NEW ENGLAND CLAM CHOWDER

MAKES 4 LUNCH PORTIONS

This Northeast staple is creamy, thick enough to coat a spoon, and absolutely brimming with chopped baby clams and tender Red Bliss potatoes. Using both the clams and their juice imparts a ton of rich flavor without overloading the soup with high-calorie heavy cream.

100 **CALORIE COUNT =**

½ **CUP**

100 Calories   ½ Cup

Recommended Serving:
LUNCH – 300 Calories = 1½ Cups

Ingredients:

1 tablespoon butter

1 cup diced onion

⅔ cup diced celery

2 teaspoons minced garlic

½ teaspoon dried thyme

2 cups chopped Red Bliss potatoes

3 (6.5-ounce) cans chopped baby clams, liquid separated

3 cups 2% milk

¾ teaspoon salt

½ teaspoon pepper

¼ teaspoon onion powder

3 tablespoons cornstarch

½ cup half-and-half

2 thick slices bacon, cooked and crumbled

1 tablespoon chopped fresh parsley

Directions:

1. Melt the butter in a stockpot over medium-high heat.

2. Add the diced onion, diced celery, garlic, and dried thyme to the stockpot, and sauté for 3 minutes, just until onions are translucent.

3. Reduce heat to medium. Add the potatoes and the clam juice from the cans of chopped clams. Cover, and let cook for 8 minutes, or until potatoes are fork-tender.

4. Stir the milk, salt, pepper, and onion powder into the pot, and bring up to a simmer.

5. Whisk the cornstarch into the half-and-half, and then stir into the pot. Bring back to a simmer, stirring until the chowder begins to thicken.

6. Stir the chopped clams, crumbled bacon, and fresh parsley into the chowder. Let cook for 2 minutes, stirring occasionally, before serving.

HELPFUL TIP:

New England Clam Chowder is traditionally served with oyster crackers, which have 50 calories per ¼ cup (about 12 crackers).

PREP TIME: 20 MINUTES • CHILL TIME: 2 HOURS

SUMMER VEGETABLE SALAD

MAKES 5 LUNCH PORTIONS

Mona's Family Favorites: Martha's Vineyard is my happy place! Every summer my family and I enjoy lazy beach days, bike rides, game nights, purchasing island-grown fruit and veggies at the farmer's market, and preparing delicious homemade meals on the porch. The cool, crisp texture of these brightly-seasoned veggies make the ideal refreshing meal for a warm summer day.

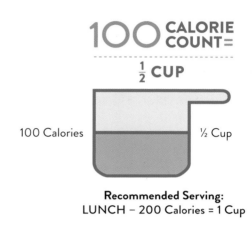

100 **CALORIE COUNT =**

½ **CUP**

100 Calories   ½ Cup

Recommended Serving:
LUNCH – 200 Calories = 1 Cup

Ingredients:

1 (10-ounce) bag frozen corn kernels, thawed (see tip)

1 pint grape tomatoes, halved

1 large zucchini, diced

½ red onion, thinly sliced

3 tablespoons red wine vinegar

2 tablespoons chopped fresh basil

1 tablespoon extra-virgin olive oil

1 teaspoon sugar

½ teaspoon dried oregano

½ teaspoon salt

¼ teaspoon pepper

Directions:

1. Place all of the ingredients in a large serving bowl, and toss to combine.
2. Cover, and refrigerate for at least 2 hours before serving.

HELPFUL TIP:

You can also make this with 3 ears of fresh corn, boiled for just 4 minutes and cooled completely before removing the kernels from the cobs to prepare the salad.

PREP TIME: 15 MINUTES

SPINACH & PEAR SALAD

MAKES 2 LUNCH PORTIONS

Anson's American Treasures: While on the set directing *Melrose Place*, I met Joanna Connell, a top makeup artist, whose clients include Madonna and Tom Cruise. JoAnna is also a well-known skincare expert, creating special products for some of the most famous faces in the world. Together, we took her formulas and started our successful company, Starmaker Products. Joanna made sure always to introduce me to new and healthy salads that the caterer would whip up for lunch. One of my favorites is this fabulous Spinach and Pear Salad. The hearty spinach and sliced pear balance each other perfectly. Red onion adds a bit of spice, walnuts add crunch, and crumbled Gorgonzola cheese, well, that's just delicious.

100 **CALORIE COUNT=**

$1\frac{1}{4}$ **CUPS**

100 Calories   1¼ Cups

Recommended Serving:
LUNCH – 200 Calories = 2½ Cups (without dressing)
300 Calories = 2½ Cups
(with 3 Tablespoons Raspberry Vinaigrette)

Ingredients:

1 (6-ounce) bag fresh spinach leaves

1 medium pear, thinly sliced

¼ cup thinly sliced red onion

¼ cup crumbled Gorgonzola cheese

3 tablespoons chopped walnuts

Directions:

1. Place the spinach leaves in a large salad bowl, or split evenly into serving bowls.
2. Top the spinach with the pear slices, red onion, Gorgonzola cheese, and walnuts.
3. Serve alongside the Raspberry Vinaigrette, page 246, or a dressing of your choice.

HELPFUL TIP:

Regular or baby spinach leaves can be used, although baby spinach is typically preferred in salads, as it contains more moisture and is slightly more tender when eaten raw.

PREP TIME: 25 MINUTES

BLT TOSSED SALAD

MAKES 3 LUNCH PORTIONS

Sure, you know the sandwich, but our combination of smoky bacon, sweet tomatoes, and creamy dressing makes a knockout salad. Blending fresh tomatoes into the dressing perfectly replicates the flavor of the mayonnaise and tomatoes mingling on a BLT sandwich. Dynamite!

100 **CALORIE COUNT =**

1 CUP

100 Calories   1 Cup

Recommended Serving:
LUNCH – 200 Calories = 2 Cups

Ingredients:

5 cups chopped iceberg lettuce

5 strips thick-cut bacon, cooked and chopped

1 cup grape tomatoes, halved

½ cup multigrain or whole-wheat croutons

¼ cup thinly sliced red onion

Dressing:

¼ cup grape tomatoes

2 tablespoons light mayonnaise*

½ teaspoon red wine vinegar

¼ teaspoon salt

¼ teaspoon pepper

Directions:

1 Place the iceberg lettuce, chopped bacon, halved grape tomatoes, croutons, and sliced onion in a large salad bowl.

2 Add all the dressing ingredients to a blender or food processor. Blend until the tomatoes are entirely smooth and the ingredients have combined.

3 Pour the dressing over the salad, and toss just before serving.

HELPFUL TIP:

One small head of iceberg lettuce will make the 5 cups of chopped lettuce needed for this recipe.

* Natural and organic light mayonnaises are in most supermarkets and are made with all natural ingredients.

PREP TIME: 20 MINUTES • CHILL TIME: 30 MINUTES

WALDORF SALAD

MAKES 3 LUNCH PORTIONS

Anson's American Treasures: Invented at the Waldorf Hotel (now the Waldorf-Astoria) in New York City, this creamy mixture of apple, celery, and walnuts is a terrific light salad or picnic side dish. Though it is traditionally made with mayonnaise, substituting Greek yogurt and honey lowers the calories and adds a unique zing to the dressing. Serve a scoop of salad in a "bowl" of large romaine, Bibb, or butter lettuce leaves.

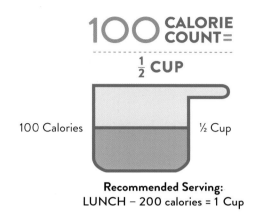

100 **CALORIE COUNT =**

½ **CUP**

100 Calories   ½ Cup

Recommended Serving:
LUNCH – 200 calories = 1 Cup

Ingredients:

1⅔ cups chopped red apple

2 teaspoons lemon juice

⅔ cup chopped celery

½ cup green grapes, halved

⅓ cup chopped walnuts

½ cup plain nonfat Greek yogurt

1 tablespoon honey

¼ teaspoon salt

⅛ teaspoon pepper

1 pinch ground nutmeg

Directions:

1. In a large mixing bowl, toss apple in lemon juice immediately after chopping.

2. Add all the remaining ingredients to the bowl, and fold together. Cover, and chill for at least 30 minutes before serving.

HELPFUL TIP:

You should be able to get 1⅔ cups chopped apple from 1 large apple. Honeycrisp apples work particularly great in this recipe, with the creamy dressing cutting their natural sweetness. For a great balanced lunch with only 320 calories, add 3 ounces of cooked and chopped chicken breast to 1 cup of the salad.

PREP TIME: 25 MINUTES

CHUNKY CHICKEN SALAD

MAKES 4 SALAD PORTIONS OR 8 SANDWICH PORTIONS

This longtime lunch classic packs a ton of protein goodness. Here's a healthy culinary trick: Use only lean white meat, but create the texture of using a whole chicken. Chop half of the breast meat, and pull the other half. Toss with a lighter creamy base, onion, celery, and grapes for great texture and big flavor, and you're left with a new and improved favorite.

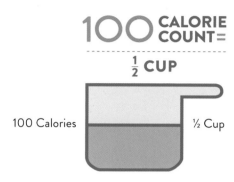

100 CALORIE COUNT =
½ CUP

100 Calories   ½ Cup

Recommended Serving:
SANDWICH – 100 Calories = ½ Cup
SALAD – 200 Calories = 1 Cup

Ingredients:

1 pound boneless, skinless chicken breasts, cooked (see tip)

¾ cup red grapes, halved

½ cup diced celery

3 tablespoons minced yellow onion

2 tablespoons chopped celery leaves

½ cup plain nonfat Greek yogurt

3 tablespoons 2% milk

2 tablespoons mayonnaise

1 teaspoon Dijon mustard

½ teaspoon salt

¼ teaspoon pepper

Directions:

1. Roughly chop half of the cooked chicken breasts, and use your hands to finely shred the other half.

2. Place the chopped and shredded chicken, grapes, celery, onion, and celery leaves in a large mixing bowl.

3. In a separate bowl, whisk together the yogurt, milk, mayonnaise, Dijon mustard, salt, and pepper to create a dressing.

4. Pour the dressing into the mixing bowl of dry ingredients, and fold together until all is well coated. Garnish with additional chopped celery leaves, if desired.

HELPFUL TIP:

The chicken breasts can be cooked in any method (even grilled). The easiest method is simply to bake in an oven preheated to 375°F for 20 minutes, or until slicing into the thickest piece reveals no pink.

PREP TIME: 5 MINUTES • COOK TIME: 5 MINUTES

LILLIAN'S GRILLED CHEESE

MAKES 1 LUNCH PORTION

Anson's American Treasures: Ahh...a warm, crispy grilled cheese sandwich reminds me of my childhood best friend Jeff Schredder who lived two doors away. His mom Lillian made the best grilled cheese ever. She took care in making them, from spreading the butter to getting the perfect flame on the stove. Gooey and buttery every time. Bob and Mona want to share their love of grilled cheese with you, too. By combining Cheddar and ultra-creamy American, they produced the perfect balance of flavor and texture ever. This recipe is filled with love and comfort.

100 CALORIE COUNT=

⅓ SANDWICH

Recommended Serving:
LUNCH – 300 Calories = 1 Sandwich

Ingredients:

2 teaspoons butter

2 slices light white bread

3 tablespoons shredded Cheddar cheese

1 slice American cheese

Directions:

1. Heat 2 teaspoons of butter in a nonstick skillet over medium heat, just until melted.

2. Place the 2 slices of white bread in the skillet to butter both slices at the same time. Remove 1 slice and set aside.

3. Sprinkle the Cheddar cheese over the bread in the skillet, and then top with the American cheese.

4. Place the reserved slice of buttered bread, buttered side up, over the top of the cheeses to make a complete sandwich.

5. Let cook for about 3 minutes on each side, or until golden brown on the outside with melted cheese on the inside.

HELPFUL TIP:

Light bread is sold in loaves in the normal bread aisle. It usually contains only 40–45 calories per slice and far more fiber than ordinary white bread.

PREP TIME: 15 MINUTES • COOK TIME: 20 MINUTES

CHICKEN QUESADILLAS

MAKES 4 QUESADILLAS OR 4 LUNCH PORTIONS

Bob's Farm to Table: Our loaded quesadillas are a meal all their own. Serve this winning combination of gooey cheese, chicken, sautéed onions, and bell peppers with our Restaurant-Style Salsa (see page 209) or Fresh Guacamole (see page 206) to really knock it out of the park.

100 **CALORIE COUNT=**

⅓ **QUESADILLA**

Recommended Serving:
LUNCH – 300 Calories = 1 Quesadilla

Ingredients:

Nonstick cooking spray

½ pound boneless, skinless chicken breasts, sliced into strips

¾ cup sliced yellow onion

½ cup diced red bell pepper

Juice of ½ lime

½ teaspoon chili powder

½ teaspoon salt

¼ teaspoon pepper

4 (10-inch) whole-wheat or multigrain flour tortillas

¾ cup shredded Cheddar Jack cheese

Directions:

1. Spray a skillet with nonstick cooking spray, and place over medium-high heat.

2. Add the chicken to the skillet, and cook until lightly browned, about 5 minutes.

3. Add the onion, bell pepper, lime juice, chili powder, salt, and pepper to the skillet, and sauté for 5 minutes, or until peppers are tender and chicken is cooked through.

4. Lay out 4 flour tortillas, and sprinkle ½ side of each with 1½ tablespoons of the cheese, leaving the other side of the tortillas clean (to fold over).

5. Spoon ¼ of the chicken and vegetables onto each flour tortilla and top with an equal amount of the remaining cheese. Fold each tortilla closed to create the quesadillas.

6. Spray a clean skillet or griddle with nonstick cooking spray, and place over medium heat.

7. Cook each quesadilla in the prepared skillet for 3 minutes on each side, or until golden brown on the outside with melted cheese on the inside.

HELPFUL TIP:

When shopping for flour tortillas, brands that are labeled as "high fiber" tend to not only contain more whole grains but are also usually as much as 30 percent lower in calories.

PREP TIME: 15 MINUTES • BAKE TIME: 5 MINUTES

OPEN-FACED TUNA MELTS

MAKES 4 LUNCH PORTIONS OR 4 TUNA MELTS

This diner classic is served open-faced to not only keep the calories down to a mere 200 per sandwich, but it also allows you to easily melt the cheese under the broiler. We top our Tuna Melts with sliced tomatoes for a hint of fresh flavor and contrasting texture, but don't forget the knife and fork!

100 CALORIE COUNT =

$\frac{1}{2}$ **TUNA MELT**

Recommended Serving:
LUNCH – 200 Calories = 1 Tuna Melt

Ingredients:

3 tablespoons light mayonnaise*

2 tablespoons minced yellow onion

2 teaspoons whole-grain mustard

2 teaspoons chopped fresh parsley

1 teaspoon lemon juice

¼ teaspoon salt

¼ teaspoon pepper

2 (5-ounce) cans chunk light tuna, drained

4 slices light wheat bread (see tip)

2 tomatoes, sliced

½ cup shredded sharp Cheddar cheese

Directions:

1. Add the light mayonnaise, onion, mustard, parsley, lemon juice, salt, and pepper to a mixing bowl, and stir to combine.

2. Add the tuna to the mixing bowl, and gently fold into the dressing to create the tuna salad.

3. Toast the wheat bread until golden brown. Transfer the toasted bread to a sheet pan.

4. Place the oven rack in the second highest position, and set the broiler to high.

5. Top each slice of toast with ¼ of the tuna salad. Arrange slices from ½ of a tomato over the top of the salad on each sandwich. Sprinkle the tomatoes with additional salt and pepper to season, if desired.

6. Sprinkle the shredded cheese evenly over the top of each sandwich.

7. Broil for just 3–5 minutes, or until cheese has melted and begins to brown.

HELPFUL TIP:

Light bread is sold in loaves in the normal bread aisle. It usually contains only 45 calories (or less) per slice and far more fiber than ordinary bread.

* Natural and organic light mayonnaises are in most supermarkets and are made with all natural ingredients.

PREP TIME: 5 MINUTES • COOK TIME: 10 MINUTES

BUILD YOUR OWN BURGER

MAKES 1 OR MORE BURGERS

Anson's American Treasures: Happy days are here again! Want it your way? Well you're in luck. Whether you want a 100 calorie slider, a grilled quarter-pound beef burger on white, or a pan-fried turkey burger on wheat, this recipe allows you to pick and choose exactly what you want for the calories you'd like to allocate. We've even included the calorie counts for all of your favorite toppings!

100 CALORIE COUNT =

1 SLIDER PATTY

Recommended Serving:
LUNCH – 200 Calories = 2 Slider Patties

Ingredients:

Sliders:

2 ½ ounces (93%) lean ground beef slider patty (100 calories)

Salt and pepper

¼ Pound Patties:

4 ounces 93% lean ground beef (165 calories)

4 ounces 85% ground beef (200 calories)

4 ounces 99% extra-lean ground turkey (120 calories)

4 ounces 93% lean ground turkey (175 calories)

Buns:

Slider bun (90 calories)

Hamburger bun (120 calories)

Light wheat bun (80 calories)

Burger Toppings:

See page 71

Directions:

① Form your burger patties, and flatten to ½ inch thick. Generously season patties with salt and pepper.

② Using nonstick cooking spray to grease the grill or pan, grill or pan-fry burgers for about 3 minutes on each side for medium-rare, 4 minutes on each side for medium, and 5 minutes on each side for medium-well. When in doubt, cut into a burger to test for doneness.

③ If adding cheese, top the burger with the cheese in the last minute of cooking, and cover the pan or close the lid of the grill to melt the cheese. Let burgers rest for 3 minutes before serving topped with your chosen toppings.

HELPFUL TIP:

For an even lower-calorie option, serve your burger and toppings over a bed of lettuce (instead of a bun) as a diner-style hamburger and salad plate.

BURGER TOPPINGS

¼ cup sautéed mushrooms or onions
(15 calories)

Lettuce, tomato, onion, and pickles
(5 calories or less)

⅕ medium avocado
(50 calories)

1 slice American cheese
(70 calories)

1 slice Cheddar or Swiss cheese
(80 calories)

2 tablespoons crumbled blue cheese
(70 calories)

1 tablespoon mayonnaise
(90 calories)

1 tablespoon low-fat mayonnaise
(35 calories)

1 tablespoon ketchup
(15 calories)

1 tablespoon mustard
(5 calories)

1 tablespoon Thousand Island dressing
(70 calories)

2 slices cooked bacon
(90 calories)

2 slices cooked turkey bacon
(50 calories)

SAUTÉED ONIONS & MUSHROOMS
¼ CUP = 15 CALORIES

LETTUCE, TOMATO, PICKLE, ONION
5 CALORIES OR LESS

CHEDDAR CHEESE
1 SLICE = 80 CALORIES

BLUE CHEESE

2 TBSP = 70 CALORIES

KETCHUP

1 TBSP = 15 CALORIES

1000 ISLAND DRESSING

1 TBSP = 70 CALORIES

LOW-FAT MAYONNAISE

1 TBSP = 35 CALORIES

COOKED BACON

2 SLICES = 90 CALORIES

MUSTARD

1 TBSP = 5 CALORIES

TURKEY BACON

2 SLICES = 50 CALORIES

AMERICAN CHEESE

1 SLICE = 70 CALORIES

MEDIUM AVOCADO

⅕ AVOCADO = 50 CALORIES

3 CASSEROLES & ONE-POT MEALS

PREP TIME: 25 MINUTES • BAKE TIME: 30 MINUTES

BAKED MAC & CHEESE

MAKES 12 LUNCH PORTIONS

Anson's American Treasures: As a kid, my family couldn't always afford great meals, but there was one night each month when everything seemed perfect. There were no arguments at the table, no worries, just my mother's amazing Baked Mac & Cheese. The fabulous recipe gurus were able to swap a little of the milk for chicken broth and sharp Cheddar cheese instead of mild to capture that great flavor I still savor. So good!

100 CALORIE COUNT =

$\frac{1}{36}$ **BAKED MAC & CHEESE**

Recommended Serving:
LUNCH – 300 Calories = 3 Sections

Ingredients:

Nonstick cooking spray

16 ounces elbow macaroni

2 tablespoons butter

2 tablespoons all-purpose flour

2 teaspoons ground mustard

1 teaspoon salt

½ teaspoon white pepper

2½ cups 2% milk

½ cup chicken broth

3 cups shredded sharp Cheddar cheese, divided

Directions:

1. Preheat the oven to 375°F. Spray a 13 x 9-inch baking dish with nonstick cooking spray.

2. Boil the macaroni just until al dente. Drain and rinse under cold water.

3. Melt the butter in a large pot over medium heat. Add the flour, ground mustard, salt, and white pepper, and stir until smooth and combined. Let cook for 2 minutes.

4. Whisk the milk and chicken broth into the pot, and continue whisking until the sauce is smooth and free of lumps.

5. Bring the sauce to a simmer, whisking constantly, cooking until it begins to thicken.

6. Remove the pot from the heat, and stir in 2¼ cups of the Cheddar cheese, stirring until melted into the sauce. Add the cooked macaroni to the pot and stir until evenly coated with the sauce.

7. Pour the macaroni and cheese sauce into the prepared baking dish, and spread to even out. Top with the remaining ¾ cup shredded Cheddar cheese.

8. Bake for 30 minutes, or until cheese is bubbly and lightly browned. Let cool for at least 5 minutes before slicing. For 100 calorie portions, slice casserole into 36 sections by cutting 4 rows by 9 rows.

PREP TIME: 5 MINUTES • COOK TIME: 20 MINUTES

STOVETOP MAC & CHEESE

MAKES 12 LUNCH PORTIONS

Creamy Stovetop Mac & Cheese doesn't just come out of a blue box; in fact, you can make it from scratch in nearly the exact same amount of time as the boxed stuff. Making an extra creamy cheese sauce from real Cheddar cheese can be difficult to do without the sauce separating, but this recipe uses both cornstarch and reduced-fat cream cheese to bind things together and keep things easy and foolproof.

100 CALORIE COUNT =

⅓ CUP

100 Calories ⅓ Cup

Recommended Serving:
LUNCH – 300 Calories = 1 Cup

Ingredients:

16 ounces elbow macaroni

2 tablespoons cornstarch

1½ cups chicken broth

1 (12-ounce) can fat-free evaporated milk

¾ teaspoon salt

4 ounces reduced-fat cream cheese

3 cups shredded sharp Cheddar cheese

1 tablespoon grated Parmesan cheese

Directions:

1. Boil the macaroni according to package directions. Drain, but do not rinse.

2. In a stockpot over medium-high heat, whisk the cornstarch into the chicken broth, until dissolved. Bring up to a simmer, and let cook for 2 minutes.

3. Whisk the evaporated milk and salt into the thickened chicken broth, and bring back up to a simmer.

4. Remove sauce from heat, and stir in cream cheese, Cheddar cheese, and Parmesan cheese, until melted and creamy.

5. Add the cooked macaroni into the cheese sauce, and stir to combine before serving.

HELPFUL TIP:

It is best to make the sauce as the macaroni is boiling, so that you can add hot macaroni into the sauce. If the finished dish has cooled too much, simply warm over medium-low heat and stir constantly, until hot throughout.

PREP TIME: 30 MINUTES • COOK TIME: 45 MINUTES

CHICKEN POT PIE

MAKES 10 LUNCH PORTIONS OR 8 DINNER PORTIONS

Bob's Farm to Table: My mom's Chicken Pot Pie was wonderful. Over the years I have learned more about how to achieve deeper, more complex flavors in my recipes. I have adapted my mom's original farm to our table recipe to make it even more delicious, while reducing the calorie count from over 550 calories per 1 cup serving to an even 300.

Featured Recipe Story: See next page.

100 CALORIE COUNT =

⅓ CUP PLUS 1 CROUTON

100 Calories   ⅓ Cup

Recommended Serving:
LUNCH – 300 Calories = 1 Cup plus 3 Croutons
DINNER – 400 Calories = 1⅓ Cups plus 4 Croutons

Ingredients:

1 sheet frozen puff pastry, thawed
1 large egg, beaten
Nonstick cooking spray
2 russet potatoes, cut into ½-inch cubes
1½ cups carrots, cut into ½-inch cubes
¾ cup celery cut into ¼-inch rounds
3 tablespoons butter
1½ pounds boneless, skinless chicken breast, cut into ½-inch cubes
¾ cup diced yellow onion
⅓ cup all-purpose flour
2 cups chicken broth
2 cups 2% milk
½ cup sliced mushrooms
1 cup frozen peas
8 ounces of frozen or fresh corn
2 tablespoons soy sauce
2 teaspoons lemon juice
2 tablespoons tomato paste
Salt and pepper to taste

Directions:

1. Preheat the oven to 400°F. Unroll the puff pastry, and use a pastry or pizza cutter to cut into 32 pieces by slicing 4 rows on the shorter end by 8 rows lengthwise. Transfer to a sheet pan, placing them 1 inch apart. Brush top of pastry with beaten egg.

2. Bake the pastry pieces for 10–12 minutes, until they are fluffy and golden brown "croutons."

3. Spray a sheet pan with nonstick cooking spray. Place chopped potatoes, carrot, and celery on sheet pan, and roast in the preheated oven for 20 minutes, just until potatoes are lightly browned. Set aside.

4. Melt the butter in a large stockpot over medium-high heat. Add the chicken to the pot and sauté for 5 minutes, lightly browning on all sides. Add the onion to the pot, and sauté for an additional 2 minutes.

5. Stir the flour into the pot, coating the chicken and onions, and let cook for 2 minutes, stirring constantly.

6. Stir the chicken broth, milk, roasted vegetables, and all of the remaining ingredients into the pot. Stir constantly as you bring the mixture to a boil. Reduce heat to medium, and let simmer for 5 minutes, stirring occasionally until sauce is smooth and creamy.

7. Season with salt and pepper to taste. Measure your perfect portion into a soup bowl, and top chicken pie mixture with croutons.

MOM'S CHICKEN POT PIE

Comfort Food At Its Best — Dinner for 400 Calories!

MY FAVORITE COMFORT FOOD GROWING UP ON our farm in Iowa was my mom's chicken pot pie. I never got tired of eating it at least once a week. But here I was, faced with Anson's challenge to make chicken pot pie taste even better with fewer calories. I was going to have to come up with some creative ideas.

The old-fashioned crust caused the biggest calorie creep. It actually accounted for over half of the calories! To reduce calories, I cut a sheet of puff pastry into small squares that I baked. I measured a cup of pie mixture into a bowl and topped it with 25 calorie puff pastry croutons. I used four for a dinner portion. I created the same buttery flavors with a lot fewer calories!

Brown 'em! As a chef, I've learned that roasting vegetables creates sweetness and richness through the browning process. So, I roasted the chopped vegetables on a sheet pan till browned, yet still crunchy, adding bold flavor, not calories.

Bite-Sized is Best! How was I going to cut the calories and still make "chicken" pot pie (and not "vegetable" pot pie)? In Mom's pie, the chicken was always in chunks, and when I think about it, all I tasted was chicken. To get balanced bites of veggies and chicken, I doubled the veggies and cut both into smaller, fork-friendly pieces. Now, I could taste all of the veggies and chicken in every mouthful.

Secret Sauce! To compensate for the added veggies, I increased the meatiness with a secret chef trick. I added mushrooms, tomato paste, and low-sodium soy sauce—all ingredients loaded with umami, a natural element that mimics meaty flavor.

1 In order to get the best flavors in every bite, I chop the chicken into diced pieces. This blends all the flavors together and adds great texture to the filling.

4 My favorite time- and calorie-saving trick is to make pot pie "croutons" from puff pastry dough. I spoon a cup of filling into bowls and place the crunchy squares on top.

2 My first flavor secret is roasting the vegetables before cooking them with the chicken and sauce. Browning the vegetables adds deeper flavor and sweetness.

3 My second flavor secret is adding mushrooms, tomato paste, and soy sauce, which all mimic meatiness. Adding the roasted vegetables and simmering blends those flavors.

5 I did it! Mona was so impressed that I met my 400 calorie goal with such flavor and richness. Anson enjoyed the crunch from the puff pastry croutons.

PREP TIME: 1 HOUR • BAKE TIME: 1 HOUR

LASAGNA

MAKES 12 LUNCH PORTIONS OR 9 DINNER PORTIONS

Our homemade Lasagna with Meat Sauce is a symphony of flavors and textures. We built layer after layer of tender noodles, robust meat sauce, and creamy, tangy ricotta cheese for a lasagna that will knock your socks off. By using ground turkey, we've been able to lighten up the lasagna (up to 100 calories less per serving) without skimping on the noodles or luxuriously smooth filling.

100 CALORIE COUNT =

$\frac{1}{36}$ **LASAGNA**

Recommended Serving:
LUNCH – 300 Calories = 3 Sections
DINNER – 400 Calories = 4 Sections

Ingredients:

Nonstick cooking spray

1 batch Ground Turkey Bolognese (see page 113)

8 ounces lasagna noodles

1 (15-ounce) container part-skim ricotta cheese

2 large egg whites, beaten

¼ cup grated Parmesan cheese

2 tablespoons chopped fresh parsley

½ teaspoon salt

½ teaspoon pepper

¼ teaspoon garlic powder

3 cups part-skim mozzarella cheese

Directions:

1. Preheat the oven to 375°F, and spray a 13 x 9-inch baking dish with nonstick cooking spray.

2. Prepare the Ground Turkey Bolognese according to the recipe's directions.

3. Boil the lasagna noodles according to the package directions, undercooking by 2 minutes (to leave them very al dente). Drain and rinse under cold water.

4. In a large mixing bowl, fold together the ricotta cheese, egg whites, Parmesan cheese, parsley, salt, pepper, and garlic powder to make the ricotta filling.

5. Start building the lasagna by spreading a thin layer of the Bolognese sauce at the bottom of the prepared baking dish. Top the sauce with ⅓ of the cooked noodles. Top the noodles with ⅓ of the ricotta cheese mixture, dropping it into the dish in small dollops. Top the ricotta cheese with ⅓ of the Bolognese sauce. Finally, top the sauce with 1 cup of mozzarella cheese to complete the layer. Repeat to create 3 full layers of ingredients.

6. Cover with aluminum foil, and bake for 40 minutes. Remove aluminum foil, and bake for an additional 20 minutes, or until sauce is bubbly hot and cheese begins to brown. Let cool for 10 minutes before slicing. For 100 calorie portions, slice Lasagna into 36 sections by cutting 6 rows by 6 rows.

PREP TIME: 50 MINUTES • BAKE TIME: 30 MINUTES

SHEPHERD'S PIE

MAKES 10 LUNCH PORTIONS OR 8 DINNER PORTIONS

Shepherd's Pie, a layered casserole of sautéed ground lamb and vegetables topped with mashed potatoes and baked until golden, is the quintessential casserole of the United Kingdom. Inspired by this fantastic combination, American Cottage Pie mirrors its predecessor except that ground beef is used in place of the lamb. Regardless of what you call it, this savory meal of meat and vegetables topped with golden brown mashed potatoes is a hearty, one-dish supper that can more than feed your whole family.

100 CALORIE COUNT =

$\frac{1}{32}$ **SHEPHERD'S PIE**

Recommended Serving:
LUNCH – 300 Calories = 3 Sections
DINNER – 400 Calories = 4 Sections

Ingredients:

Nonstick cooking spray

1 batch Home-Style Mashed Potatoes (see page 221)

1 tablespoon canola oil

2 pounds (96%) extra lean ground beef

1 cup diced yellow onion

1 cup diced carrots

¾ cup diced celery

¾ teaspoon salt

½ teaspoon pepper

¼ teaspoon garlic powder

2 tablespoons all-purpose flour

1 cup beef broth

2 teaspoons Worcestershire sauce

1¼ cups frozen peas

Directions:

1. Preheat the oven to 375°F, and spray a 13 x 9-inch baking dish with nonstick cooking spray.

2. Prepare the Home-Style Mashed Potatoes (page 221) according to the recipe's directions.

3. Heat the canola oil in a large skillet or Dutch oven over medium-high heat. Add the ground beef to the skillet, and brown well, crumbling the beef as it cooks.

4. Add the onion, carrots, celery, salt, pepper, and garlic powder to the skillet, and sauté for 5 minutes, or until onions are translucent and celery begins to soften. Stir the flour into the beef and vegetables, and sauté for 1 minute.

5. Add the beef broth, Worcestershire sauce, and peas to the skillet, and bring to a simmer. Let simmer for 5 minutes, or until the sauce has slightly thickened and the carrots are tender.

6. Spread the beef and sauce mixture evenly across the bottom of the prepared baking dish. Spoon the Home-Style Mashed Potatoes over the top of the beef, and spread to even out.

7. Bake, uncovered, for 30 minutes, or until the top of the potatoes has lightly browned. Let cool for 10 minutes before slicing. For 100 calorie portions, slice into 32 sections by cutting 4 rows by 8 rows.

PREP TIME: 25 MINUTES • COOK TIME: 1 HOUR

EGGPLANT PARMESAN CASSEROLE

MAKES 9 LUNCH PORTIONS OR 6 DINNER PORTIONS

Breading the eggplant in bread crumbs and Parmesan cheese gives you not only nutty, cheesy flavor, but also crunchy texture. No need to pan-fry! Simply transfer the eggplant to a baking sheet, and pop them in a hot oven so you can get the rest of dinner done. Once our eggplant and sauce are ready to go, we quickly layer them with creamy mozzarella, and bake for a mere 20 minutes. Bubbling, gooey, and brimming with big flavor, this Italian classic should not be missed!

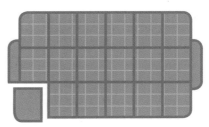

100 CALORIE COUNT =

$\frac{1}{18}$ **EGGPLANT PARMESAN CASSEROLE**

Recommended Serving:
LUNCH – 200 Calories = 2 Sections
DINNER – 300 Calories = 3 Sections

Ingredients:

Nonstick cooking spray

2 large eggplants

1 large egg

2 large egg whites

½ teaspoon salt

½ teaspoon pepper

¼ teaspoon garlic powder

1½ cups Italian bread crumbs

½ cup grated Parmesan cheese

1 batch Tuscan Tomato Sauce (see page 249)

1 cup shredded part-skim mozzarella cheese

Directions:

1. Preheat the oven to 400°F, and spray 2 sheet pans with nonstick cooking spray.

2. Peel the eggplants, and slice into ½-inch-thick discs.

3. In a wide bowl, whisk together the egg, egg whites, salt, pepper, and garlic powder. In a separate wide bowl, combine the Italian bread crumbs and Parmesan cheese.

4. Dip the eggplant slices into the egg mixture and then the bread crumb mixture, fully coating on both sides. Transfer the breaded eggplant to the prepared sheet pans.

5. Bake the breaded eggplant for 40 minutes, flipping halfway through.

6. As the eggplant is baking, prepare the Tuscan Tomato Sauce (page 249) according to the recipe's directions. Cover, and let sit over warm heat.

7. Spray a 13 x 9-inch baking dish with nonstick cooking spray. Spread 2 cups of the Tuscan Tomato Sauce at the bottom of the baking dish. Top with ½ of the breaded eggplant, then 2 more cups of the tomato sauce, and finally ½ of the cheese. Repeat with another layer of eggplant, sauce, and then cheese.

8. In preheated oven (400°F), bake the casserole for 20 minutes, or until the cheese is melted and the sauce is bubbly hot. For 100 calorie portions, slice into 18 sections by cutting 3 rows by 6 rows.

PREP TIME: 40 MINUTES • BAKE TIME: 30 MINUTES

TURKEY TETRAZZINI

MAKES 8 LUNCH PORTIONS OR 6 DINNER PORTIONS

Turkey, egg noodles, and peas wrapped in a mushroom-studded cream sauce and topped with toasty bread crumbs...what's not to love? Lucky for us this creamy comfort casserole isn't relegated to leftover holiday turkey anymore. Enjoy it any time by buying small precooked turkey breasts.

100 CALORIE COUNT =

$\frac{1}{24}$ **TURKEY TETRAZZINI**

Recommended Serving:
LUNCH – 300 Calories = 3 Sections
DINNER – 400 Calories = 4 Sections

Ingredients:

Nonstick cooking spray

6 ounces egg noodles

1 tablespoon butter

8 ounces sliced baby bella mushrooms

¾ cup diced yellow onion

½ cup diced celery

¼ cup all-purpose flour

2 ½ cups 2% milk

1 cup chicken stock

½ teaspoon fresh thyme

½ teaspoon salt

¼ teaspoon pepper

3 cups cooked and chopped turkey breast

½ cup grated Parmesan cheese

1 cup frozen peas

½ cup panko bread crumbs

Directions:

1. Preheat the oven to 350°F, and spray a 13 x 9-inch baking dish with nonstick cooking spray.

2. Cook the egg noodles according to package directions, and drain well, rinsing under cold water to stop the cooking process.

3. Place the butter in a stockpot over medium-high heat, cooking until melted.

4. Add the mushrooms, onion, and celery to the pot, and sauté until the mushrooms are tender, about 5 minutes. Reduce heat to medium.

5. Whisk the flour into a mixture of the milk and chicken stock, and add to the pot, stirring constantly, until the mixture comes to a simmer and begins to thicken. Add the thyme, salt, and pepper, and let simmer for 3 minutes.

6. Remove the sauce from the heat. Stir in the chopped turkey, Parmesan cheese, peas, and cooked egg noodles.

7. Pour the finished casserole mixture into the prepared baking dish, and top with the panko bread crumbs. Lightly spray the bread crumbs with nonstick cooking spray to moisten.

8. Bake for 30 minutes, just until the edges are beginning to brown and the sauce is bubbly hot. For 100 calorie portions, slice the casserole into 24 portions by cutting 6 rows by 4 rows.

PREP TIME: 30 MINUTES · BAKE TIME: 30 MINUTES

ENCHILADA BAKE

MAKES 12 LUNCH PORTIONS OR 8 DINNER PORTIONS

Authentic enchiladas are time consuming, as they require filling and rolling delicate individual tortillas. We capture the same flavors and textures in a fraction of the time by assembling the tortillas, beef mixture, and cheese as a family-friendly Mexican lasagna. It's hard to beat good food that's also easy to make! Olé!

100 CALORIE COUNT=

$\frac{1}{24}$ **ENCHILADA BAKE**

Recommended Serving:
LUNCH – 200 Calories = 2 Sections
DINNER – 300 Calories = 3 Sections

Ingredients:

Nonstick cooking spray

1 pound (96%) extra lean ground beef

1 cup diced yellow onion

½ cup diced green bell pepper

2 teaspoons minced garlic

1 teaspoon chili powder

¾ teaspoon salt

½ teaspoon pepper

1½ cups picante sauce (such as Pace)

1 (15-ounce) can black beans, drained

1 cup frozen corn kernels

2 tomatoes, diced

½ cup sliced black olives

2 tablespoons chopped cilantro

10 (6-inch) soft corn tortillas, halved

1 cup shredded Cheddar Jack cheese

Directions:

1. Preheat the oven to 375°F, and spray a 13 x 9-inch baking dish with nonstick cooking spray. Spray a large sauce pot with nonstick cooking spray, and place over medium-high heat.

2. Add the ground beef to the pot, and cook until well browned, crumbling the beef as it cooks.

3. Add the onion, bell pepper, garlic, chili powder, salt, and pepper to the pot, and sauté for 3 minutes, just until onions are translucent.

4. Add the picante sauce, black beans, corn, diced tomatoes, black olives, and cilantro to the pot. Bring to a simmer, and then remove from the heat.

5. Build the casserole by layering ½ of the corn tortillas on the bottom of the prepared baking dish. Top the tortillas with ½ of the ground beef mixture. Top the ground beef mixture with ½ of the shredded cheese.

6. Repeat the last step to create a second layer using the remaining tortillas, ground beef mixture, and cheese.

7. Cover with aluminum foil, and bake for 20 minutes.

8. Remove aluminum foil, and bake for an additional 10 minutes, or until bubbly hot. Let cool for 10 minutes before slicing. For 100 calorie portions, slice casserole into 24 sections by cutting 4 rows by 6 rows.

PREP TIME: 30 MINUTES • BAKE TIME: 30 MINUTES

CHICKEN, BROCCOLI & RICE CASSEROLE

MAKES 10 LUNCH PORTIONS OR 8 DINNER PORTIONS

This crowd-pleasing recipe has it all, vegetables, protein, some rice, and rich cheese flavor. We opt for lean white meat but infuse rich chicken flavor throughout by simmering the rice in the chicken broth.

100 **CALORIE COUNT=**

$\frac{1}{32}$ **CHICKEN, BROCCOLI & RICE CASSEROLE**

Recommended Serving:
LUNCH – 300 Calories = 3 Sections
DINNER – 400 Calories = 4 Sections

Ingredients:

Nonstick cooking spray

3 cups chicken broth

1½ cups uncooked white rice

1 tablespoon butter

1½ pounds chicken tenderloins, chopped

½ cup diced yellow onion

3 tablespoons all-purpose flour

3 cups 2% milk

½ teaspoon salt

¼ teaspoon white pepper

¼ teaspoon onion powder

1 (16-ounce) bag frozen broccoli florets, thawed

1½ cups shredded sharp Cheddar cheese, divided

Directions:

1. Preheat the oven to 350°F, and spray a 13 x 9-inch baking dish with nonstick cooking spray.

2. In a medium-size sauce pot, bring the chicken broth to a boil. Add the rice, cover, and reduce heat to low. Let simmer for 15–20 minutes, just until all the water has been absorbed. Remove from heat and let cool for 5 minutes before fluffing with a fork.

3. Melt the butter in a large stockpot over medium-high heat.

4. Add the chicken to the pot, and sauté for 5 minutes, browning well on all sides. Add the diced onion to the pot, and sauté for an additional 2 minutes.

5. Stir the flour into the pot, coating the chicken and onions, and let cook for 1 minute.

6. Stir the milk, salt, white pepper, and onion powder into the pot, and bring to a simmer. Reduce heat to low, and let simmer for 2 minutes.

7. Remove the pot from the heat, and stir in the broccoli, 1 cup Cheddar cheese, and cooked rice. Transfer to the prepared baking dish, and top with the remaining ½ cup of cheese.

8. Bake for 25–30 minutes, or until cheese has melted and sauce is bubbly hot. Let cool for 7 minutes before serving. For 100 calorie portions, slice into 32 sections by cutting 4 rows by 8 rows.

PREP TIME: 20 MINUTES • BAKE TIME: 30 MINUTES

TUNA NOODLE CASSEROLE

MAKES 10 LUNCH PORTIONS OR 8 DINNER PORTIONS

This fantastic update on the iconic tuna casserole replaces stodgy canned soup with a homemade milk sauce seasoned with tangy Dijon, rich Worcestershire, and robust Old Bay Seasoning. We add broccoli and red pepper for fresh bite and heft, but the finishing cheesy cracker crust sends this one-dish meal off the charts.

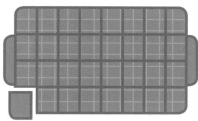

100 CALORIE COUNT =

$\frac{1}{32}$ **TUNA NOODLE CASSEROLE**

Recommended Serving:
LUNCH – 300 Calories = 3 Sections
DINNER – 400 Calories = 4 Sections

Ingredients:

Nonstick cooking spray

12 ounces elbow macaroni

1 tablespoon butter

1 cup diced red onion

½ cup diced red bell pepper

¼ cup all-purpose flour

3¼ cups 2% milk

2 teaspoons Worcestershire sauce

2 teaspoons Dijon mustard

1 teaspoon Old Bay Seasoning

½ teaspoon each, salt and pepper

1¼ cups shredded sharp Cheddar cheese, divided

¼ cup grated Parmesan cheese

1 (16-ounce) bag frozen broccoli florets, thawed

2 (5-ounce) cans chunk light tuna, drained

½ cup crushed saltine crackers

Directions:

1. Preheat the oven to 350°F, and spray a 13 x 9-inch baking dish with nonstick cooking spray.

2. Boil the elbow macaroni just until al dente; drain well, rinsing under cold water to stop the cooking process.

3. Place the butter in a stockpot over medium heat, cooking until melted. Add the onion and bell pepper to the pot, and sauté until onions are translucent, about 4 minutes.

4. Whisk the flour into the milk, and add to the pot, stirring constantly, until the mixture comes to a simmer and begins to thicken. Add the Worcestershire sauce, Dijon mustard, Old Bay Seasoning, salt, and pepper, and let simmer for 3 minutes.

5. Remove the sauce from the heat. Stir in ½ cup of the Cheddar cheese and all the Parmesan cheese. Stir the broccoli florets and cooked macaroni into the sauce before gently folding in the drained tuna.

6. Pour the finished casserole mixture into the prepared baking dish; top with the remaining ¾ cup of Cheddar cheese and then the crushed saltines. Lightly spray the saltines with nonstick cooking spray to moisten.

7. Bake for 30 minutes, just until the edges are beginning to brown and the sauce is bubbly hot. Let cool for 5 minutes before slicing. For 100 calorie portions, slice casserole into 32 sections by cutting 4 rows by 8 rows.

PREP TIME: 25 MINUTES • COOK TIME: 30 MINUTES

CHICKEN & DUMPLINGS

MAKES 8 LUNCH PORTIONS OR 6 DINNER PORTIONS

Bob's Farm to Table: The dumplings in this recipe are so easy to prepare, and grow in size to make such a satisfying and filling dish. Our rich, lightly thickened broth is chock-full of vegetables, and our dumplings puff up, and are lightened up, thanks to reduced-fat milk and baking powder.

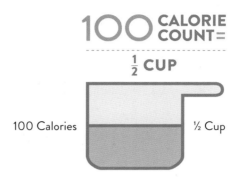

100 CALORIE COUNT =

½ **CUP**

100 Calories   ½ Cup

Recommended Serving:
LUNCH – 300 Calories = 1½ Cups
DINNER – 400 Calories = 2 Cups

Ingredients:

1 tablespoon butter

1½ pounds boneless, skinless chicken thighs, chopped in large pieces

1 yellow onion, chopped

1½ cups chopped carrots

1 cup chopped celery

2 tablespoons all-purpose flour

6 cups chicken broth

¼ cup half-and-half

1 cup frozen peas

1¼ teaspoons dried thyme

¾ teaspoon pepper

Dumplings:

1½ cups all-purpose flour

¼ cup chopped fresh parsley

1½ teaspoons baking powder

¾ teaspoon salt

⅔ cup 2% milk

1 tablespoon butter, melted

Directions:

1. Melt the butter in a large stockpot over medium-high heat.

2. Add the chicken to the pot, and sauté for 5 minutes, browning well on all sides.

3. Add the onion, carrots, and celery to the pot, and sauté for an additional 2 minutes.

4. Stir the flour into the pot, coating the chicken and vegetables, and let cook for 2 minutes, stirring constantly.

5. Stir the chicken broth and all of the remaining ingredients into the pot. Stir constantly, and bring the mixture to a boil. Reduce heat to low, and let simmer for 5 minutes as you prepare the dumplings.

6. Create the dumplings by combining the flour, parsley, baking powder, and salt in a mixing bowl. Add the milk and melted butter, and mix just until a batter is formed. Do not overmix!

7. Drop heaping teaspoons of the dumpling batter into the simmering stew until all the batter has been used up.

8. Cover, and let simmer for 15 minutes. Season the broth with salt to taste, and serve.

PREP TIME: 30 MINUTES • BAKE TIME: 1 HOUR

RATATOUILLE & SAUSAGE BAKE

MAKES 4 LUNCH PORTIONS OR 3 DINNER PORTIONS

While ratatouille is traditionally stewed on the stove, this recipe roasts the medley of fresh vegetables for an even more robust flavor. Adding Italian chicken sausage to the dish makes this a complete entrée that you can pair with steamed white rice (100 calories per ½ cup) or brown rice (110 calories per ½ cup) for a complete meal.

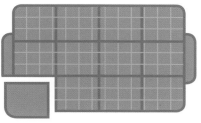

100 CALORIE COUNT =

$\frac{1}{12}$ **RATATOUILLE & SAUSAGE BAKE**

Recommended Serving:
LUNCH – 300 Calories = 3 Sections
DINNER – 400 Calories = 4 Sections

Ingredients:

4 links fully cooked Italian chicken sausage, sliced (see tip)

1 medium eggplant (unpeeled), chopped

2 zucchini, chopped

2 yellow squash, chopped

1 red onion, chopped

1 red bell pepper, chopped

1 (14.5-ounce) can diced tomatoes, drained

2 tablespoons tomato paste

2 tablespoons extra virgin olive oil

1 tablespoon red wine vinegar

1 tablespoon minced garlic

2 teaspoons sugar

2 teaspoons Italian seasoning

1 teaspoon salt

¾ teaspoon pepper

Directions:

1. Preheat the oven to 375°F.

2. Place all the ingredients in a very large mixing bowl, and toss to combine.

3. Transfer the combined ingredients to a 13 x 9-inch baking dish, and spread to even out the top. It is alright if the baking dish is nearly overflowing, as the vegetables will cook down.

4. Bake, uncovered, for 1 hour. Serve immediately (though this tastes even better when reheated the next day). For 100 calorie portions, slice casserole into 12 sections by cutting 3 rows by 4 rows.

HELPFUL TIP:

The chicken sausage used in this recipe is the fully cooked variety that they sell near the hot dogs. Al Fresco brand "Sweet Italian Chicken Sausage" is recommended and used in the nutritional information, though you can use any brand and flavor.

PREP TIME: 25 MINUTES • COOK TIME: 2 HOURS

BEEF STEW

MAKES 8 LUNCH OR 6 DINNER PORTIONS

Anson's American Treasures: My close friend, who loves to cook, turns his home into a dining experience once a month. He made a beef stew last year that was to die for. Bob and Mona reviewed the recipe, did their magic again, and created the masterpiece below! By increasing the volume of hearty vegetables and slightly reducing the beef, they made it possible to truly eat what you love, and more of it! So good!

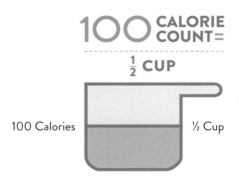

100 **CALORIE COUNT =**

½ **CUP**

100 Calories   ½ Cup

Recommended Serving:
LUNCH – 300 Calories = 1½ Cups
DINNER – 400 Calories = 2 Cups

Ingredients:

1 tablespoon canola oil

1 tablespoon butter

2 pounds beef stew meat, trimmed of excess fat

Salt and pepper

1 cup chopped onions

8 ounces mushrooms, quartered

5 cups beef broth

1 cup dry red wine (see tip)

2 tablespoons tomato paste

4 sprigs fresh thyme

½ teaspoon garlic powder

1 pound Red Bliss potatoes, chopped

1½ cups sliced carrots

3 tablespoons all-purpose flour

2 medium tomatoes, chopped

Directions:

1. Heat the oil and butter in a stockpot over medium-high heat.

2. Generously season the stew meat with the salt and pepper. Add the seasoned meat to the pot, and brown well.

3. Add the onions and mushrooms to the pot, and sauté until onions are translucent, about 5 minutes.

4. Add the beef broth, red wine, tomato paste, thyme, garlic powder, and ½ teaspoon each of salt and pepper to the pot, and bring to a boil. Reduce heat to low, cover, and let simmer for 1 hour.

5. Add the potatoes and carrots to the stew, cover, and let simmer for 45 additional minutes, or until both meat and vegetables are tender.

6. Raise heat to medium. Ladle ¼ cup of the broth into a bowl, and let cool for 1 minute. Whisk the flour into the broth, and then stir into the pot of stew.

7. Add the chopped tomatoes to the stew, and let simmer for 5 minutes before serving.

HELPFUL TIP:

An additional cup of beef broth, 2 teaspoons of red wine vinegar, and 2 teaspoons of sugar can be substituted in place of the red wine.

PREP TIME: 25 MINUTES • COOK TIME: 40 MINUTES

MONA'S SOUTHWESTERN CHILI

MAKES 5 LUNCH OR 4 DINNER PORTIONS

Mona's Family Favorites: This chili may look like it contains a lot of ingredients, but many of them are staples that you most likely already have in your pantry and fridge. Everyone has their own secret ingredient for their chili recipes, and mine is freshly chopped basil! I find it adds even more herbaceous punch than the cilantro you'd typically use in a Southwestern dish.

Featured Recipe Story: See next page.

100 CALORIE COUNT =

½ CUP

100 Calories   ½ Cup

Recommended Serving:
LUNCH – 300 Calories = 1½ Cups
DINNER – 400 Calories = 2 Cups

Ingredients:

1 tablespoon olive oil

1 pound 93% lean ground beef

2 cups chopped bell peppers

1 cup chopped yellow onion

1 jalapeño, seeded and diced

1 tablespoon minced garlic

1 (28-ounce) can diced tomatoes, with liquid

1 (15-ounce) can tomato sauce

2 tablespoons chopped fresh basil

1 tablespoon light brown sugar

1 tablespoon chili powder

1 teaspoon ground cumin

¾ teaspoon salt

¾ teaspoon pepper

1 (15-ounce) can black beans, drained

¾ cup frozen corn kernels

Directions:

1 Heat the olive oil in a stockpot over medium-high heat.

2 Brown the ground beef until fully cooked. Add the bell peppers, onion, jalapeño, and garlic. Sauté for 5 minutes, just until the onion and peppers begin to soften.

3 Add the diced tomatoes, tomato sauce, basil, brown sugar, chili powder, cumin, salt, and pepper to the pot, and stir to combine. Bring to a simmer, reduce heat to low, cover, and let simmer for 30 minutes.

4 Add the black beans and corn to the chili, and simmer for an additional 5 minutes before serving.

HELPFUL TIP:

Topping a bowl of this chili with 1 tablespoon of sour cream will add 30 calories. Topping it with 1 tablespoon of reduced-fat sour cream will add around 25 calories, depending on the brand.

MONA'S SOUTHWESTERN CHILI

Game Day Winner — A Super Bowl Full of Goodness

WHAT'S GREAT ABOUT MAKING CHILI IS THAT, with its combination of veggies, ground meat, and beans, it's a one-bowl meal. Since I am always assigned by my friends to bring the "good stuff" to the tailgate parties, I use my culinary tricks to make it healthier, yet delicious. I like to use lower fat ground beef. To make it more flavorful, I add a generous amount of sautéed vegetties to add extra flavor (and more fiber) with fewer calories. Making my own chili seasoning adds bold flavor without the added sodium you usually find in the pre-packed stuff. Using smaller black beans gives the chili distinct texture without making it too mealy. My big secret? I use fresh basil instead of cilantro for great aromatics. Its sweet, peppery taste adds the right herb note. This chili makes any day a winning one!

Bump up the Veggies! Don't be stingy with the veggies. Peppers and onions are standard fare here, but I like the sweetness and pop of frozen corn kernels as well.

Keep it Fresh! Don't use pre-packaged seasoning mixes. They are usually full of sodium and sugar. I make my own with chili powder, cumin, and brown sugar.

Skip the Cilantro! While cilantro is traditional here, I found that basil adds more powerful herb flavor.

For the next tailgate, I urge you to throw together this chili, and bring it to the game. At only 400 calories for 2 full cups, they'll be so satisfied they won't guess it's good for them!

1 Adding lots of aromatic vegetables adds so much flavor. I love using different colored peppers. Use a food processor to shortcut the chopping!

4 It's so delicious to eat right out of the pot! Or add a piece of Savory Southern-Style Cornbread (found on p. 169)!

2 Add all the veggies to the pot once the meat is browned. Then sauté until the veggies are softened.

3 Simmer for a good 30 minutes to intensify flavors. Adding frozen corn creates a colorful dish and adds little bursts of sweetness.

5 Thumbs up! Everyone who tried the chili at this photo shoot loved it! Not a spoonful was left...be prepared! I'm sure you will enjoy it too.

4 EVERYDAY MEALS

PREP TIME: 15 MINUTES • COOK TIME: 45 MINUTES

MEATBALLS MARINARA

MAKES 6 DINNER PORTIONS

Mona's Family Favorites: It's so great when you can bring a fantastic vacation memory home with you by preparing a traditional weeknight meal. And even better, this meal is delicious, simple to make, and has a healthy twist! We combine my spinach-packed Tuscan Tomato Sauce (see page 249) with the meatballs for a great blend of protein and greens. By using leaner meat and baking the meatballs, you save on calories without any compromise on flavor. The trick is in the simmering, which makes the meatballs nice and tender. Thanks, Chef Luca! Serve over spaghetti (100 calories per ½ cup cooked).

Featured Recipe Story: See next page.

100 CALORIE COUNT =

2 MEATBALLS WITH 3 TABLESPOONS SAUCE

Recommended Serving:
DINNER – 300 Calories =
6 Meatballs with ½ Cup Sauce

Ingredients:

1 batch Tuscan Tomato Sauce (see page 249)

Nonstick cooking spray

1½ pounds (93%) lean ground beef

1 large egg, beaten

1 large egg white, beaten

¼ cup minced yellow onion

¼ cup Italian bread crumbs

1 tablespoon grated Parmesan cheese

1 tablespoon chopped fresh basil

2 teaspoons minced garlic

1½ teaspoons dried oregano

1 teaspoon salt

½ teaspoon pepper

Directions:

1. Prepare the Tuscan Tomato Sauce according to the recipe's directions. Cover, and let sit over warm heat.

2. Preheat the oven to 400°F, and spray a large sheet pan with nonstick cooking spray.

3. In a large mixing bowl, use your hands to combine all of the remaining ingredients to make the meatball mixture.

4. Form the meatball mixture into 36 meatballs that are 1 inch tall (about the size of a ping-pong ball). Place on the prepared sheet pan.

5. Bake the meatballs for 15 minutes.

6. Raise the heat on the tomato sauce to a simmer, and add the baked meatballs into the sauce.

7. Cover, and let the meatballs simmer in the sauce for 10 minutes before serving.

HELPFUL TIP:

Using extra lean (98%) ground turkey in place of the ground beef will lower the calories in this recipe to only 85 calories per 2 meatballs with sauce.

MEATBALLS MARINARA

The Tuscan Experience— Six Meatballs and Sauce for Just 300 Calories!

MY FAMILY AND I CELEBRATED MY DAUGHTER Rachel's college graduation, and my 25th wedding anniversary, in Tuscany. In addition to the vino tastings and gorgeous hikes, I had always wanted to take a family cooking class to learn how to make traditional red sauce that would be REALLY easy to make. Dream come true! Thanks to Chef Luca and our host, Stefania, at Villa Poggiano, we learned how to make the best sauce ever with just six ingredients, including fresh spinach! I've also added my favorite meatball recipe to make a complete meal. Read on for my own little trick for adding moistness without extra fat.

The Right Ingredients! Sautéing fresh garlic in olive oil and adding fresh basil creates the best aromatics for this sauce. We've also added these fresh ingredients to the meatballs.

Sneaky Spinach! Adding fresh spinach into the sauce adds a healthy veggie to the meal and adds texture and earthiness.

Bake First, Simmer Second! Baking the meatballs allows any extra fat to pool on the sheet tray—not in the sauce! Simmering the cooked meatballs in the Tuscan Tomato Sauce allows the meat to soak in all the delicious flavors.

You can use this great sauce to make all of your favorite Italian dishes at home.

1 Add fresh spinach leaves to the sauce during the last few minutes of cooking. They will quickly wilt and add texture and freshness to the sauce.

4 Serve the meatballs and sauce on top of cooked pasta. A ½-cup portion of cooked plain pasta is only 100 calories!

2 When making Meatballs Marinara, add the meatballs to the sauce after baking them in the oven for 15 minutes.

3 Make sure the meatballs are covered in sauce during the simmering process to ensure they season the sauce and vice versa.

5 So simple to prepare. My critics approve! Bob loves the meatball texture, and Anson loves the fresh flavor of the sauce. Delicioso!

PREP TIME: 25 MINUTES • BAKE TIME: 1 HOUR

CLASSIC MEATLOAF

MAKES 6 DINNER PORTIONS

Our culinary tricks were at work with this recipe to make it better for you without compromising on flavor. We used extra lean ground beef, but added minced zucchini and onion to make it moist. Plus, we added some extra veggies to your dinner! Shh, the kids will never know!

100 CALORIE COUNT =

½-INCH SLICE

Recommended Serving:
Dinner – 300 Calories = 3 Slices or 1 1½-Inch Slice

Ingredients:

Nonstick cooking spray

1½ pounds (93%) lean ground beef

2 large eggs

½ cup Italian bread crumbs

½ cup minced yellow onion

½ cup minced zucchini

¼ cup grated Parmesan cheese

2 tablespoons tomato paste

1 tablespoon Worcestershire sauce

2 teaspoons minced garlic

1¼ teaspoons salt

1 teaspoon Italian seasoning

¾ teaspoon pepper

½ cup ketchup

Directions:

1 Preheat the oven to 350°F. Spray a 9 x 5-inch loaf pan with nonstick cooking spray.

2 In a large mixing bowl, use your hands to mix all the ingredients except the ketchup, folding until well combined.

3 Spread the meatloaf mixture into the prepared loaf pan, and pat it down to smooth out the top. Spread the ketchup over the top of the entire loaf.

4 Bake for 1 hour. Let rest for 8 minutes before slicing into ½-inch-thick slices.

HELPFUL TIP:

Mincing the yellow onion and zucchini can be done quickly in a food processor, though you can also grate the zucchini using a cheese grater.

PREP TIME: 20 MINUTES • COOK TIME: 20 MINUTES

GROUND BEEF STROGANOFF

MAKES 6 DINNER PORTIONS

While traditional Hungarian Stroganoff calls for chunks of stew meat, our spin on this classic comfort food calls for extra lean ground beef as a quick and healthy alternative. Then add a rich mushroom gravy and tender egg noodles to the mix, and you're left with an unbelievably delicious single skillet meal.

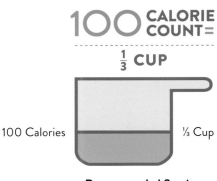

100 CALORIE COUNT =

⅓ CUP

100 Calories   ⅓ Cup

Recommended Serving:
DINNER – 400 Calories = 1⅓ Cups

Ingredients:

12 ounces egg noodles

1 tablespoon butter

12 ounces (white) button mushrooms, sliced

1 yellow onion, diced

¾ cup diced celery

2 teaspoons minced garlic

1¼ pounds 93% lean ground beef

¾ teaspoon dried thyme

¾ teaspoon salt

½ teaspoon pepper

½ teaspoon onion powder

1 cup beef broth

1 tablespoon chopped fresh tarragon (see tip)

1 cup plain nonfat Greek yogurt

Directions:

1. Cook the egg noodles according to the package directions. Drain, and set aside.

2. Melt the butter in a very large skillet or Dutch oven over medium-high heat.

3. Add the mushrooms, onion, celery, and garlic to the skillet, and sauté for 3 minutes, just until mushrooms begin to cook down.

4. Add the ground beef, thyme, salt, pepper, and onion powder to the skillet, and sauté for 8–10 minutes, or until the meat is browned and crumbled.

5. Add the beef broth and tarragon to the skillet, and bring to a simmer. Cook for 3 minutes, or until liquid has reduced by ⅓.

6. Stir the Greek yogurt and cooked egg noodles into the skillet before serving.

HELPFUL TIP:

Fresh tarragon has a slight hint of licorice flavor that goes well with the creamy yogurt. Chopped fresh parsley can be substituted if you have an aversion to licorice.

PREP TIME: 20 MINUTES • COOK TIME: 1 HOUR

GROUND TURKEY BOLOGNESE

MAKES 6 DINNER PORTIONS

Bob's Farm to Table: I love Bolognese sauce. Our version of this classic Italian meat sauce swaps healthful ground turkey in place of beef and produces unexpectedly bold flavors and a tender, silky texture. Starting the sauce with chopped carrots adds sweetness and earthiness to complement the tomatoes and the meat. This sauce is sure to become a family favorite! Serve over spaghetti, ziti, or penne pasta (each about 100 calories per ½ cup cooked).

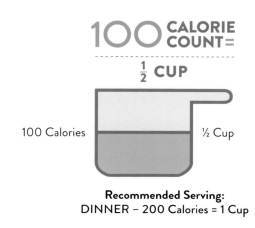

100 CALORIE COUNT =

½ CUP

100 Calories   ½ Cup

Recommended Serving:
DINNER – 200 Calories = 1 Cup

Ingredients:

1 tablespoon olive oil

1 pound (93%) lean ground turkey

1 yellow onion, diced

½ cup finely chopped carrot

¼ cup finely diced celery

1 tablespoon minced garlic

1 (28-ounce) can crushed tomatoes

½ cup chicken broth

3 ounces (½ can) tomato paste

2 tablespoons chopped fresh basil

2 teaspoons sugar

1 teaspoon balsamic vinegar

1 teaspoon Italian seasoning

¾ teaspoon salt

½ teaspoon pepper

Directions:

1. Heat the olive oil in a stockpot over medium-high heat.

2. Brown the ground turkey until fully cooked. Add the onion, carrot, celery, and garlic. Sauté for 5 minutes, just until carrot begins to soften.

3. Add the crushed tomatoes, chicken broth, tomato paste, basil, sugar, balsamic vinegar, Italian seasoning, salt, and pepper to the pot, and stir to combine.

4. Bring to a simmer, reduce heat to low, cover, and let simmer for 45 minutes.

5. Remove the cover, and simmer for an additional 10 minutes (to allow the sauce to slightly thicken) before serving.

HELPFUL TIP:

Italian-seasoned ground turkey works great in this sauce, adding the fennel flavor you get in Italian sausage.

PREP TIME: 30 MINUTES • BAKE TIME: 15–45 MINUTES

OVEN-FRIED CHICKEN

MAKES 14 CHICKEN TENDERS OR 8 PIECES FRIED CHICKEN

Bob's Farm to Table: We were able to create moist and tender chicken with a satisfying crunchy crust without a single drop of oil! The secret is using a thick buttermilk marinade and a substantial coating of ground cornflakes and flour. This recipe can be prepared three ways: as 100 calorie chicken tenders, traditional fried chicken, or as oven-fried chicken without the skin for even lower calories.

100 **CALORIE COUNT =**

1 CHICKEN TENDER

Recommended Serving:
DINNER – 300 Calories = 3 Chicken Tenders or
1–2 Pieces Fried Chicken

BREAST – Skinless = 335 Calories; with Skin = 435 Calories
THIGH – Skinless = 200 Calories; with Skin = 260 Calories
DRUM – Skinless = 150 Calories; with Skin = 195 Calories
WING – Skinless = 105 Calories; with Skin = 180 Calories

Ingredients:

Chicken:

2 pounds chicken tenderloins

or

1 whole chicken (3½–4 pounds), split into 8 pieces (with or without skin)

Breading:

¾ cup low-fat buttermilk

1 tablespoon hot pepper sauce (Tabasco)

1¼ teaspoons salt, divided

1 teaspoon pepper, divided

½ teaspoon dried thyme

½ teaspoon paprika

¼ teaspoon garlic powder

¼ teaspoon onion powder

3 cups cornflakes

¾ cup flour

Directions:

1. Place the chicken in a large bowl or food storage container. Add the buttermilk, hot pepper sauce, ½ teaspoon salt, ½ teaspoon pepper, thyme, paprika, garlic powder, and onion powder, and toss to fully coat the chicken. Cover, and refrigerate for at least 2 hours to marinate.

2. Preheat the oven to 425°F, and place a rack in a roasting pan for the crispiest results.

3. In a food processor, pulse the cornflakes until finely ground. Transfer to a wide bowl; combine with flour and the remaining ¾ teaspoon salt and ½ teaspoon pepper.

4. Flip the marinated chicken in the buttermilk to ensure that it is well coated before pressing each piece into the cornflake mixture, breading on all sides. Place on the rack inside the roasting pan. For crispier chicken, lightly spray the breading with nonstick cooking spray.

FOR CHICKEN TENDERS: Bake for 15 minutes, flipping halfway through. Check for doneness by slicing into the thickest tender to reveal no pink.

FOR WHOLE CHICKEN PIECES: Bake for 20 minutes, and flip. Reduce heat to 375°F, and continue baking for 25–30 additional minutes, or until a meat thermometer inserted into the thickest piece registers 165°F.

PREP TIME: 20 MINUTES • BAKE TIME: 20 MINUTES

LEMON & HERB ROASTED CHICKEN THIGHS

8 LUNCH PORTIONS OR 4 DINNER PORTIONS

We use a slew of fresh herbs and spices for our exceptionally moist Lemon and Herb Roasted Chicken Thighs. Not only is this recipe delicious, it's a snap to cook, because we only have to monitor evenly sized chicken thighs rather than temping a whole chicken. We save calories by removing the chicken skin, but using the dark meat ensures that each piece is nice and tender. No question, this is our new go-to comfort roast chicken.

Recommended Serving:
LUNCH – 200 Calories = 1 Chicken Thigh
DINNER – 400 Calories = 2 Chicken Thighs

Ingredients:

8 boneless, skinless chicken thighs (about 2 pounds)

1 tablespoon butter, melted

Juice from 1 lemon

½ teaspoon light brown sugar

4 cloves garlic, sliced

2 tablespoons chopped fresh thyme leaves

2 tablespoons chopped fresh sage

1 teaspoon lemon zest

½ teaspoon Italian seasoning

½ teaspoon salt

½ teaspoon pepper

¼ teaspoon paprika

Directions:

1. Preheat the oven to 425°F. Place the chicken thighs in a roasting pan.

2. In a small bowl, combine the butter, lemon juice, and brown sugar, and then drizzle over the chicken thighs.

3. Sprinkle the garlic, thyme, sage, lemon zest, Italian seasoning, salt, pepper, and paprika evenly over the chicken thighs.

4. Bake for 20 minutes, or until a meat thermometer inserted into the thickest piece registers 165°F. Serve immediately.

PREP TIME: 15 MINUTES • COOK TIME: 20 MINUTES

CHICKEN PICCATA

MAKES 4 DINNER PORTIONS

Mona's Family Favorites: I love to make this recipe when entertaining and it always gets a "Wow!" from friends and family. Here's the culinary trick, timing! Lemon juice and chicken broth are simmered together before whisking in rich butter off the heat to emulsify or thicken the sauce just before serving. We found that 2½ tablespoons of butter was enough to thicken the liquid and make this sauce delicious. I usually serve it over pasta or on a bed of sautéed spinach.

Recommended Serving:
DINNER – 400 Calories = 1 Chicken Breast with Sauce

Ingredients:

4 (6-ounce) boneless, skinless chicken breasts, pounded thin

Salt and pepper

½ cup all-purpose flour

2 tablespoons olive oil

2 tablespoons finely diced red onion

½ cup chicken stock

Juice of 1 large lemon

2 tablespoons capers, drained

2 ½ tablespoons butter

2 tablespoons chopped fresh parsley

Directions:

1. Season both sides of the chicken breasts with salt and pepper. Place the flour on a wide plate, adding a pinch of salt and pepper.

2. Dredge the chicken in the seasoned flour, pressing down to coat on all sides before shaking off any excess.

3. Add olive oil to a large skillet over medium-high heat, and heat until oil thins and coats the skillet.

4. Place the dredged chicken into the skillet, and cook for 4–5 minutes on each side, until browned. Remove the skillet from the heat, and transfer the chicken to a plate.

5. Add the red onion to the skillet, and return to the heat, just until sizzling. Deglaze the pan with chicken stock and lemon juice, scraping any browned chicken from the bottom. Bring the sauce to a simmer, and let reduce to about half.

6. Add the capers to the sauce before returning the chicken to the pan to cook for an additional 2 minutes.

7. Remove the skillet from the heat, and stir in butter to thicken the sauce. Serve garnished with chopped fresh parsley.

PREP TIME: 40 MINUTES • BAKE TIME: 20 MINUTES

CHICKEN CORDON BLEU

MAKES 4 DINNER PORTIONS

Our Chicken Cordon Bleu delivers a winning golden brown, crisp exterior and gooey, pinwheeled interior without the guilt. Instead of using extra oil for pan-frying, we bake our bread crumb-coated chicken bundles on a baking sheet sprayed with cooking spray at a high temperature.

100 CALORIE COUNT =

¼ **CHICKEN BREAST + 2 TEASPOONS SAUCE**

Recommended Serving:
DINNER – 400 Calories = 1 Chicken Breast +
2 Teaspoons Sauce

Ingredients:

Nonstick cooking spray

4 (6-ounce) boneless, skinless chicken breasts

Salt and pepper

⅛ pound (2 ounces) thinly sliced lean deli ham

4 slices Swiss cheese

1 large egg

1 tablespoon water

1 cup Italian bread crumbs

¼ cup 2% milk

2 tablespoons prepared yellow mustard

½ teaspoon honey

¼ teaspoon dried thyme

Directions:

1. Preheat the oven to 400°F, and generously spray a sheet pan with nonstick cooking spray.

2. Place the chicken breasts between 2 sheets of plastic wrap, and use a meat mallet or rolling pin to pound each chicken breast to about ⅓ inch thick. Lightly season both sides of the pounded chicken with salt and pepper.

3. Place ¼ of the ham and 1 slice of the Swiss cheese over the top of each pounded chicken breast. Roll the chicken, ham, and cheese up into 4 tight pinwheels. Tuck the sides of each chicken breast underneath the bulk of the pinwheel, and secure with toothpicks to retain this shape.

4. In a wide bowl, whisk the egg and water. Place the bread crumbs in a second wide bowl.

5. Roll each stuffed chicken breast in the egg mixture and then the bread crumbs, coating with bread crumbs on all sides. Place on the prepared sheet pan, seam-side down.

6. Bake for 20 minutes, or until the breading is lightly browned and slicing into the top of a stuffed chicken breast reveals no pink.

7. Meanwhile, prepare the honey mustard sauce by whisking the milk, mustard, honey, and thyme in a small sauce pot over medium-low heat to warm through. Let the chicken breasts rest for 7 minutes before removing the toothpicks, slicing, and serving drizzled with the honey mustard sauce. Slice each breast into 8 pieces.

PREP TIME: 25 MINUTES • COOK TIME: 10 MINUTES

CHICKEN & VEGETABLE STIR-FRY

MAKES 4 DINNER PORTIONS

Mona's Family Favorites: This is my go-to weekday dinner and it takes only 25 minutes to prepare! My stir-fry is packed with "fresh from the farm" chicken, broccoli, peppers, and carrots (not to mention that it can be on your table in the amount of time spent waiting for takeout). For a full meal, serve over steamed white rice (100 calories per ½ cup) or, my preference, whole-grain brown rice (110 calories per ½ cup).

100 **CALORIE COUNT =**

$\frac{2}{3}$ **CUP**

100 Calories   ⅔ Cup

Recommended Serving:
DINNER – 300 Calories = 2 Cups

Ingredients:

1 pound boneless, skinless chicken breasts

2 tablespoons cornstarch, divided

1 tablespoon sesame oil

1 yellow onion, chopped

1 red bell pepper, sliced

1 cup thinly sliced carrots

1 teaspoon minced garlic

16 ounces frozen broccoli florets, thawed

3 tablespoons soy sauce (can use reduced-sodium)

2 teaspoons honey

¼ teaspoon ground ginger

¾ cup chicken broth

Directions:

1. Cut the chicken breasts into ¾-inch chunks, and then toss in 1 tablespoon of the cornstarch to lightly coat on all sides.

2. Heat the sesame oil in a large skillet or wok over high heat. Add the coated chicken to the skillet, and sauté for 3 minutes, or until it begins to brown.

3. Add the onion, bell pepper, carrots, and garlic to the skillet, and sauté for 3 minutes.

4. Add the broccoli florets, and reduce the heat to medium.

5. Whisk the soy sauce, honey, ginger, and the remaining 1 tablespoon of cornstarch into the chicken broth, and then stir into the skillet, stirring until the sauce begins to simmer and thicken.

6. Sauté for an additional 3 minutes, or until the sauce is thick and the carrots are tender.

HELPFUL TIP:

Chopped fresh broccoli can be used in place of the frozen broccoli florets, but it should be boiled or steamed for 4 minutes, just until crisp-tender, before adding to the stir-fry.

PREP TIME: 15 MINUTES • BAKE TIME: 3 HOURS

BONELESS BBQ RIBS

MAKES 4 DINNER PORTIONS

Bob's Farm to Table: Most pork ribs are riddled with fat, however boneless "country- style ribs" are cut from the pork loin, making them a far leaner, healthier option. We cook them low and slow, first coated with a spice rub and covered, and finally smeared with barbecue sauce and uncovered to caramelize. These sticky, sweet ribs "melt in your mouth" every time, just the way mom used to make them for Saturday night dinners on the farm!

100 CALORIE COUNT =

1½ OUNCES RIBS WITH SAUCE

Recommended Serving:
DINNER – 400 Calories = 6 Ounces Ribs

Ingredients:

2 pounds boneless loin country-style ribs

1 tablespoon olive oil

1 tablespoon lemon juice

2 teaspoons paprika

½ teaspoon onion powder

¼ teaspoon garlic powder

¼ teaspoon salt

¼ teaspoon pepper

1 batch Blue Ribbon Barbecue Sauce (see page 248)

Directions:

1. Preheat the oven to 250°F.

2. In a large mixing bowl, use your hands to toss ribs in the olive oil, lemon juice, paprika, onion powder, garlic powder, salt, and pepper, rubbing the oil and spices into the meat.

3. Transfer the rubbed ribs to a sheet pan, cover with aluminum foil, and bake for 2 hours.

4. Drain the pan of all liquid, and coat the ribs with the Blue Ribbon Barbecue Sauce. Return to the oven, and bake, uncovered, for 1 additional hour before serving.

HELPFUL TIP:

The nutritional information in this recipe was calculated for country-style ribs cut from the pork loin, not the shoulder. The pork loin variety is the most popular and easiest to find, though some stores will sell both varieties.

PREP TIME: 20 MINUTES • COOK TIME: 8½ HOURS

PULLED PORK

MAKES 16 SLIDER PORTIONS OR 8 SANDWICH PORTIONS

Bob's Farm to Table: Our Pulled Pork is made using lean pork tenderloin rather than the high-calorie pork shoulder or butt roasts used in most other recipes. We found that a gentle, lengthy cook in a slow cooker made the already tender tenderloin fall right apart, just like a barbecued fattier cut of meat would. Once the meat is pulled and tossed with sauce, you'd be hard-pressed to ever tell the difference. Serve as is over rice, or on slider or sandwich buns.

Recommended Serving:
SLIDER – 100 Calories = ⅓ Cup
LUNCH (SANDWICH) – 200 Calories = ⅔ Cup

Ingredients:

1 tablespoon butter

1 large yellow onion, diced

2 teaspoons minced garlic

1 teaspoon paprika

2 pounds pork tenderloin

Salt and pepper

1 cup beef broth

1 batch Blue Ribbon Barbecue Sauce (see page 248)

Directions:

1. Place the butter in a large skillet over medium-high heat, and cook until melted.

2. Add the onion, garlic, and paprika to the skillet and sauté for 3–4 minutes, just until the onions begin to cook down. Transfer the cooked onions to a slow cooker.

3. Lightly season the pork tenderloin with salt and pepper, and place in the skillet, browning on all sides before transferring to the slow cooker.

4. Pour the beef broth into the slow cooker, set the cooker to low, cover, and let cook for 8 hours.

5. Drain the liquid from the slow cooker, and use 2 forks to shred the pork tenderloin. When you pour the liquid from the slow cooker, it is best to use a mesh strainer, saving any bits of meat and onion to add back to the pork.

6. Fold the Blue Ribbon Barbecue Sauce into the shredded pork, set the slow cooker to high, and cook for 30 additional minutes before serving.

HELPFUL TIP:

When you drain the liquid from the slow cooker, it is best to use a mesh strainer to remove the most liquid while saving any bits of meat and onion to add back to the pork.

PREP TIME: 20 MINUTES • COOK TIME: 15 MINUTES

PORK CHOPS WITH APPLES & ONIONS

MAKES 4 DINNER PORTIONS

Apples are a pork chop's best friend, and everybody knows it. Though most people have served pork chops with applesauce at some point, large, tender slices of sautéed apple are an even better addition. Caramelized onions and seasonings bring savory depth to the dish, combining with the apples to make a warm slaw you serve piled right over each pork chop. Home cooking at its finest!

Recommended Serving:
DINNER – 400 Calories = 1 Pork Chop

Ingredients:

1 tablespoon olive oil

1½ pounds, 4–6 ounce pork loin chops

Salt and pepper

½ teaspoon thyme

1 large yellow onion, thinly sliced

2 apples, cored and thinly sliced (see tip)

2 tablespoons butter, divided

⅓ cup chicken stock

1 tablespoon light brown sugar

2 teaspoons cider vinegar

¼ teaspoon ground mustard

⅛ teaspoon ground allspice

2 tablespoons chopped fresh sage

Directions:

1 Add the olive oil to a large skillet over medium-high heat, and heat until the oil thins and coats the skillet.

2 Generously season both sides of the pork chops with the salt, pepper, and thyme.

3 Place the seasoned chops into the skillet, and cook for 3–4 minutes on each side, until browned, and slicing into the thickest chop reveals no pink. Remove from skillet, and cover with aluminum foil.

4 Reduce heat to medium, and add the onion, apples, and 1 tablespoon of butter to the skillet. Sauté for 5 minutes, or until onions are lightly caramelized.

5 Deglaze the skillet with the chicken stock, scraping any browned pork and onions from the bottom. Once deglazed, add the brown sugar, cider vinegar, mustard, and allspice. Sauté for an additional 4–5 minutes, or until apples are tender.

6 Remove the skillet from heat, and stir in chopped sage and the remaining 1 tablespoon of butter. Return the pork chops to the skillet, and cover with the apples and onions before serving.

HELPFUL TIP:

It is not necessary to peel the apples in this recipe. Not only does the final dish look better with the peel on, but there are tons of nutrients contained within that peel!

PREP TIME: 15 MINUTES • COOK TIME: 20 MINUTES

PORK TENDERLOIN WITH DIJON GRAVY

MAKES 4 DINNER PORTIONS

Pork tenderloin is not only the most tender cut of pork, but it is also the leanest. Its mild flavor and lack of fat mean that you need to pair it with a powerhouse of a sauce, and that is exactly what you'll find here. With only five ingredients, the Dijon sauce may seem simple, but it packs a punch of flavor and a little bit of heat as well.

100 CALORIE COUNT =

$\frac{1}{8}$ **PORK TENDERLOIN PLUS**
$1\frac{1}{2}$ **TABLESPOONS GRAVY**

Recommended Serving:
DINNER – 200 Calories = 2 Slices + 3 Tablespoons Gravy

Ingredients:

2 teaspoons olive oil

1 (16-ounce) pork tenderloin

½ teaspoon dried rosemary

¼ teaspoon salt

¼ teaspoon pepper

½ cup chicken stock

2 tablespoons Dijon mustard

1 teaspoon minced garlic

¼ teaspoon dried thyme

2 tablespoons butter

Directions:

1. Preheat oven to 450°F. Heat oil in a large skillet over high heat.

2. Season all sides of the pork tenderloin with rosemary, salt, and pepper, and add to the hot skillet, browning on all sides.

3. Transfer pork to a sheet pan, and bake for 12–15 minutes, or until a meat thermometer registers 145°F. Cover with aluminum foil, and let rest for 10 minutes before slicing thin.

4. Meanwhile, return the skillet you browned the pork in to the heat, and add the chicken stock to deglaze, scraping any browned bits from the bottom of the pan.

5. Add the Dijon mustard, garlic, and thyme to the skillet, and let the sauce reduce by about ⅓.

6. Remove sauce from heat, and stir in butter until slightly thickened.

7. Slice the pork tenderloin into 8-100 calorie slices. Serve each portion of the sliced pork drizzled with 1½ tablespoons of the sauce.

HELPFUL TIP:

Whole-grain (sometimes labeled "coarse" or "deli") mustard goes incredibly well in place of the Dijon in this sauce. It has a bit less spice than the Dijon if you want to keep things mild.

CHILL TIME: 1 HOUR • COOK TIME: 10 MINUTES

GRILLED GREEK PORK CHOPS

MAKES 4 DINNER PORTIONS

Bob's Farm to Table: Inspired by the traditional pork souvlaki found in Greek diners, we marinate lean boneless pork chops in a medley of Mediterranean seasonings. We love the smoky char that grilling lends to these chops, but they can also be pan-fried over high heat in the same amount of time. Top the chops with a dollop of Tzatziki Sauce (see page 247) for a tangy, creamy finish.

$\frac{1}{2}$ **PORK CHOP**

Recommended Serving:
DINNER – 200 Calories = 1 Pork Chop

Ingredients:

4 (4-ounce) boneless, center-cut pork loin chops

1 tablespoon olive oil

1 tablespoon lemon juice

½ teaspoon lemon zest

1½ teaspoons dried oregano

1½ teaspoons minced garlic

¼ teaspoon onion powder

¼ teaspoon salt

¼ teaspoon pepper

Directions:

1. Add pork chops and all the remaining ingredients to a large food storage bag or mixing bowl, and toss to thoroughly coat chops. Marinate for 1 hour in the refrigerator.

2. Preheat a grill or grill pan to high heat.

3. Shake excess marinade from chops, and grill for 4–5 minutes on each side, just until the internal temperature reaches 145°F, or slicing into the thickest chop reveals meat that is opaque with juices that run clear.

4. Let rest for 5 minutes before serving topped with Tzatziki Sauce (page 247), if desired.

HELPFUL TIP:

Though the usual rule of thumb is that you can leave meat in a marinade overnight and get even better results, that is not recommended with a marinade with this much acid (from lemon juice). An hour or two is all you need; after that, the lemon juice will begin to cook the outside of the pork.

PREP TIME: 25 MINUTES • BAKE TIME: 2½ HOURS

POT ROAST

MAKES 6 DINNER PORTIONS

Anson's American Treasures: The best Pot Roast that I've ever eaten was years ago at a small restaurant in Albany, New York, at the end of a grueling concert tour. After all that time away from home, you can really use some comfort, and there isn't any meal more comforting than Pot Roast. This restaurant's Pot Roast was just like Grandma's, only somehow better. When I asked the waitress the secret, she said they added vinegar to the broth to help tenderize the meat as it cooks. Remembering that little tip after all these years ought to show you just how good it was!

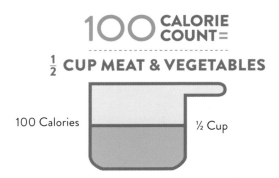

100 CALORIE COUNT =

½ **CUP MEAT & VEGETABLES**

100 Calories   ½ Cup

Recommended Serving:
DINNER – 400 Calories = 2 Cups Meat & Vegetables

Ingredients:

1½ tablespoons canola oil

3 pounds beef chuck roast, trimmed of excess fat

Salt and pepper

2 cups chopped onions

1 tablespoon minced garlic

3 cups beef broth

1 tablespoon balsamic vinegar

2 teaspoons Worcestershire sauce

2 bay leaves

½ teaspoon dried thyme

½ teaspoon dried rosemary

2 pounds Yukon Gold potatoes, chopped in large chunks

2 cups baby carrots

2 cups large chopped celery

Directions:

1. Preheat the oven to 350°F. Heat the oil in a Dutch oven over medium-high heat.

2. Generously season the chuck roast with the salt and pepper. Place the roast in the Dutch oven, and brown on all sides. Remove, and set aside.

3. Add the onion and garlic to the Dutch oven, and sauté until onions are translucent, about 5 minutes.

4. Place the browned chuck roast over the onions in the Dutch oven.

5. Add the beef broth, balsamic vinegar, Worcestershire sauce, bay leaves, thyme, rosemary, and ½ teaspoon each of salt and pepper to the Dutch oven, and bring to a boil. Remove from heat.

6. Cover the Dutch oven, and bake for 1½ hours.

7. Add the potatoes, carrots, and celery to the Dutch oven, cover, and bake for 1 additional hour. Break meat into chunks before serving alongside vegetables drizzled in juices from the pan.

HELPFUL TIP:

For thicker gravy, use a ladle to transfer 2 cups of the cooking liquid to a saucepan over medium-high heat. Whisk 2 tablespoons of cornstarch into another ladle of gravy and then whisk into the pan. Bring to a simmer, and cook until thickened.

PREP TIME: 30 MINUTES • COOK TIME: 20 MINUTES

CHICKEN-FRIED STEAK

MAKES 4 LUNCH OR DINNER PORTIONS

Here's an easy culinary trick: Soak the steaks in a mixture of acidic buttermilk and egg whites to maximize tenderness. Plus, we found that a mere tablespoon of oil was enough to sizzle up a perfectly crisp, golden brown Chicken-Fried Steak. Delicious, with less fat and fewer calories! Can't beat that!

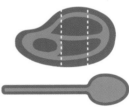

100 CALORIE COUNT =

$\frac{1}{3}$ **STEAK WITH 1 TABLESPOON GRAVY**

Recommended Serving:
LUNCH OR DINNER – 300 Calories =
1 Steak and 3 Tablespoons Gravy

Ingredients:

⅓ cup low-fat buttermilk

2 large egg whites

4 (4-ounce) cubed steaks

1 cup all-purpose flour

¾ teaspoon baking powder

¾ teaspoon salt

¾ teaspoon pepper

½ teaspoon onion powder

½ teaspoon garlic powder

1 tablespoon canola oil

Gravy:

2 tablespoons all-purpose flour

½ cup 2% milk

¼ cup low-fat buttermilk

¼ teaspoon salt

½ teaspoon cracked black pepper

Directions:

1. In a mixing bowl, whisk together the buttermilk and egg whites. Add the cubed steaks, cover, and refrigerate for 30 minutes.

2. In a wide bowl, combine the flour, baking powder, salt, pepper, onion powder, and garlic powder.

3. Flip the marinated steaks in the buttermilk mixture to ensure that they are well coated, and then press into the flour mixture, breading them on both sides.

4. Heat the canola oil in a skillet over medium-high heat until nearly smoking hot.

5. Place the breaded steaks into the pan, and fry for 5–7 minutes, or until golden brown on the bottom. Flip and cook for an additional 5 minutes, or until browned on both sides. Transfer to a plate, and cover with aluminum foil.

6. Create the gravy by stirring the 2 tablespoons of flour into any drippings in the skillet. Cook for 2 minutes, stirring constantly.

7. Whisk the milk, buttermilk, salt, and pepper into the skillet and bring to a boil, whisking constantly. Let simmer for 2 minutes before serving over the steaks.

HELPFUL TIP:

Marinating the steaks for 30 minutes can be skipped, though this time allows the buttermilk to tenderize the meat.

PREP TIME: 45 MINUTES • BAKE TIME: 30 MINUTES

STUFFED FLANK STEAK

MAKES 4 DINNER PORTIONS

This show-stopping roast is the perfect protein for a special-occasion meal at home. We fill tender flank steak with a hearty mixture of spinach, bread crumbs, and Parmesan cheese and roll it up, producing an impressive, flavor-packed spiral when sliced. This is a dinner your guests or family won't soon forget, and they don't need to know how easy it is!

100 CALORIE COUNT=

$\frac{1}{2}$-INCH SLICE

Recommended Serving:
DINNER –400 Calories = 4 Slices

Ingredients:

1 ½ pounds flank steak, trimmed of fat

Salt and pepper

Paprika

Stuffing:

10 ounces frozen chopped spinach, thawed

¼ cup grated Parmesan cheese

1 large egg white, beaten

2 tablespoons Italian bread crumbs

2 tablespoons diced pimentos

2 teaspoons minced garlic

½ teaspoon Italian seasoning

¼ teaspoon onion powder

¼ teaspoon salt

¼ teaspoon pepper

1 tablespoon olive oil

Directions:

1. Preheat the oven to 375°F.

2. With your free hand over the top of the flank steak, carefully slice horizontally through the middle of the steak, leaving ⅓ inch of one end intact (so you can unfold the two halves of the steak as you would open a book). If it does not lay perfectly flat along the seam, use a meat mallet to pound the steak into a flat rectangle.

3. Lightly season both sides of the steak with the salt, pepper, and paprika.

4. Squeeze any excess liquid from the thawed spinach. Combine all the stuffing ingredients, except the olive oil, to create the filling.

5. Spread the filling evenly across the surface of the steak, leaving 1 inch clean on the top and bottom (the shorter sides) of the rectangle. Starting on the bottom, tightly roll the steak and filling into a large pinwheel. Tie the stuffed steak with baker's twine in at least 4 places to hold it together.

6. Add the olive oil to a large skillet over high heat. Place the stuffed steak into the skillet, seam-side down first, and brown on all sides.

7. Transfer the browned steak to the oven, and bake for 30 minutes, or until a meat thermometer inserted into the thickest part registers 135°F. Let rest for at least 5 minutes before slicing into 16- ½ inch slices.

PREP TIME: 20 MINUTES • COOK TIME: 20 MINUTES

STEAK TIPS

MAKES 4 LUNCH OR DINNER PORTIONS

Inspired by slow-cooked Beef Burgundy, our quick sauté delivers tender chunks of top sirloin steak in a rich, mushroom-studded red wine sauce. Though the alcohol in the wine cooks out, see the tip below to prepare this without any wine at all. Serve over egg noodles or steamed white rice (100 calories per ½ cup).

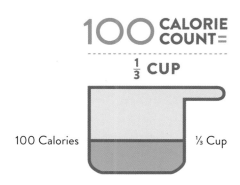

100 **CALORIE COUNT =**

⅓ **CUP**

100 Calories   ⅓ Cup

Recommended Serving:
DINNER – 300 Calories = 1 Cup

Ingredients:

1¼ pounds top sirloin steak

Salt and pepper

2 teaspoons olive oil

1½ tablespoons butter, divided

8 ounces sliced baby bella mushrooms

¾ cup diced red onion

2 teaspoons minced garlic

3 tablespoons all-purpose flour

1¼ cups beef broth

½ cup dry red wine (see tip)

4 sprigs fresh thyme

2 tablespoons chopped fresh parsley

Directions:

1. Trim any fat from the sirloin steak, and then cut steak into ¾-inch chunks. Season generously with salt and pepper.

2. Add the olive oil to a large skillet over high heat, and heat until the oil thins and coats the skillet.

3. Place the seasoned steak in the skillet, and sauté for 5 minutes, browning on all sides. Transfer the browned steak to a plate, and cover with aluminum foil.

4. Reduce heat to medium, and add ½ tablespoon of the butter to the skillet. Add the mushrooms, onion, and garlic, and sauté for 5 minutes, or until the mushrooms have begun to brown.

5. Stir the flour into the skillet, coating the mushrooms and onions, and sauté for 1 minute.

6. Stir the beef broth, red wine, and fresh thyme into the skillet, and raise heat to medium-high. Bring to a simmer, and let cook for 3–4 minutes, or until the sauce has thickened.

7. Remove the skillet from the heat, and stir in the cooked steak, chopped parsley, and remaining 1 tablespoon of butter. Remove the thyme sprigs, and season the sauce with salt and pepper to taste before serving.

HELPFUL TIP:

An additional ½ cup of beef broth, 2 teaspoons of balsamic vinegar, and 1 teaspoon of sugar can be used in place of the red wine.

PREP TIME: 20 MINUTES • COOK TIME: 6 MINUTES

SHRIMP SCAMPI

MAKES 6 LUNCH PORTIONS OR 4 DINNER PORTIONS

Shrimp Scampi has become one of America's most popular seafood restaurant dishes, though most people have no idea just how quick and easy it is to prepare at home. We sauté an entire julienned zucchini with the shrimp to turn this into a stand-alone dish you don't even need to serve over pasta.

3 SHRIMP WITH SAUCE

Recommended Serving:
LUNCH – 200 Calories = 6 Shrimp
DINNER – 300 Calories = 9 Shrimp

Ingredients:

1 tablespoon olive oil

2 ½ tablespoons butter

2 tablespoons minced garlic

1 ½ pounds extra large raw shrimp, peeled and deveined

1 large zucchini, thinly julienned

⅓ cup dry white wine (see tip)

Juice of 1 fresh lemon

2 tablespoons chopped fresh parsley

Salt and pepper

Directions:

1 Heat oil, butter, and garlic in a large sauté pan over medium-high heat, and bring up to a sizzle.

2 Add the shrimp and julienned zucchini to the pan, and sauté for 1 minute, tossing to cook evenly.

3 Add the white wine and lemon juice, bring to a simmer, and continue sautéing for 3 minutes, or until shrimp are pink on the outside and opaque on the inside.

4 Remove from heat, toss with chopped fresh parsley, and season with salt and pepper to taste.

HELPFUL TIP:

Though white wine is traditional in a scampi sauce, you can substitute ¼ cup water and a tiny pinch of sugar, if desired.

PREP TIME: 30 MINUTES • COOK TIME: 25 MINUTES

SHRIMP & GRITS

MAKES 4 DINNER PORTIONS

Classic Shrimp and Grits is an out-of-this-world meal for any time of day. Creamy cheese grits topped with a fresh tomato sauce studded with tender, flavor-packed shrimp and vegetables...what's not to love? "Yellow grits" (not "quick cooking" or "instant") are most often used in this dish and can usually be found in the organic grains section. That being said, you can also prepare this with the white "old-fashioned" grits sold in the breakfast aisle.

100 CALORIE COUNT =

¼ **CUP GRITS + 2 SHRIMP**

100 Calories   ¼ Cup + 2 Shrimp

Recommended Serving:
DINNER – 400 Calories = 1 Cup + 8 Shrimp

Ingredients:

4 cups water

½ teaspoon salt, divided

½ teaspoon pepper, divided

1 cup stone-ground grits

1 tablespoon olive oil

1¼ pounds extra large raw shrimp, peeled and deveined

1 cup diced yellow onion

½ cup diced green bell pepper

2 teaspoons minced garlic

1 large tomato, diced

1 tablespoon tomato paste

2 teaspoons lemon juice

½ teaspoon dried thyme

2 tablespoons butter

¼ cup shredded sharp Cheddar cheese

2 tablespoons chopped fresh parsley

Directions:

1 In a sauce pot over high heat, bring the 4 cups of water, ¼ teaspoon of the salt, and ¼ teaspoon of the pepper to a boil. Add the grits, cover, and reduce heat to low. Let cook for 20–25 minutes, or until all water is absorbed.

2 Meanwhile, start preparing the shrimp by placing the olive oil in a large skillet over medium-high heat.

3 Add the shrimp, onion, bell pepper, and garlic to the skillet, and sauté for 2 minutes.

4 Stir the diced tomato, tomato paste, lemon juice, thyme, the remaining ¼ teaspoon salt, and the remaining ¼ teaspoon pepper into the shrimp, and continue sautéing for 3 minutes, or until the shrimp are pink on the outside and opaque on the inside.

5 Once the grits have finished cooking, remove from heat, and stir in the butter and Cheddar cheese.

6 Serve the cheese grits topped with the shrimp and vegetables, sprinkled with the chopped fresh parsley.

HELPFUL TIP:

For a little heat, add a pinch of crushed red pepper flakes or a splash of hot sauce in step 4.

PREP TIME: 10 MINUTES • COOK TIME: 10 MINUTES

BLACKENED COD

MAKES 4 LUNCH OR DINNER PORTIONS

Why turn to butter or mayonnaise-based sauces to flavor cooked fish when you can infuse big flavor without the guilt? We "blacken" our fish with a quick coating of spice rack staples and pan-sear until toasty and cooked through.

100 CALORIE COUNT=
½ FILLET

Recommended Serving:
LUNCH OR DINNER – 200 Calories = 1 Fillet

Ingredients:

½ teaspoon paprika

½ teaspoon pepper

¼ teaspoon thyme

¼ teaspoon ground cayenne pepper

¼ teaspoon garlic powder

¼ teaspoon onion powder

¼ teaspoon salt

4 (6-ounce) cod fillets

1 tablespoon olive oil

1 tablespoon butter

Directions:

1. In a small bowl, combine the paprika, pepper, thyme, cayenne pepper, garlic powder, onion powder, and salt to create a blackening spice.

2. Generously coat both sides of each cod fillet with the blackening spice, pressing the spices into the fish.

3. Heat the oil and butter in a large skillet over medium-high heat, until butter is almost sizzling.

4. Place the seasoned cod into the skillet, and cook for 4 minutes on each side, or until the fish is easily flaked with a fork. Serve immediately, garnished with fresh lemon, if desired.

HELPFUL TIP:

This combination of spices cooked at a high heat will create a lot of smoke (this is completely normal), so be sure to turn your overhead exhaust fan on as you cook.

PREP TIME: 15 MINUTES • BAKE TIME: 12 MINUTES

PARMESAN-CRUSTED TILAPIA

MAKES 4 LUNCH OR DINNER PORTIONS

These tilapia fillets have a hint of lemon and a savory crust of Parmesan bread crumbs that bakes up crispy without the need to fry the fish in oil. It makes for an impressive entrée that you can prepare in only minutes using just a handful of pantry staples. Though the nutritional information was calculated for tilapia, this technique will work well with any mild white fish. The calorie count should also be comparable.

100 **CALORIE COUNT =**

½ **FILLET**

Recommended Serving:
LUNCH OR DINNER – 200 Calories = 1 Fillet

Ingredients:

4 (4-ounce) tilapia fillets

1 tablespoon olive oil

2 teaspoons lemon juice

⅓ cup grated Parmesan cheese

3 tablespoons Italian bread crumbs

1 tablespoon parsley flakes

¼ teaspoon garlic powder

¼ teaspoon salt

¼ teaspoon pepper

Directions:

1. Preheat the oven to 400°F, and line a sheet pan with aluminum foil.

2. In a mixing bowl, toss the tilapia fillets with the olive oil and lemon juice to coat.

3. In a separate bowl, combine all the remaining ingredients to create a breading mixture.

4. Press the top of each coated tilapia fillet into the breading mixture to fully crust the fish on one side, and then place on the prepared sheet pan, crust-side up.

5. Bake for 10–12 minutes, or until the crust is golden brown and the fish easily flakes with a fork.

HELPFUL TIP:

Any additional breading mixture that is left over after crusting the fish can be sprinkled over the top of the fish before baking for an even thicker crust.

PREP TIME: 15 MINUTES • COOK TIME: 15 MINUTES

BAKED FISH PACKETS WITH DILL

MAKES 4 LUNCH OR DINNER PORTIONS

Cooking fish in sealed parchment paper packets, or in papillote, not only makes for a beautiful presentation but also allows the fish to steam in its own juices instead of using extra butter or oil for sautéing. The fish stays incredibly moist, and its flavor can really shine!

100 CALORIE COUNT=

$\frac{1}{2}$ **FILLET**

Recommended Serving:
LUNCH OR DINNER – 200 Calories = 1 Fillet

Ingredients:

4 (4-ounce) tilapia fillets

Juice of ½ lemon

2 tablespoons butter, divided

2 teaspoons minced garlic, divided

Salt and pepper

4 sprigs fresh dill

Directions:

1. Preheat oven to 400°F, and lay out 4 large squares of parchment paper.

2. Place a tilapia fillet in the center of each square of paper, and then squeeze fresh lemon juice over the top.

3. Top each fillet with ½ tablespoon butter, and then sprinkle each with ½ teaspoon of minced garlic.

4. Lightly season each fillet with salt and pepper, and then top with a full sprig of dill.

5. Fold the sides of the paper up and over the fish, and then fold the edges over each other to fully seal. Place on a sheet pan, seam-side down.

6. Bake for 15 minutes, and let rest for 3 minutes before serving.

HELPFUL TIP:
You can also make this in aluminum foil rather than parchment paper. It is far easier to seal the packets this way.

PREP TIME: 5 MINUTES • BAKE TIME: 20 MINUTES

HONEY MUSTARD SALMON

MAKES 4 LUNCH OR DINNER PORTIONS

Mona's Family Favorites: This recipe is one of my weekday dinner secrets that I must share! The sweet and sour combination of honey, mustard, and dill produces an outstanding glaze for fresh salmon. And with only five minutes of prep time, you don't get any easier than this, at least not with results that taste this good! The glaze is also great on chicken breasts too!

100 CALORIE COUNT =

½ FILLET

Recommended Serving:
LUNCH OR DINNER – 200 Calories = 1 Fillet

Ingredients:

2 tablespoons Dijon mustard

2 tablespoons honey

Juice of 1 lemon

2 teaspoons chopped fresh dill

¼ teaspoon salt

¼ teaspoon pepper

4 (4-ounce) salmon fillets

Nonstick cooking spray

Directions:

1. In a large mixing bowl, stir together the Dijon mustard, honey, lemon juice, dill, salt, and pepper to create a glaze.

2. Place the salmon fillets in the glaze, and toss until evenly coated. Cover, and refrigerate for 30 minutes to marinate.

3. Preheat the oven to 400°F, and spray a sheet pan with nonstick cooking spray.

4. Place the marinated salmon fillets on the sheet pan, and drizzle any remaining glaze over top.

5. Bake for 15–20 minutes, just until the thickest fillet flakes with a fork.

HELPFUL TIP:

You can also use this exact same method and glaze recipe to prepare 4 (6-ounce) boneless, skinless chicken breasts by simply increasing the bake time to 20–25 minutes. Each chicken breast will contain 280 calories.

5 SIDE DISHES

PREP TIME: 10 MINUTES • COOK TIME: 10 MINUTES

CREAMED CORN

MAKES 5 SIDE DISH PORTIONS

We make our Creamed Corn from scratch using real ingredients by sautéing corn with butter and onions and then simmering it in a slightly sweetened, thickened milk. We like to add just a few drops of vanilla extract to the sauce to secretly enhance the flavor and the sweetness of the corn. You will taste a huge difference compared to what comes out of the can!

100 **CALORIE COUNT=**

½ **CUP**

100 Calories　　½ Cup

Recommended Serving:
SIDE DISH – 200 Calories = 1 Cup

Ingredients:

2 tablespoons butter

¼ cup minced yellow onion

20 ounces frozen corn kernels

2 tablespoons cornstarch

1½ cups 2% milk

2 tablespoons sugar

½ teaspoon salt

¼ teaspoon pepper

⅛ teaspoon vanilla extract

Directions:

1 Melt the butter in a medium sauce pot over medium-high heat. Add the minced onion, and sauté for 3 minutes, just until they are translucent.

2 Add the frozen corn, and sauté for 2 minutes, stirring constantly.

3 Whisk the cornstarch into the milk and then stir into the pot, stirring until the milk begins to thicken.

4 Reduce the heat to low, and stir the sugar, salt, pepper, and vanilla extract into the pot. Cover, and let cook for 3 minutes. Remove from the heat, and let cool for 2 minutes before serving.

PREP TIME: 20 MINUTES • COOK TIME: 10 MINUTES

GREEN BEANS ALMONDINE

MAKES 3 SIDE DISH PORTIONS

Green beans and almonds may seem like a simple combination, but we up the ante by slightly browning the beans in butter, olive oil, and seasonings in a skillet. This sauté develops flavor that you can't get from a steamed or boiled bean. Delicious!

100 **CALORIE COUNT=**

$\frac{1}{2}$ **CUP**

100 Calories   ½ Cup

Recommended Serving:
SIDE DISH – 200 Calories = 1 Cup

Ingredients:

1 pound green beans, ends snapped

1 tablespoon olive oil

1 tablespoon butter

1½ teaspoons minced garlic

1 teaspoon lemon juice

¼ teaspoon onion powder

¼ teaspoon salt

¼ teaspoon pepper

⅓ cup slivered almonds, toasted (see tip)

Directions:

1. Place the green beans in a large pot of boiling water, and boil until crisp-tender, no more than 3 minutes. Drain and rinse under cold water.

2. Heat the oil and butter in a large skillet over medium-high heat, until the butter has melted.

3. Add the boiled green beans, garlic, lemon juice, onion powder, salt, and pepper to the skillet, and sauté for 4–5 minutes, or until some of the green beans get a light browning.

4. Remove the skillet from the heat, and stir in the toasted almonds before serving.

HELPFUL TIP:

The easiest way to toast slivered almonds is in a heavy skillet over medium heat. Simply shake them around the pan as they cook, until the almonds are light brown and fragrant, about 5 minutes.

PREP TIME: 10 MINUTES • CHILL TIME: 1 HOUR

COLESLAW

MAKES 4 SIDE DISH PORTIONS

Our creamy Coleslaw strikes the perfect balance of tangy and sweet, and thanks to the convenience of pre-shredded cabbage, you can whip it up in a matter of minutes. Our healthy swap of yogurt and a little milk to supplement the mayonnaise as the creamy base lets you eat more of what you love!

100 CALORIE COUNT =

$\frac{2}{3}$ CUP

100 Calories   ⅔ Cup

Recommended Serving:
SIDE DISH – 100 Calories = ⅔ Cup

Ingredients:

1 (16-ounce) bag shredded coleslaw cabbage (with carrots)

¼ cup sliced green onions

¼ cup plain nonfat Greek yogurt

2 tablespoons mayonnaise

1½ tablespoons cider vinegar

1 tablespoon 2% milk

1 tablespoon sugar

¼ teaspoon celery salt

¼ teaspoon pepper

Directions:

1 Place the shredded coleslaw mix and green onions in a large mixing bowl or food storage container.

2 In a small mixing bowl, whisk together all the remaining ingredients to create the dressing.

3 Fold the dressing into the cabbage mixture, cover, and chill for at least 1 hour before serving.

HELPFUL TIP:

You can also make this from one small head of green cabbage, shredded fresh, and add ½ cup of julienned carrots for extra crunch.

PREP TIME: 15 MINUTES • BAKE TIME: 20 MINUTES

ROASTED BRUSSELS SPROUTS

MAKES 4 SIDE DISH PORTIONS

In this recipe, Brussels sprouts gain a sweet, almost nutty flavor when roasted in a high-temperature oven. First, tossing them with balsamic vinegar and a touch of brown sugar enhances their flavor and helps the sprouts caramelize even more. The sprouts will continue to crisp as they cook so roast until very deep brown.

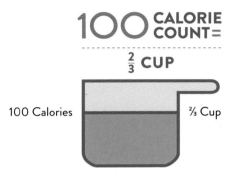

100 CALORIE COUNT =

⅔ CUP

100 Calories   ⅔ Cup

Recommended Serving:
SIDE DISH – 100 Calories = ⅔ Cup

Ingredients:

1 pound Brussels sprouts, trimmed and halved

1½ tablespoons olive oil

1 teaspoon minced garlic

1 teaspoon balsamic vinegar

1 teaspoon light brown sugar

¼ teaspoon salt

¼ teaspoon pepper

Directions:

1 Preheat the oven to 425°F.

2 In a large mixing bowl, toss Brussels sprouts in all of the remaining ingredients, until well coated.

3 Spread the coated Brussels sprouts on a sheet pan in a single layer, and bake for 20 minutes, stirring halfway through. Sprouts are done when well caramelized and fork-tender.

HELPFUL TIP:

Brussels sprouts can vary in size quite a bit. If you have a few sprouts that are larger than the others, to cut those into quarters to ensure that they cook through as quickly as the smaller, halved sprouts.

PREP TIME: 10 MINUTES • COOK TIME: 10 MINUTES

LEMON & GARLIC BROCCOLI SAUTÉ

MAKES 4 SIDE DISH PORTIONS

Whether you prepare this ultra-simple side dish from fresh or frozen broccoli (directions are provided for either choice), you are sure to produce a nutritious addition to any meal. While you'll get a good amount of vitamin C from the lemon in this recipe, surprisingly, broccoli actually contains more vitamin C than citrus!

100 **CALORIE COUNT=**

⅔ **CUP**

100 Calories — ⅔ Cup

Recommended Serving:
SIDE DISH – 100 Calories = ⅔ Cup

Ingredients:

16 ounces broccoli florets, fresh or frozen

2 tablespoons butter

2 teaspoons minced garlic

Juice of ½ lemon

2 teaspoons lemon zest

1 teaspoon light brown sugar

¼ teaspoon salt

¼ teaspoon pepper

2 tablespoons diced pimentos

Directions:

1. If using fresh broccoli florets, place a pot of water over high heat, and bring to a boil.

2. Boil the fresh broccoli for 4 minutes. Drain and rinse under cold water. If using frozen broccoli florets, cover, and microwave for 1–2 minutes, just until thawed.

3. Melt the butter in a large skillet over medium-high heat. Add the prepared broccoli florets, minced garlic, lemon juice, lemon zest, brown sugar, salt, and pepper, and sauté for 5 minutes, stirring only occasionally to let the broccoli brown slightly.

4. Remove from heat and stir in diced pimentos before serving.

HELPFUL TIP:

Many stores sell fresh broccoli florets that you can microwave to steam right in the bag, allowing you to skip straight to step 3. Microwave for 90 seconds less than the package directions to ensure the broccoli doesn't overcook as you sauté.

PREP TIME: 15 MINUTES • COOK TIME: 5 MINUTES

SMASHED CAULIFLOWER

MAKES 4 SIDE DISH PORTIONS

Bob's Farm to Table: Move over mashed potatoes! Smashed cauliflower is a low-calorie and low-carbohydrate alternative that looks and tastes a whole lot like your standard mashed spud. Like potatoes, cauliflower loves to soak up the flavor of other ingredients, so the secret is to season the smash just as you would season your mash. Say that five times fast!

100 **CALORIE COUNT=**

¾ **CUP**

100 Calories   ¾ Cup

Recommended Serving:
SIDE DISH – 100 Calories = ¾ Cup

Ingredients:

24 ounces frozen cauliflower

2 tablespoons sour cream

2 tablespoons 2% milk

2 tablespoons grated Parmesan cheese

1 tablespoon butter, melted

1 teaspoon minced garlic

¼ teaspoon onion powder

¼ teaspoon salt

¼ teaspoon pepper

1 tablespoon chopped chives

Directions:

1. In a large microwave-safe bowl, cover, and microwave cauliflower for 3 minutes, just until warmed throughout.

2. Add the warmed cauliflower, sour cream, milk, Parmesan cheese, butter, garlic, onion powder, salt, and pepper to the bowl of a food processor, and process until almost entirely smooth.

3. Return to the microwave-safe bowl, cover, and microwave for 2 minutes, or until hot. Stir in the chopped chives, and serve.

HELPFUL TIP:

This can also be made with an average-sized head of fresh cauliflower, cut into florets and steamed until very tender, 8–10 minutes. Drain well, and pat dry with paper towels before proceeding to step 2 of the recipe.

PREP TIME: 20 MINUTES • BAKE TIME: 15 MINUTES

ASPARAGUS GRATIN

MAKES 6 SIDE DISH PORTIONS

We pair creamy, flavor-packed Gorgonzola and a dusting of crisp panko bread crumbs with asparagus for a refined, yet rich and satisfying gratin. Just a small reduction of the cheese and butter still gives you great flavor without the extra calories!

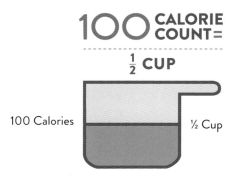

100 **CALORIE COUNT=**

$\frac{1}{2}$ **CUP**

100 Calories   ½ Cup

Recommended Serving:
SIDE DISH – 100 Calories = ½ Cup

Ingredients:

1½ pounds asparagus

1 tablespoon butter, melted

1 teaspoon minced garlic

¼ teaspoon salt

¼ teaspoon pepper

½ cup crumbled Gorgonzola cheese

¼ cup panko bread crumbs

Nonstick cooking spray

Paprika

Directions:

1. Preheat the oven to 400°F. Place a pot of water over high heat, and bring to a boil.

2. Trim 1 inch from the bottoms of the asparagus stalks, and discard. Cut each stalk of asparagus into 3 pieces, each 2–3 inches long.

3. Boil the asparagus for 2 minutes if pencil-thin or 3–4 minutes if any thicker. Drain, and transfer to a baking dish.

4. Add the butter, garlic, salt, and pepper to the baking dish, and toss the asparagus to fully coat.

5. Top the asparagus with the Gorgonzola cheese and then the panko bread crumbs. Lightly spray the bread crumbs with nonstick cooking spray to moisten, and then sprinkle a pinch of paprika over the top, for color.

6. Bake for 12–15 minutes, just until the bread crumbs begin to brown. Serve immediately.

HELPFUL TIP:

If you like your cooked asparagus to have more of a crisp snap to it, pencil-thin asparagus can be made into this gratin without preboiling.

PREP TIME: 20 MINUTES • COOK TIME: 15 MINUTES

GLAZED CARROTS

MAKES 6 SIDE DISH PORTIONS

Forget about sticky sweet glazes. These carrots are cooked with honey and brown sugar to coat them in a light glaze. Butter, lemon juice, and nutmeg help offset the sweetness, ensuring that these carrots will pair with any entrée.

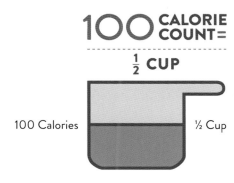

100 CALORIE COUNT =

½ CUP

100 Calories   ½ Cup

Recommended Serving:
SIDE DISH – 100 Calories = ½ Cup

Ingredients:

1 pound carrots, peeled and sliced into ¼-inch-thick discs

½ teaspoon salt, divided

2½ tablespoons butter

2 tablespoons light brown sugar

1 tablespoon honey

2 teaspoons lemon juice

⅛ teaspoon ground nutmeg

1 tablespoon chopped fresh parsley

Directions:

1. Place the carrots in a sauce pot over high heat, and cover with water. Add ¼ teaspoon of the salt. Bring to a boil, and reduce heat to medium. Simmer for 7–10 minutes, or until carrots are fork-tender. Drain well.

2. Add the butter, brown sugar, honey, lemon juice, nutmeg, and the remaining ¼ teaspoon salt to a sauté pan over medium heat, and cook, stirring constantly, until butter is melted and sugar has dissolved.

3. Add the carrots to the sauté pan and fold into the sauce. Continue cooking for 2–3 minutes, or until carrots are well coated and the glaze has thickened. Top with chopped parsley before serving.

HELPFUL TIP:

You can also use 1 pound of baby carrots in this recipe in place of sliced carrots. For thicker baby carrots, you may need to boil for 2–3 minutes longer in step 1 to ensure that they are fork-tender.

PREP TIME: 15 MINUTES • COOK TIME: 45 MINUTES

BROWN RICE PILAF

MAKES 5 SIDE DISH PORTIONS

Compared to its white counterpart, whole-grain brown rice is the more healthful choice because it's packed with hearty nutrients and extra fiber, which keeps you feeling full longer. It has an excellent and nutty flavor that we bring out by toasting the rice in butter and oil before gently simmering it into the chicken broth.

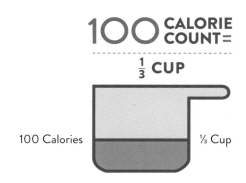

100 CALORIE COUNT =

$\frac{1}{3}$ **CUP**

100 Calories   ⅓ Cup

Recommended Serving:
SIDE DISH – 200 Calories = ⅔ Cup

Ingredients:

1 tablespoon butter

1 tablespoon olive oil

¾ cup diced carrot

½ cup diced yellow onion

1 ½ teaspoons minced garlic

1 cup long-grain brown rice

2 cups chicken broth

½ teaspoon thyme

¼ teaspoon salt

¼ teaspoon pepper

1 tablespoon chopped fresh parsley

Directions:

1 Heat the butter and oil in a sauce pot over medium-high heat, just until the butter is almost sizzling.

2 Add the carrot, onion, and garlic to the pot, and sauté for 3 minutes, or until the onions are translucent.

3 Add the rice to the pot, and sauté for an additional 2 minutes. Add the chicken broth to the rice mixture.

4 Stir the thyme, salt, and pepper into the rice and broth, and bring to a boil. Reduce heat to low, cover, and let for simmer 35–40 minutes, or until rice has absorbed all liquid.

5 Stir the chopped parsley into the rice, and fluff with a fork before serving.

HELPFUL TIP:

Brown rice is naturally more "toothsome" than white rice, which may lead you to believe the rice is slightly undercooked, but that is completely normal.

PREP TIME: 10 MINUTES • COOK TIME: 30 MINUTES

VEGETABLE FRIED RICE

MAKES 6 SIDE DISH PORTIONS

You can make authentic fried rice that rivals anything found in a cardboard takeout container with only a few ingredients. While we often like to cook with fresh vegetables, frozen peas and carrots mix is perfectly sized for an excellent quick and easy fried rice. With this recipe, the only thing missing is the chopsticks, and maybe a fortune cookie!

100 **CALORIE COUNT=**

⅓ **CUP**

100 Calories   ⅓ Cup

Recommended Serving:
SIDE DISH – 200 Calories = ⅔ Cups

Ingredients:

2 cups water

¼ teaspoon salt

1 cup long-grain white rice, rinsed

2 tablespoons sesame oil

½ cup diced yellow onion

1½ cups frozen peas and carrots

1 large egg, beaten

3 tablespoons soy sauce

⅓ cup sliced green onions

Directions:

1 In a medium sauce pot, bring the water and salt to a boil. Add the rice, cover, and reduce heat to low. Let simmer for 15–20 minutes, just until all the water has been absorbed. Remove from heat, and let cool for 5 minutes before fluffing with a fork.

2 Heat the sesame oil in a large skillet or wok over medium-high heat. Add the onion to the skillet, and sauté for 1 minute.

3 Add the cooked rice and frozen vegetables to the skillet, and toss with the oil and onions. Sauté for 2 minutes, stirring constantly.

4 Create a hole in the center of the rice to pour the beaten egg, allowing it to reach the surface of the skillet. Let cook for 1 minute before breaking up the cooked egg and stirring it into the rice.

5 Add the soy sauce and sliced green onions to the skillet, and sauté, stirring constantly, for another 2 minutes before serving.

HELPFUL TIP:

For even more flavor, add ¼ teaspoon of Chinese five-spice powder (sold in either the spice aisle or the Asian food section) to the hot oil when you add the onion in step 2.

PREP TIME: 15 MINUTES • BAKE TIME: 25 MINUTES

SAVORY SOUTHERN-STYLE CORNBREAD

MAKES 8 SIDE DISH PORTIONS

Some cornbreads are just as sweet, if not more sweet, than dessert. Real southern cornbread is far more savory. While we don't call for baking our cornbread in the traditional cast-iron skillet, our cornbread's deep corn flavor and tender crumb has all the other qualities of a fantastic, authentic southern cornbread. And we don't have to fret about seasoning our skillet!

100 **CALORIE COUNT =**

$\frac{1}{16}$ **CORNBREAD**

Recommended Serving:
SIDE DISH – 200 Calories = 2 Sections

Ingredients:

Nonstick cooking spray

1 cup yellow cornmeal

1 cup all-purpose flour

¼ cup sugar

1½ teaspoons baking powder

½ teaspoon baking soda

1 teaspoon salt

2 large eggs

1 cup buttermilk

3 tablespoons butter, melted

Directions:

1 Preheat the oven to 400°F, and spray a 9 x 9-inch baking dish with nonstick cooking spray.

2 In a large mixing bowl, stir together the cornmeal, flour, sugar, baking powder, baking soda, and salt.

3 In a separate mixing bowl, whisk together the eggs, buttermilk, and butter.

4 Add the wet ingredients into the dry ingredients, mixing together just until combined into a batter.

5 Spread the batter in the prepared baking dish, and smooth out the top.

6 Bake for 20–25 minutes, or until the top has lightly browned and a toothpick inserted into the center comes out mostly clean. Let cool for 10 minutes before slicing. For 100 calorie portions, slice into 16 sections by cutting 4 rows by 4 rows.

HELPFUL TIP:

When preparing a quick-bread such as this (as well as biscuits and muffins), it is always best to lightly mix the batter, as overdoing it can make the final bread more dense. A few lumps in the batter are perfectly alright!

PREP TIME: 15 MINUTES • BAKE TIME: 20 MINUTES

CRISPY BAKED BABY POTATOES

MAKES 4 SIDE DISH PORTIONS

We toss baby potatoes with a little olive oil and herbs and bake them at a high temperature for a deep brown, crisp exterior and creamy interior. A sprinkle of Parmesan cheese and fresh parsley before serving adds a well-seasoned, savory flavor.

100 CALORIE COUNT=

$\frac{1}{2}$ **CUP**

100 Calories   ½ Cup

Recommended Serving:
SIDE DISH – 200 Calories = 1 Cup

Ingredients:

2 pounds baby potatoes, halved (see tip)

2 tablespoons olive oil

½ teaspoon dried thyme

½ teaspoon dried rosemary

½ teaspoon salt

¼ teaspoon pepper

¼ teaspoon garlic powder

2 tablespoons chopped fresh parsley

1 tablespoon grated Parmesan cheese

Directions:

1. Preheat the oven to 450°F.

2. In a large mixing bowl, toss the halved potatoes in a mixture of the olive oil, thyme, rosemary, salt, pepper, and garlic powder.

3. Spread the coated potatoes on a sheet pan in a single layer, and bake for 20 minutes, stirring halfway through. Potatoes are done when browned on the outside and fork-tender.

4. Sprinkle with chopped fresh parsley and grated Parmesan cheese before serving.

HELPFUL TIP:

Baby potatoes are usually sold in small bags near the regular potatoes. You can usually find Yukon Gold baby potatoes or mixed potatoes with gold, purple, and red all in the same bag. They taste nearly identical, but the multicolored potatoes make for a nicer presentation.

PREP TIME: 35 MINUTES • BAKE TIME: 1 HOUR

SCALLOPED POTATOES

MAKES 8 SIDE DISH PORTIONS

Bob's Farm to Table: A traditional Scalloped Potato recipe is a simple baked casserole of thinly sliced potatoes in a creamy, savory white sauce. Over time, cooks started topping their Scalloped Potatoes with lots of cheese, turning them into potatoes au gratin. We re-created the original comfort food classic of creamy, well-seasoned potatoes, the perfect side-dish. For perfectly sliced potatoes, use a mandolin food slicer or the slicing disc of a food processor.

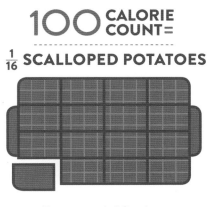

100 **CALORIE COUNT=**

$\frac{1}{16}$ **SCALLOPED POTATOES**

Recommended Serving:
SIDE DISH – 200 Calories = 2 Sections

Ingredients:

Nonstick cooking spray

3 pounds russet potatoes, scrubbed

1¼ teaspoons salt, divided

3 tablespoons butter

2 tablespoons all-purpose flour

2½ cups 2% milk

3 tablespoons chopped fresh chives

1 teaspoon onion powder

½ teaspoon pepper

½ teaspoon garlic powder

Paprika

Directions:

1. Preheat the oven to 350°F. Spray a 13 x 9-inch baking dish with nonstick cooking spray.

2. Slice the potatoes into thin slices, about ⅛ inch thick, placing them into a pot of water as you go (to prevent browning). Add ½ teaspoon of the salt to the water.

3. Ensure that the potatoes are fully covered with water before placing the pot over high heat. Bring to a boil, and let boil for just 1 minute.

4. Drain the potatoes, and let cool for at least 5 minutes (do not rinse). Add the cooled potatoes into the prepared pan, arranging them in overlapping layers.

5. Melt the butter in a sauce pot over medium-high heat. Add the flour, and stir until smooth and combined. Let cook for 1 minute.

6. Whisk the milk, chives, onion powder, pepper, garlic powder, and remaining ¾ teaspoon salt into the pot, and continue whisking until the sauce is smooth and free of lumps. Bring the sauce to a simmer, whisking constantly, before removing from the heat.

7. Pour the sauce over the potatoes in the baking dish, and press down on the potatoes until they are mostly submerged. Lightly sprinkle the tops of the potatoes with paprika, for color.

8. Bake for 1 hour, or until the top is golden brown and potatoes are fork-tender. Let cool for at least 5 minutes before slicing. For 100 calorie portions, slice into 16 sections by cutting 4 rows by 4 rows.

PREP TIME: 15 MINUTES • COOK TIME: 10 MINUTES

GRILLED SWEET POTATO WEDGES

MAKES 4 SIDE DISH PORTIONS

Fried sweet potato wedges have become a popular alternative to their starchy counterpart, but we turn to the grill for a new twist. A little oil and the high heat of the grill produces the same crisp, golden exterior and creamy interior without the deep-frying! And a final dusting of mildly sweet seasoned salt knocks these wedges out of the park.

100 CALORIE COUNT=

5 WEDGES OR ½ SWEET POTATO

Recommended Serving:
SIDE DISH – 200 Calories = 1 Sweet Potato or 10 Wedges

Ingredients:

4 large sweet potatoes, scrubbed

1 tablespoon olive oil

1 teaspoon light brown sugar

½ teaspoon seasoning salt

¼ teaspoon ground cinnamon

¼ teaspoon smoked paprika (optional)

Directions:

1. Slice sweet potatoes in half lengthwise, and then slice each half into 5 long wedges.

2. Preheat a grill or grill pan to high heat.

3. Toss the potato wedges in olive oil before placing on the grill horizontally (to prevent them from falling through the grate). Grill for 8–10 minutes, turning halfway through. Wedges are done when they easily bend with pressure from your grilling tongs.

4. In a small mixing bowl, combine brown sugar, seasoning salt, cinnamon, and smoked paprika, if desired. Sprinkle evenly over the grilled wedges before serving.

HELPFUL TIP:

Smoked paprika adds a great flavor to the sweet potato wedges that is reminiscent of barbecue potato chips. If you do not have any on hand, or are not a fan of that smoky flavor, you can simply omit it.

PREP TIME: 30 MINUTES • CHILL TIME: 1 HOUR

MACARONI SALAD

MAKES 6 SIDE DISH PORTIONS

For our take on this classic picnic side, we use a combination of mayonnaise and Greek yogurt to deliver a creamy salad with far fewer calories than using mayonnaise alone. Then we really punch up the flavor with celery, red bell pepper, sweet relish, mustard, and celery salt, in place of ordinary salt.

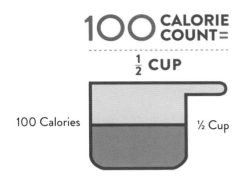

100 CALORIE COUNT =

½ **CUP**

100 Calories   ½ Cup

Recommended Serving:
SIDE DISH – 200 Calories = 1 Cup

Ingredients:

8 ounces elbow macaroni

¾ cup diced celery

⅓ cup finely diced red bell pepper

6 ounces plain nonfat Greek yogurt

2 tablespoons mayonnaise

2 tablespoons sweet relish

1 tablespoon chopped fresh parsley

1 tablespoon yellow mustard

1 tablespoon cider vinegar

1 teaspoon celery salt

¼ teaspoon onion powder

¼ teaspoon pepper

Directions:

1. Cook the elbow macaroni according to the package directions. Drain and rinse under cold water before adding to a large mixing bowl.

2. Add all the remaining ingredients to the mixing bowl, and fold together until all is well combined.

3. Cover, and refrigerate for at least 1 hour before serving.

HELPFUL TIP:

For the perfect macaroni consistency, cook the pasta 1 minute less than you normally would, testing to see that it is just slightly more al dente than you prefer. The mustard and vinegar will continue cooking the pasta as it chills in the fridge, letting the dressing actually absorb into the macaroni itself.

PREP TIME: 20 MINUTES • COOK TIME: 8 HOURS

BOSTON BAKED BEANS

MAKES 12 SIDE DISH PORTIONS

Good things come to those that wait. Baked beans are often served up mushy and ultra sweet. We used the gentle heat of the slow cooker to produce perfectly creamy beans that strike a winning balance of sweetness and rich smoke flavor.

100 **CALORIE COUNT =**

¼ CUP

100 Calories   ¼ Cup

Recommended Serving:
SIDE DISH – 200 Calories = ½ Cup

Ingredients:

1 pound dry Great Northern beans

1½ teaspoons salt, divided

3 thick-cut slices bacon, raw, chopped

1 yellow onion, diced

3 cups water

½ cup ketchup

¼ cup light brown sugar

3 tablespoons molasses

2 tablespoons Dijon mustard

2 teaspoons Worcestershire sauce

½ teaspoon onion powder

½ teaspoon pepper

Directions:

1. Place the beans in a large bowl or pot, and cover with 2 inches of water. Stir in 1 teaspoon of salt. Soak overnight.

2. Drain and rinse the soaked beans.

3. Add the chopped bacon and onion to the bottom of a slow cooker set to low heat. Top with the rinsed beans.

4. In a mixing bowl, whisk together the water, ketchup, brown sugar, molasses, Dijon mustard, Worcestershire sauce, onion powder, pepper, and the remaining ½ teaspoon of salt. Pour the mixture on top of all the ingredients in the slow cooker.

5. Cover, and let cook for 8 hours, or until beans are tender.

HELPFUL TIP:

Most people believe that adding salt to beans as they cook will result in undercooked beans with a tough skin; however, soaking the beans in salted water to "brine" them (as is done in this recipe) has been shown to have the exact opposite effect, making for creamy and tender beans.

6 ENTERTAINING

PREP TIME: 20 MINUTES • COOK TIME: 20 MINUTES

SWEET & SOUR MEATBALLS

MAKES 24 MEATBALLS OR 6 APPETIZER PORTIONS

Our moist and tender party meatballs hit all the parts of your taste buds, keeping you coming back for more. We boost the flavor of these miniature morsels by generously seasoning the meat with bold ingredients and then simmering them in a rich and tangy sauce. To keep the meatballs warm on a party buffet, simply serve them in a slow cooker set to low heat.

100 CALORIE COUNT =

2 MEATBALLS

Recommended Serving:
APPETIZER – 200 Calories = 4 Meatballs

Ingredients:

1 pound 93% lean ground beef

1 large egg, beaten

3 tablespoons minced yellow onion

3 tablespoons bread crumbs

2 teaspoons Worcestershire sauce

2 teaspoons parsley flakes

¼ teaspoon garlic powder

¼ teaspoon salt

¼ teaspoon pepper

1 tablespoon canola oil

Sauce:

½ cup ketchup

⅓ cup light brown sugar

1 tablespoon cider vinegar

2 teaspoons soy sauce

½ teaspoon onion powder

Directions:

1. In a large mixing bowl, use your hands to combine all meatball ingredients, except the canola oil.

2. Form the meatball mixture into 24 meatballs that are 1 inch in size (about the size of a ping-pong ball).

3. Heat the canola oil in a large skillet over medium-high heat.

4. Add the meatballs to the skillet, and brown on all sides, about 5 minutes.

5. Add all the sauce ingredients to a large sauce pot over medium heat and stir to combine.

6. Transfer the browned meatballs into the sauce ,and toss to coat. Cover, and let cook for 15 minutes, stirring occasionally. Serve stuck with toothpicks to easily pick up.

HELPFUL TIP:

These can also be made with extra lean (99% fat-free) ground turkey, if you prefer, though the final result will have nearly the same amount of calories.

PREP TIME: 20 MINUTES • COOK TIME: 10 MINUTES

MARYLAND CRAB CAKES

MAKES 8 CRAB CAKES OR 4 APPETIZER PORTIONS

Anson's American Treasures: There are times in life when a food experience becomes an everlasting moment of bonding. This is how I felt when I shared my first true Maryland Crab Cake with my daughter Hannah in Baltimore. After settling Hannah (then only 15 years old) into her summer dorm at John Hopkins University, we set out for dinner. With a teenage daughter, you get too few moments to sit and enjoy a meal together, and this particular one remains one of my most special ones. Bob and Mona created a great "no-filler" crab cake, spiced perfectly, with just enough egg and bread crumb to hold it together. The perfect portion that still creates perfect memories!

1 CRAB CAKE

Recommended Serving:
APPETIZER – 200 Calories = 2 Crab Cakes

Ingredients:

1 large egg

1 tablespoon mayonnaise

2 teaspoons Old Bay Seasoning

1 teaspoon Dijon mustard

1 teaspoon Worcestershire sauce

1 pound lump crabmeat, drained

⅓ cup panko bread crumbs

1 tablespoon minced red bell pepper

1 tablespoon finely chopped fresh parsley

1 tablespoon canola oil

1 tablespoon butter

Fresh lemon wedges

Directions:

1. Line a sheet pan with parchment paper.

2. In a large mixing bowl, whisk together the egg, mayonnaise, Old Bay Seasoning, Dijon mustard, and Worcestershire sauce.

3. Add the crabmeat, bread crumbs, bell pepper, and parsley to the bowl, and gently fold together to create the crab cake batter.

4. Form the batter into 8 crab cakes, using about ⅓ cup of batter for each cake. Transfer to the prepared sheet pan. For best results, cover, and refrigerate for 1 hour before cooking.

5. Add the canola oil and butter to a large nonstick skillet or griddle over medium heat, and bring up to a sizzle.

6. Place the chilled crab cakes into the pan, and cook until golden brown, about 4 minutes on each side. Serve with fresh lemon wedges to squeeze over top.

HELPFUL TIP:

Lump crabmeat is sold in refrigerated tubs in the seafood section of your grocery store. You should always carefully check for any pieces of shell before cooking with it.

PREP TIME: 30 MINUTES • BAKE TIME: 20 MINUTES

STUFFED MUSHROOMS

MAKES 20 MUSHROOMS OR 5 APPETIZER PORTIONS

This classic entertaining appetizer is literally stuffed with bold, fresh Italian flavors that your guests won't forget. Not only do these little beauties taste fantastic, you can enjoy four satisfying whole mushrooms for only 100 calories!

100 CALORIE COUNT=

4 MUSHROOMS

Recommended Serving:
APPETIZER – 100 Calories = 4 Mushrooms
LUNCH – 200 Calories = 8 Mushrooms

Ingredients:

16 ounces white (button) mushrooms (about 20 mushrooms)

1 tablespoon olive oil

1 tablespoon butter

3 tablespoons minced red onion

1½ teaspoons minced garlic

½ teaspoon Italian seasoning

¼ teaspoon salt

¼ teaspoon pepper

3 tablespoons shredded Parmesan cheese

1 tablespoon chopped fresh parsley

2 tablespoons Italian bread crumbs

Directions:

1. Preheat the oven to 375°F.

2. Pull the stems from the mushrooms, and finely mince the stems. In a mixing bowl, toss the mushroom caps in olive oil, and set aside.

3. Heat the butter in a large skillet over medium-high heat until almost sizzling. Add the chopped mushroom stems, minced onion, garlic, Italian seasoning, salt, and pepper, and sauté for 4 minutes, or until mushroom stems are tender.

4. Remove the skillet from heat, and stir in the Parmesan cheese, parsley, and bread crumbs to create the filling.

5. Stuff each mushroom cap with an equal amount of the filling, and place on a sheet pan. Bake for 20 minutes, or until mushrooms are tender and the filling is beginning to brown. Garnish with additional chopped fresh parsley, if desired.

HELPFUL TIP:

For even more mushroom flavor, you can prepare these with brown cremini mushrooms, or "baby bella" mushrooms, as they are often labeled in stores.

PREP TIME: 15 MINUTES • BAKE TIME: 50 MINUTES

BUFFALO WINGS

MAKES MAKES 32 WINGS/DRUMETTES OR 16 APPETIZER PORTIONS

No need to deep-fry your wings anymore to get that amazing crunch and flavor. You can get the same result by tossing the wings with a mere tablespoon of oil and roasting them in a hot oven, leaving them golden brown, crisp, and unbelievably delicious. Be sure to serve them with cut celery sticks and our Chunky Bleu Cheese Dressing (see page 243).

Recommended Serving:
APPETIZER – 200 Calories = 2 Wings or Drumettes

Ingredients:

3 pounds chicken wing sections (wings and drumettes)

1 tablespoon canola oil

½ teaspoon salt

½ teaspoon pepper

¼ teaspoon garlic powder

3 tablespoons butter, melted

2 tablespoons Louisiana Hot Sauce

Directions:

1 Preheat the oven to 400°F. If necessary, split wings from drumettes by cutting at the joint. If wing tips (see tip) are intact, cut tips at the joint and discard.

2 In a large mixing bowl, toss the wings in a mixture of the canola oil, salt, pepper, and garlic powder.

3 Spread the wings in a single layer on a sheet pan, and bake for 45–50 minutes, or until the skin is browned and crispy, and cutting into the largest drumette reveals juices that run clear.

4 Combine butter and hot sauce in a large mixing bowl. Add the baked wings, and toss to coat with the sauce before serving.

HELPFUL TIP:

Whole chicken wings have three distinct sections: the drumette, the wing, and the wing tip. Wing tips are the smallest of the three sections and are almost entirely bone and skin. They are best discarded or saved for making chicken stock.

PREP TIME: 25 MINUTES • COOK TIME: 25 MINUTES

OVEN-FRIED GREEN TOMATOES

MAKES 16 TOMATO SLICES OR 8 APPETIZER PORTIONS

Fried green tomatoes are a southern staple made from firm, and somewhat tart, unripe tomatoes that cook up soft inside of a breading of flour and cornmeal. While the tomatoes in this recipe are actually baked, instead of fried, they still cook up crispy and golden brown. For the perfect dipping sauce, serve alongside our Buttermilk Ranch Dressing (see page 245).

100 CALORIE COUNT=

2 FRIED GREEN TOMATO SLICES

Recommended Serving:
APPETIZER – 100 Calories = 2 Tomato Slices

Ingredients:

Nonstick cooking spray

4 medium green tomatoes

2 large eggs

½ cup buttermilk

1 cup all-purpose flour

½ cup cornmeal

½ teaspoon onion powder

½ teaspoon salt

½ teaspoon pepper

¼ teaspoon garlic powder

Directions:

1. Preheat the oven to 400°F, and spray a sheet pan with nonstick cooking spray.

2. Trim ends from the tomatoes, and discard. Slice each tomato into 4 thick slices.

3. In a wide bowl, whisk the eggs and buttermilk until well combined.

4. In a second wide bowl, combine the flour, cornmeal, onion powder, salt, pepper, and garlic powder.

5. Dip each slice of tomato into the flour mixture, then the egg mixture, and then back into the flour mixture to fully coat before placing on the prepared sheet pan.

6. Bake for 12 minutes before flipping the breaded tomatoes. Bake for an additional 10–13 minutes, or until the breaded tomatoes are crisp and lightly browned. If desired, sprinkle lightly with additional salt as soon as you remove them from the oven.

HELPFUL TIP:

If you can't find green tomatoes, this recipe can also be prepared with 1 large zucchini cut at a slight angle to make ½-inch-thick ovals. This reduces the calories to 95 calories per two breaded zucchini slices.

PREP TIME: 40 MINUTES • COOK TIME: 8 MINUTES

PESTO CHICKEN SKEWERS

MAKES 10 APPETIZER PORTIONS

We transform boneless chicken breasts and a variety of vegetables into a scrumptious and colorful appetizer. Our quick, flavor-packed Pesto Sauce (see page 251) is a winning solution to jazzing up these Pesto Chicken Skewers. Serve them as a festive party appetizer or have 2 or 3 skewers as an entrée, served over rice or alongside Crispy Baked Baby Potatoes (see page 170).

100 **CALORIE COUNT=**

1 SKEWER

Recommended Serving:
APPETIZER – 100 Calories = 1 Skewer

Ingredients:

Bamboo skewers

1 pound boneless, skinless chicken breasts

2 yellow squash

1 large zucchini

16 ounces small white (button) mushrooms

1 batch Pesto Sauce, divided (see page 251)

Directions:

1. Soak the bamboo skewers in water for 1 hour before preparing (to prevent charring).

2. Preheat a grill or grill pan to high heat.

3. Chop the chicken breasts, yellow squash, and zucchini into uniform 1-inch cubes.

4. Thread a cube of chicken onto a soaked skewer, then a cube of yellow squash, a whole mushroom, and finally a cube of zucchini. Repeat to thread another set of the ingredients on the same skewer. Finally, add a third cube of chicken to top the skewer off. Repeat until you've made 10 skewers and you are out of cubed ingredients.

5. Brush the skewers with ½ of the Pesto Sauce.

6. Place the pesto skewers on the grill, and cook for 5 minutes. Flip, and cook for an additional 3 minutes on the opposite site, just until the vegetables are tender and slicing into a cube of chicken reveals no pink.

7. Using a clean brush, brush the remaining ½ of the Pesto Sauce over the cooked skewers before serving.

HELPFUL TIP:

These can also be cooked under a broiler set to high by placing the oven rack in the second-highest position. Broil for 10 minutes, flipping halfway through.

PREP TIME: 45 MINUTES • COOK TIME: 10 MINUTES

CLAMS CASINO

MAKES 36 CLAMS OR 12 APPETIZER PORTIONS

These bacon and bread crumb–stuffed clams on the half shell are a New England staple that makes for an impressive, flavor-packed appetizer. Plus, you can eat three for 100 calories! This recipe starts by lightly steaming the clams to loosen the shells for far easier shucking.

100 CALORIE COUNT =

3 STUFFED CLAMS

Recommended Serving:
APPETIZER – 100 Calories = 3 Stuffed Clams

Ingredients:

36 littleneck clams, shells scrubbed

5 strips bacon, diced

¼ cup minced red onion

¼ cup minced red bell pepper

1½ teaspoons minced garlic

½ cup panko bread crumbs

3 tablespoons grated Parmesan cheese

2 tablespoons lemon juice

1 tablespoon chopped fresh parsley

¼ teaspoon salt

¼ teaspoon pepper

Directions:

1. Place the clams in a steamer basket over boiling water, and steam for 2–3 minutes, just until the shells are barely beginning to open.

2. Shuck the partially steamed clams by inserting a small paring knife into the shells and twisting to pop them open. Run the knife over the top of the clam inside to disconnect the muscle connecting it to the top shell. Discard the tops of the shells. Run the paring knife underneath the clam to disconnect the muscle connecting it to the bottom shell, leaving the clams in the bottom shell.

3. Place the diced bacon in a skillet over medium-high heat, and sauté for 2 minutes before adding the onion, bell pepper, and garlic. Continue sautéing until bacon is crispy. Do not drain the bacon grease.

4. Remove the skillet from the heat, and stir in the bread crumbs, Parmesan cheese, lemon juice, parsley, salt, and pepper to create the stuffing.

5. Place the oven rack in the second-highest position, and set the broiler to high.

6. Top each shucked clam with a heaping teaspoon of the stuffing, and place on a sheet pan.

7. Broil stuffed clams for 3–5 minutes, just until stuffing is well browned. Serve hot.

HELPFUL TIP:

When making any clam recipe, you should always discard any open or cracked ones before cooking.

PREP TIME: 25 MINUTES • COOK TIME: 10 MINUTES

PORK POTSTICKERS

MAKES 24 POTSTICKERS OR 12 APPETIZER PORTIONS

Anson's American Treasures: When I was directing the television series *Melrose Place,* dim sum restaurants were popping up all over Hollywood, and I quickly fell in love with Chinese dumplings. For our recipe, we used lean ground pork, egg white, pungent green onion, and aromatic ginger for an outstanding pork dumpling you don't have to go to Hollywood to enjoy.

2 POTSTICKERS

Recommended Serving:
APPETIZER – 100 Calories = 2 Potstickers

Ingredients:

⅓ pound lean ground pork

1 large egg white, beaten

2 tablespoons minced green onion

1 tablespoon reduced-sodium soy sauce

¼ teaspoon ground ginger

¼ teaspoon pepper

24 (3-inch) wonton wrappers

2 tablespoons canola oil

Dipping Sauce:

⅓ cup reduced-sodium soy sauce

2 tablespoons minced green onion

1 tablespoon cider vinegar

1 tablespoon light brown sugar

1 teaspoon sesame oil

Directions:

1. In a mixing bowl, use your hands to combine the ground pork, egg white, green onion, soy sauce, ginger, and pepper to form the potsticker filling.

2. Lay out 24 wonton wrappers, and place a heaping teaspoon of the potsticker filling into the center of each.

3. Use the tip of your finger dipped into a bowl of water to wet all 4 edges of each wonton. Fold wonton over, and press hard to fully seal.

4. Cook the potstickers in 2 batches of 12, or cook in 2 nonstick skillets at the same time. Place 1 tablespoon of canola oil in each skillet over medium-high heat.

5. Add the potstickers to the skillet, and brown for 2 minutes on each side.

6. Add ⅓ cup of water to the skillet, cover, and let steam for 5 minutes, or until cutting into a potsticker reveals the wonton is tender and the filling is not pink.

7. Combine all of the dipping sauce ingredients, whisking until the sugar has dissolved. Serve dipping sauce at room temperature, alongside the potstickers.

HELPFUL TIP:

Wonton wrappers can usually be found in the produce section, refrigerated near the tofu and organic items.

PREP TIME: 20 MINUTES • BAKE TIME: 12 MINUTES

SUPREME FLATBREAD PIZZA

MAKES 4 FLATBREAD PIZZAS OR 6 APPETIZER PORTIONS

We double the serving size of the average slice by using flatbread for our supreme pizzas! Cut the flatbreads at alternating angles for a sophisticated-looking appetizer that you know your guests will love. Enjoy a whole delicious flatbread pizza for lunch!

Featured Recipe Story: See next page.

100 CALORIE COUNT=

⅓ **FLATBREAD**

Recommended Serving:
APPETIZER – 200 Calories = ⅔ Flatbread

Ingredients:

4 flatbread pizza crusts (see tip)

1 cup prepared pizza sauce

1⅓ cups shredded part-skim mozzarella cheese

32 slices turkey pepperoni

¾ cup sliced baby bella mushrooms

½ cup diced green bell pepper

¼ cup sliced black olives

½ teaspoon Italian seasoning

Directions:

1. Preheat the oven to 400°F, and place the pizza crusts on sheet pans.

2. Spread ¼ cup of the pizza sauce over each pizza crust.

3. Top the pizza sauce on each crust with ⅓ cup of mozzarella cheese.

4. Arrange 8 slices of turkey pepperoni and an equal amount of the mushrooms, bell peppers, and olives on each pizza. Sprinkle lightly with Italian seasoning.

5. Bake for 8–12 minutes, just until the cheese is bubbly and the pepperoni is crisp.

HELPFUL TIP:

Many brands now sell low-calorie flatbread pizza crusts (usually located in the deli, near the pita bread Standard sizes are 5 x 13 or 7 x 9 inches).

FLATBREAD PIZZA

More Pizza with Fewer Calories— Only 100 Calories a Slice!

NO BONES ABOUT IT, WE LOVE PIZZA. The combination of crunchy crust, melted cheese, and a boatload of toppings is irresistible. However, we almost always feel guilty by how much we eat. Anson asked us, "Can you create a pizza recipe with 'the works'—meat and veggies—but fewer calories than those take-out joints?" To us, that didn't mean just cutting down on size. We wanted a pizza recipe that would give us a real meal (300 calories) and the option for a 200-calorie appetizer or snack.

Crust Buster! We first figured out that by using flatbread-style crusts, you can reduce your calories in half of standard crusts.

Have your meat and eat it too! "The works" means meat, not just veggie toppings. Namely pepperoni or sausage, which are both high in fat and calories. We subbed in turkey sausage and pepperoni for the pork—a lot fewer calories without a taste difference with all the other ingredients.

Pile on the Veggies! Adding veggies not only adds texture, but lots of bold flavor. In this recipe, we added fresh peppers, mushrooms, and olives...but have a good time adding your own fresh vegetables or herbs. Go crazy! The more veggies, the more flavor. It'll be more filling too!

Cheese, and Sauce Please! What's a pizza without cheese? In this recipe, we used part skim mozzarella cheese. It has enough fat to provide that cheesiness we all love, without the added calories. For a quick prep, we recommend using pre-made pizza sauce. Check the label! Some sauces add lots of sugar and salt. The best are available for 100 calories per cup.

With these simple changes, we reached our goal of 100 calories per ⅓ flatbread, and 300 calories for a WHOLE flat-bread pizza. Perfect size for a meal. More great pizza with fewer calories.

1 For a quick prep, we recommend using pre-made pizza sauce. Check the label! Some sauces add lots of sugar and salt. The best are available for around 100 calories per cup.

4 Experiment with different veggie toppings—savory vegetables like garlic, onions, and peppers go well with broccoli, spinach, and zucchini. Use lean proteins too.

2 Be creative with your toppings. Adding fresh herbs, like fresh basil, adds no calories and a lot of flavor. Be creative with your vegetable choices too.

3 One whole Flatbread Pizza is 300 calories. Cut it into pieces for a great appetizer for entertaining.

5 Flatbread Pizzas are seriously delicious. One-third of a pizza is only 100 calories. Have 1-2 slices as a healthier, afternoon pick-me up. Yum!

PREP TIME: 20 MINUTES

TURKEY & HERBED CHEESE PINWHEELS

MAKES 24 PINWHEELS OR 8 APPETIZER PORTIONS

Sandwich pinwheels are a party and potluck staple, because they are easy to make, filling, and hold up well throughout the party. We take our pinwheels to another level by making our own flavor-packed cream cheese spread, while fresh spinach and shredded carrots add crunch and bulk.

3 PINWHEELS

Recommended Serving:
APPETIZER – 100 Calories = 3 Pinwheels

Ingredients:

Herbed Cheese:

4 ounces (½ brick) fat-free cream cheese, softened

2 tablespoons chopped fresh chives

2 tablespoons chopped fresh parsley

1 tablespoon 2% milk

½ teaspoon minced garlic

¼ teaspoon salt

¼ teaspoon pepper

Pinwheels:

3 (10-inch) multigrain flour tortillas

½ pound sliced deli turkey breast

1½ cups fresh spinach leaves

¾ cup shredded carrots

Directions:

1. Place all of the herbed cheese ingredients in a food processor and pulse until combined.

2. Lay out 3 flour tortillas, and spread ⅓ of the herbed cheese across the entire surface of each.

3. Place ⅓ of the turkey breast over the top of the cheese on each tortilla, keeping the turkey to one side of the tortilla to allow for easier rolling of the pinwheels.

4. Place ½ cup of spinach leaves and ¼ cup of shredded carrots on top of the turkey on each tortilla.

5. Starting on the ends that are topped with the ingredients, roll each tortilla into a tight wrap, using the herbed cheese to seal the edges.

6. Slice each wrap into 8 pinwheels that are about 1¼ inch thick. Serve immediately, or cover, and chill until ready to serve.

HELPFUL TIP:

Refrigerating the full wraps for 1 hour before slicing will allow you to make cleaner cuts to the pinwheels, as the herbed cheese will have hardened.

PREP TIME: 20 MINUTES • COOK TIME: 6 MINUTES

SHRIMP COCKTAIL

MAKES 42-50 SHRIMP OR 6 APPETIZER PORTIONS

In cooking, it's important to infuse flavor whenever you can. Before adding the shrimp, we season and boil our cooking water along with a tablespoon of Old Bay, bright lemon juice, and an earthy bay leaf for a show-stopping cocktail shrimp. Also, our homemade cocktail sauce is simple but stellar thanks to the addition of lemon zest, Tabasco sauce, and a generous amount of horseradish, of course. With only 100 calories for four jumbo shrimp with sauce, this recipe will surely please your party guests without weighing them down.

100 CALORIE COUNT=

4 SHRIMP WITH SAUCE

Recommended Serving:
APPETIZER – 200 Calories = 8 Shrimp with Sauce

Ingredients:

1 lemon, halved

1 tablespoon Old Bay Seasoning

1 bay leaf

2 pounds jumbo (size 21/25) raw shrimp, peeled and deveined

Cocktail Sauce:

1 cup ketchup

2 tablespoons lemon juice

1 tablespoon prepared horseradish (see tip)

1 teaspoon lemon zest

½ teaspoon hot pepper sauce (Tabasco)

Directions:

1. Fill a large pot with at least 3 quarts of water, and place over high heat.

2. Add the lemon, Old Bay Seasoning, and bay leaf to the pot, and bring to a boil. Cover, and let boil for 3 minutes to season the water.

3. Add the shrimp to the pot, and let boil for 3 minutes, or until bright pink. Drain and rinse under cold water. To serve immediately, transfer to a large bowl of ice water to cool the shrimp further.

4. Prepare the sauce by mixing all cocktail sauce ingredients until well combined.

5. For the best temperature and flavor, cover, and refrigerate both the shrimp and the sauce for 1 hour before serving.

HELPFUL TIP:

Prepared horseradish is sold in glass jars, usually near the mustard, but sometimes below the seafood counter as well.

PREP TIME: 40 MINUTES • COOK TIME: 20 MINUTES

100 CALORIE DEVILED EGGS

MAKES 12 APPETIZER PORTIONS

Deviled eggs are a popular party option that packs much more protein than other snacks. We stick to a fairly classic preparation but uniquely salt the egg whites before filling them to ensure that every bite is well seasoned. This recipe allows you to have two deviled eggs (one whole egg) for 100 calories, only 30 more calories than a plain hard-boiled egg!

Recommended Serving:
APPETIZER – 100 Calories = 1 Whole Egg

Ingredients:

12 large eggs

¼ cup mayonnaise

1 tablespoon sweet relish

1 tablespoon prepared yellow mustard

⅛ teaspoon pepper

Salt

Paprika, for garnish

Chopped chives, for garnish

Directions:

1. Place eggs in a large pot, and fill with enough cold water to cover the eggs by 2 inches.

2. Place pot over high heat, and bring up to a rolling boil. Cover, remove from heat, and let stand for 15 minutes.

3. Drain eggs, and fill pot with ice water to cool down. Let cool for at least 5 minutes.

4. Peel and halve eggs, scooping the yolks into a mixing bowl or food processor and placing the whites on a serving platter as you go.

5. Mash together (or food process) the egg yolks, mayonnaise, relish, yellow mustard, and pepper.

6. Lightly sprinkle the entire platter of egg white halves with salt before filling each with an equal amount of the yolk filling. Refrigerate for at least 30 minutes before serving. Garnish with a sprinkling of paprika and chopped fresh chives, if desired.

HELPFUL TIP:

For the best presentation, use a pastry bag with a star-shaped tip to pipe the yolk filling into the whites.

PREP TIME: 30 MINUTES

GUACAMOLE-STUFFED CHERRY TOMATOES

MAKES 24 TOMATOES OR 6 APPETIZER PORTIONS

100 CALORIE COUNT=

4 TOMATOES

Recommended Serving:
APPETIZER – 100 Calories = 4 Tomatoes

Mona's Family Favorites: Not all party finger foods have to be heavy, greasy "calorie bombs." These little "cherry bombs" are a simple and satisfying alternative for your guests. With only 25 calories in each filled tomato, you can go back for a second, or third, or fourth without any guilt!

Featured Recipe Story: See next page.

Ingredients:

24 large cherry tomatoes (about 2 pints)

1 lime, halved

Salt

1 cup Fresh Guacamole (see page 206)

6 corn tortilla chips, crushed

Chili powder

Fresh cilantro

Directions:

1 Slice the tops and bottoms off each cherry tomato, cutting just a thin sliver from the bottoms for the tomatoes to stand upright.

2 Use a melon baller or grapefruit spoon to remove and discard the pulp and seeds from each tomato, placing them on a serving dish as you finish.

3 Squeeze the lime over all the tomatoes on the serving dish, and then lightly sprinkle with salt.

4 Fill each tomato with 2 teaspoons of the Fresh Guacamole, letting it pile up and out of the tomato.

5 Top the filled tomatoes with crushed tortilla chips, and then sprinkle lightly with chili powder. Garnish each with a leaf of fresh cilantro and serve.

HELPFUL TIP:
Stores are often overstocked with (oval) grape tomatoes and have very few (round) cherry tomatoes. If you are having trouble finding them, don't forget to check the organic produce section. They may even have both yellow and red cherry tomatoes to make a multicolored platter!

GUACAMOLE-STUFFED CHERRY TOMATOES

The Perfect Portion for Any Party—Four Fun-Filled Tomatoes for 100 Calories!

HOLIDAY PARTIES CAN DEFINITELY CAUSE CALORIE creep with all the fattening dips and appetizers. And veggies and dip are so boring. What I love about these guacamole-stuffed tomatoes is knowing I have the right portion of guacamole and tomato in each bite. Plus, by using an assortment of different colored tomatoes, I can serve a beautiful and impressive-looking platter at my next party. The added crunch of the crushed tortilla chips makes me feel like I'm getting chips and guacamole in one! The best part is that I can eat four, and it's only 100 calories!

Foolproof Portion! The flavorful guacamole is measured into a cherry tomato—a built-in portion cup that makes calorie counting a snap!

Easy Filling! Cut a slice off the bottom of each tomato so they stand up. Then, use a melon baller to scoop the insides out. To fill, use a teaspoon measure or, for a fancier look, a plastic bag and decorating tip.

Kick and Crunch! A little spice from chili powder and crunch from tortilla chip crumbs work together to re-create your favorite Mexican chip and dip combo!

You can also try this recipe with mini peppers!

1 Use a small measuring spoon to add the guacamole—two teaspoons per tomato.

4 Using different colored tomatoes to impress your guests definitely creates a WOW appetizer.

2 Leave a smooth surface on the top so the tortilla crumbs can easily adhere to the guacamole.

3 Break up the tortilla chips with your hands in a small plastic bag, or use a small food processor. Don't break them up too much—you want that crunch!

5 Experiment with different displays. I like a zig-zag look to show off all of the different tomato colors.

PREP TIME: 10 MINUTES

FRESH GUACAMOLE

3 DIP PORTIONS OR 6 TOPPING PORTIONS

Avocados are known to be an expensive, temperamental fruit, so it's no wonder that store-bought guacamole is often loaded with fillers and preservatives to bulk it up and prolong the shelf life. Yet the one thing they don't seem to bulk up guacamole products with is flavor! We vastly prefer homemade! The best time to make guacamole is when avocados go on sale, as they're not only less expensive, but they're typically at their peak as well.

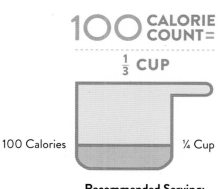

100 **CALORIE COUNT=**

$\frac{1}{3}$ **CUP**

100 Calories   ¼ Cup

Recommended Serving:
DIP – 200 Calories = ½ Cup
TOPPING – 100 Calories = ¼ Cup

Ingredients:

2 medium Haas avocados, halved and pitted

Juice of ½ lime

2 tablespoons chopped fresh cilantro

2 tablespoons minced red onion

1 tablespoon seeded and minced jalapeño

¼ teaspoon salt

Directions:

1. Use a large spoon to scoop the avocado out of the peel, then roughly chop.

2. Place the chopped avocado in a medium-size mixing bowl, and toss with lime juice.

3. Use a heavy fork or potato masher to mash the avocado until creamy and mostly smooth.

4. Stir in the remaining ingredients. Serve immediately, or cover tightly and refrigerate for 1 hour to let the flavors combine.

HELPFUL TIP:

A ripe Haas avocado has brown skin, is slightly soft to the touch, and reveals green when the short stem on the top is pulled out. Hard avocados should be ripened at room temperature. Ripe avocados can be kept in the fridge for 2-3 days before using.

PREP TIME: 10 MINUTES

HOMEMADE HUMMUS

MAKES 4 DIP PORTIONS OR 8 SPREAD PORTIONS

Though store-bought versions are fine in a pinch, our Homemade Hummus is out of this world! We toss chickpeas, tahini paste, and a few seasonings into a food processor, and this silky, intensely flavored, nutrient-packed dip whirls up in a matter of seconds. It's hard to compete with that! Hummus makes a great and healthier spread on sandwiches or wraps in place of mayonnaise.

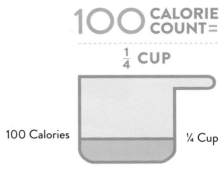

100 **CALORIE COUNT=**

$\frac{1}{4}$ **CUP**

100 Calories   ¼ Cup

Recommended Serving:
DIP – 200 Calories = ½ Cup
SPREAD – 100 Calories = ¼ Cup

Ingredients:

3 tablespoons tahini paste (see tip)

2 tablespoons lemon juice

1 (15-ounce) can chickpeas (garbanzo beans), drained and rinsed

3 tablespoons water

1 tablespoon extra virgin olive oil

2 teaspoons minced garlic

¼ teaspoon ground cumin

¼ teaspoon salt

Directions:

1. Place the tahini and lemon juice in a food processor, and process for 2 minutes, until it is light and fluffy.

2. Add all the remaining ingredients, and process until all is smooth and combined. Serve immediately.

HELPFUL TIP:

Tahini is a smooth sesame paste that can be found in the ethnic foods section. Roasted tahini is essential to the flavor of hummus, so be sure not to purchase tahini that is labeled as "raw."

PREP TIME: 30 MINUTES • CHILL TIME: 1 HOUR

RESTAURANT-STYLE SALSA

MAKES 2 APPETIZER PORTIONS OR 8 TOPPING PORTIONS

Most homemade salsa recipes are made by either dicing tomatoes for a very chunky, pico de gallo style or by puréeing them to a thin, tomato sauce-like consistency. This recipe uses both techniques to give you a variety of fresh flavors and textures in every bite.

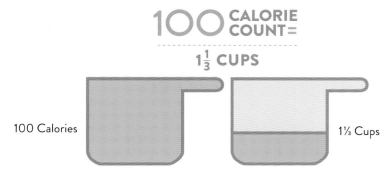

100 CALORIE COUNT =

1⅓ CUPS

100 Calories   1⅓ Cups

Recommended Serving:
APPETIZER – 100 Calories = 1⅓ Cup
TOPPING – 25 Calories = ⅓ Cup

Ingredients:

1½ pounds plum tomatoes, halved

½ red onion, finely diced

½ cup chopped fresh cilantro

¼ cup finely diced green bell pepper

1 large jalapeño pepper, finely diced, with seeds

Juice of 1 lime

¼ teaspoon chili powder

¼ teaspoon ground cumin

¼ teaspoon pepper

¼ teaspoon salt, or more to taste

Directions:

1. Core, seed, and dice the plum tomatoes, and place in a large mixing bowl.

2. Add all the remaining ingredients, and toss to combine, adding any additional salt to taste.

3. Transfer ⅓ of the salsa to a food processor, and process until very finely minced and almost smooth.

4. Fold the puréed salsa back into the diced salsa, cover, and refrigerate for at least 1 hour to let the flavors combine before serving.

HELPFUL TIP:

For a milder salsa, discard the seeds of the jalapeño, as that is where most of the heat comes from. Or simply omit the jalapeño and increase the diced green bell pepper from ¼ cup to ⅓ cup.

PREP TIME: 15 MINUTES • BAKE TIME: 25 MINUTES

SPINACH & ARTICHOKE DIP

MAKES 5 APPETIZER PORTIONS

This popular restaurant appetizer is known for being not only delicious, but also high in calories. By substituting thick and creamy Greek yogurt for the cream cheese or mayonnaise that is typically used, we've been able to keep the flavor you love while allowing for a larger protein and calcium-packed portion size. For the least-calorie dippers, serve with celery and carrot sticks.

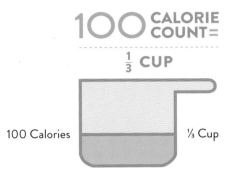

100 CALORIE COUNT=

⅓ CUP

100 Calories   ⅓ Cup

Recommended Serving:
APPETIZER – 200 Calories = ⅔ Cup

Ingredients:

1 (10-ounce) package frozen chopped spinach, thawed

1 (14-ounce) can artichoke hearts, drained and chopped

8 ounces nonfat plain Greek yogurt

1¼ cups shredded Parmesan cheese

¼ cup finely diced red onion

2 tablespoons finely diced red bell pepper

2 teaspoons minced garlic

¼ teaspoon Worcestershire sauce

¼ teaspoon onion powder

¼ teaspoon salt

¼ teaspoon pepper

Directions:

1. Preheat oven to 375°F.

2. In a fine mesh strainer, squeeze as much water from the thawed spinach as possible.

3. Place the drained spinach in a large mixing bowl, and add all the remaining ingredients, stirring to combine.

4. Transfer the dip to a 1½-quart baking dish, and bake for 20–25 minutes, or until hot and bubbly. Serve warm.

HELPFUL TIP:

Using shredded Parmesan cheese adds that gooey cheese texture that you can't quite get from grated; however, you can substitute 1 cup of grated Parmesan in a pinch.

PREP TIME: 30 MINUTES • CHILL TIME: 1 HOUR

FRENCH ONION DIP

MAKES 9 APPETIZER PORTIONS

Forget about packaged powdered dips. We build layers of phenomenal flavor by first caramelizing onions and then mixing in bold seasonings. Cool, creamy, and loaded with onion flavor, this is a dip that you won't want to wait to dive into!

100 **CALORIE COUNT=**

$\frac{1}{3}$ **CUP**

100 Calories   ⅓ Cup

Recommended Serving:
APPETIZER – 100 Calories = ⅓ Cup

Ingredients:

1 tablespoon olive oil

2 cups diced yellow onions

18 ounces plain nonfat Greek yogurt

¼ cup mayonnaise

2 tablespoons chopped fresh chives

1½ teaspoons Worcestershire sauce

1 teaspoon sugar

¾ teaspoon onion powder

½ teaspoon salt

¼ teaspoon garlic powder

¼ teaspoon white pepper

Directions:

1. Place the olive oil in a skillet over medium heat. Add the onions, and cook until well caramelized, about 15 minutes. Let cool.

2. In a mixing bowl, combine the cooled onions and all the remaining ingredients, folding until well mixed.

3. Cover, and refrigerate for at least 1 hour before serving garnished with additional chives, if desired.

HELPFUL TIP:

Two cups of diced yellow onions is about the yield of two medium onions. Sweet yellow (Vidalia) onions are recommended over Spanish onions, as the natural sugars in the Vidalia onions will help them caramelize in step 1.

SMART DIPPING

1 cup sugar snap peas
(35 calories)

1 cup sliced radishes
(20 calories)

1 cup celery sticks
(15 calories)

1 cup broccoli florets
(20 calories)

1 cup baby carrots
(70 calories)

1 cup sliced cucumber
(15 calories)

1 cup sliced zucchini or squash
(20 calories)

1 cup sliced bell pepper
(20 calories)

½ cup Oven-Fried Potato Chips, page 275
(100 calories)

7 whole-wheat pita chips
(100 calories)

10 pretzel chips
(100 calories)

6 reduced-fat woven wheat crackers
(100 calories)

8 multigrain tortilla chips
(100 calories)

SNAP PEAS
1 CUP =
35
CALORIES

SLICED RADISHES
1 CUP =
20
CALORIES

BROCCOLI FLORETS
1 CUP =
20
CALORIES

SLICED ZUCCHINI
1 CUP =
20
CALORIES

SLICED SQUASH
1 CUP =
20
CALORIES

CELERY STICKS
1 CUP = 15 CALORIES

WHOLE WHEAT PITA CHIPS
7 = 100 CALORIES

BAKED POTATO CHIPS
½ CUP = 100 CALORIES

SLICED CUCUMBER
1 CUP = 15 CALORIES

PRETZEL CHIPS
10 = 100 CALORIES

REDUCED-FAT WHEAT CRACKERS
6 = 100 CALORIES

BABY CARROTS
1 CUP = 70 CALORIES

MULTI-GRAIN TORTILLA CHIPS
8 = 100 CALORIES

BELL PEPPERS
1 CUP = 20 CALORIES

7 HOLIDAY FAVORITES

PREP TIME: 15 MINUTES • BAKE TIME: 3 HOURS

ROASTED TURKEY

MAKES 12 DINNER PORTIONS

Thanksgiving wouldn't be the same without a turkey, but as I'm sure you know, roasting them can be daunting. Many recipes spell success by loading on the butter, covering the turkey with an entire stick, or two! We use only 2 tablespoons of butter, and to make sure the bird is crispy, we baste the pan drippings onto the skin during cooking. If you have an eye on the clock and a meat thermometer, you don't need a ton of butter to keep a turkey moist. The real secret is to simply not overcook it!

100 CALORIE COUNT =

$2\frac{1}{2}$ **OUNCES WHITE MEAT (SKINLESS)**
2 OUNCES WHITE MEAT WITH SKIN
2 OUNCES DARK MEAT (SKINLESS)
$1\frac{1}{2}$ **OUNCES DARK MEAT WITH SKIN**

Recommended Serving:
DINNER – 300 Calories
7½ Ounces White Meat (Skinless)
6 Ounces White Meat with Skin
6 Ounces Dark Meat (Skinless)
4½ Ounces Dark Meat with Skin

Ingredients:

1 (12-pound) young turkey, thawed

2 tablespoons butter, softened

Juice of ½ lemon

1 tablespoon chopped fresh sage

1 tablespoon chopped fresh thyme leaves

1 teaspoon salt

¾ teaspoon pepper

¼ teaspoon paprika

Directions:

1. Preheat the oven to 350°F. Place a rack into a roasting pan.

2. Remove the neck and giblets from the turkey cavity (if included), and discard (or save) to add flavor to the Turkey Gravy (on the next page). Rinse the turkey inside and out with cold water, and pat dry with paper towels. Transfer to the roasting pan.

3. Place the butter, lemon juice, sage, thyme, salt, pepper, and paprika in a food processor or blender, and pulse only a few times, just until combined.

4. Use your hands to rub the butter mixture over the entire surface of the bird.

5. Bake for 2½–3 hours, basting every 45 minutes with juices from the roasting pan. Turkey is done when a meat thermometer inserted into the thigh registers 165°F.

6. Transfer to a carving board, and let rest for at least 20 minutes before slicing.

HELPFUL TIP:

Many people truss their turkey by tying the legs together with baking twine. This makes for a neater presentation, but can cause uneven cooking and is entirely unnecessary.

PREP TIME: 15 MINUTES • COOK TIME: 5 MINUTES

TURKEY GRAVY

MAKES 8 PORTIONS

Let's face it, gravy is about as high in calories as it gets, but we've been able to significantly lower them and keep the same rich, savory taste. We skim the turkey grease off the very flavorful pan juices, reduce the juices to super concentrate them, and then stir in a little creamy Greek yogurt for a silky smooth finish. Guilt-free gravy? We think we've done it!

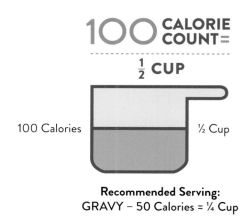

100 **CALORIE COUNT =**

½ **CUP**

100 Calories   ½ Cup

Recommended Serving:
GRAVY – 50 Calories = ¼ Cup

Ingredients:

Roasting pan juices from a cooked turkey (about 1 cup)

1 tablespoon chopped fresh sage

½ teaspoon light brown sugar

1 tablespoon cornstarch

1 cup (or more, if needed) chicken broth, divided

3 ounces plain nonfat Greek yogurt

Salt and pepper

Directions:

1. Scrape any browned bits from the bottom of your turkey roasting pan.

2. Pour all of the cooking liquid and browned turkey bits from the roasting pan into a tempered glass measuring cup (or other narrow container). This should be at least 1 cup of liquid. If less, add additional chicken stock in step 6.

3. Place the measuring cup into the freezer, and chill for 15 minutes. (This will allow the fat to separate from the liquid and begin to harden.)

4. Use a spoon to skim all of the fat that has floated to the top of the measuring cup; discard.

5. Add the skimmed cooking liquid, chopped sage, brown sugar, and ¾ cup of the chicken broth to a sauce pot over medium-high heat, and bring to a boil. Boil until liquid has reduced by about ⅓.

6. Whisk the cornstarch into the remaining ¼ cup chicken broth, and then whisk into the pot. Bring back up to a boil, and let simmer, stirring constantly, for 2 minutes, or until thickened.

7. Remove from heat, and stir in the Greek yogurt to thicken further before seasoning with salt and pepper to taste.

HELPFUL TIP:

For even more flavor, you can brown the turkey giblets and neck in the sauce pot before creating the gravy; however, there is more than enough turkey flavor to make gravy from just the pan juices used in this recipe.

PREP TIME: 15 MINUTES • COOK TIME: 18 MINUTES

HOME-STYLE MASHED POTATOES

MAKES 8 SIDE DISH PORTIONS

Some would say that you can't have a holiday meal without perfect mashed potatoes! Yukon Golds are our preferred potato for mashing because of their natural creamy, buttery texture. And since half of their fiber is in the skin, we leave the skins on for our mash, giving you the maximum nutrients at a fraction of the work. What could be better than that?

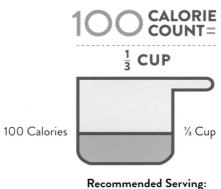

100 **CALORIE COUNT =**

$\frac{1}{3}$ **CUP**

100 Calories   ⅓ Cup

Recommended Serving:
SIDE DISH – 200 Calories = ⅔ Cup

Ingredients:

3 pounds Yukon Gold potatoes

1½ teaspoons salt, divided

½ cup sour cream

¼ cup butter

½ teaspoon onion powder

¼ teaspoon garlic powder

¼ teaspoon pepper

2 tablespoons chopped chives

Directions:

1. Chop potatoes (with skin, unless undesired) into 1-inch pieces, and add to a large pot.

2. Add 1 teaspoon of the salt to the pot, and fill with enough water to cover potatoes.

3. Place over high heat, and bring to a boil. Cover, and cook for 15–18 minutes, or until potatoes are fork-tender. Drain well, and return the potatoes to the pot.

4. Add sour cream, butter, onion powder, garlic powder, pepper, and the remaining ½ teaspoon of salt to the potatoes, and mash with a potato masher, just until mostly smooth.

5. If potatoes have cooled, place the pot over medium-low heat and cook, stirring occasionally, just until hot. Stir in chopped chives before serving.

HELPFUL TIP:

You can also use a food processor or hand blender to "mash" the potatoes, though you should be careful not to overprocess them, as they can become gummy.

PREP TIME: 10 MINUTES • BAKE TIME: 1½ HOURS

MAPLE-GLAZED HAM

MAKES 12 DINNER PORTIONS

Forget about those corn syrupy "glaze" packets that come with hams. We wanted the real deal for our holiday stunner. We make a thickened glaze of maple syrup, apple juice, brown sugar, coarse mustard, and cloves and coat our ham not once, but twice, for a fabulous looking and tasting ham.

100 CALORIE COUNT =

2 OUNCES GLAZED HAM

Recommended Serving:
DINNER – 300 Calories = 6 Ounces Glazed Ham

Ingredients:

1 semi-boneless lean smoked half ham, about 6 pounds

¼ cup pure maple syrup

¼ cup apple juice

¼ cup light brown sugar

1 tablespoon whole-grain deli mustard

2 teaspoons cornstarch

⅛ teaspoon ground cloves

Directions:

1. Preheat the oven to 325°F.

2. Use a sharp knife to slice a patchwork pattern across the skin of the ham, only slicing ⅛ inch into the meat of the ham.

3. Place the scored ham in a roasting pan lined with aluminum foil, and bake for 1 hour.

4. Whisk the maple syrup, apple juice, brown sugar, mustard, cornstarch, and cloves in a small sauce pot over medium-high heat. Bring up to a boil, reduce heat to low, and let simmer for 3 minutes to create the glaze.

5. Spoon half of the glaze over the entire surface of the ham, and return the ham to the oven. Bake for 15 minutes.

6. Top the ham with the remaining glaze, and bake for an additional 15 minutes. Let the ham rest for 15 minutes before slicing.

HELPFUL TIP:

Lining your roasting pan with aluminum foil or using a disposable pan is highly recommended for easy cleanup.

PREP TIME: 20 MINUTES • BAKE TIME: 55 MINUTES

THANKSGIVING STUFFING

MAKES 8 SIDE DISH PORTIONS

Mona's Family Favorites: On Thanksgiving my family always gets together to not only give thanks, but also to celebrate my father's birthday. His smile and infectious laugh are still with us around the dinner table. I can't help but think of the holidays shared with him when I serve this dish. I've lightened up my recipe over the years by using less butter and leaving out egg yolks. The fresh and dried herbs and seasonings makes for a fantastic, flavor-packed stuffing.

100 CALORIE COUNT =

$\frac{1}{16}$ **THANKSGIVING STUFFING**

Recommended Serving:
SIDE DISH – 200 Calories = 2 Sections

Ingredients:

1 (1-pound) loaf French bread

Nonstick cooking spray

1 cup diced yellow onion

1 cup diced celery

2 cups chicken broth

2 tablespoons chopped fresh sage

½ teaspoon dried thyme

½ teaspoon onion powder

½ teaspoon salt

½ teaspoon pepper

¼ teaspoon poultry seasoning

2 large egg whites

2 tablespoons butter, melted

Directions:

1. Preheat the oven to 400°F. Cut the French bread into ½-inch cubes. Arrange the cubes in a single layer on 2 sheet pans.

2. Bake the bread cubes for 10 minutes, or until lightly browned. Let cool.

3. Reduce the oven temperature to 375°F. Spray a 13 x 9-inch baking dish with nonstick cooking spray.

4. Spray a skillet with nonstick cooking spray, and place over medium-high heat.

5. Add the onion and celery to the skillet, and sauté for 5 minutes, or until onions are translucent and celery is almost tender.

6. In a large mixing bowl, combine the chicken broth, sage, thyme, onion powder, salt, pepper, and poultry seasoning. Add the toasted bread cubes to the bowl, and quickly toss until nearly all the liquid has been soaked up by the bread.

7. Add the sautéed vegetables to the cubed bread in the mixing bowl, and toss to combine. Transfer to the prepared baking dish.

8. In a small bowl, whisk together the egg whites and melted butter. Drizzle over the stuffing in the baking dish.

9. Cover with aluminum foil and bake for 25 minutes. Remove aluminum foil and bake for an additional 20 minutes, or until the top of the stuffing begins to brown. Let cool for 5 minutes before slicing. For 100 calorie portions, slice into 12 sections by cutting 3 rows by 4 rows.

PREP TIME: 15 MINUTES • BAKE TIME: 30 MINUTES

ROSEMARY ROASTED BEEF TENDERLOIN

MAKES 8 DINNER PORTIONS

Why not serve beef tenderloin for your next special occasion? Though this large roast might look imposing, it's actually incredibly easy to cook. We coat our tenderloin with salt, pepper, fresh rosemary, and garlic for winning savory depth. We recommended cooking the roast to medium-rare for optimum juicy tenderness, but we've included instructions for other temperatures as well.

100 CALORIE COUNT =

2 OUNCE SLICE BEEF TENDERLOIN

Recommended Serving:
DINNER – 300 Calories = 6 Ounces Beef Tenderloin

Ingredients:

1 (3-pound) center-cut beef tenderloin roast

¾ teaspoon salt

¾ teaspoon pepper

½ teaspoon dried rosemary

1 tablespoon olive oil

2 teaspoons minced garlic

6 sprigs fresh rosemary

Directions:

1. Preheat the oven to 400°F.

2. Season the tenderloin roast on all sides with the salt, pepper, and dried rosemary.

3. Place the olive oil in a large skillet over high heat. Add the seasoned roast to the skillet and brown on all sides. Transfer the browned roast to a roasting pan.

4. Spread the minced garlic over the top of the roast, and press 3 sprigs of rosemary over the top. Tuck the remaining 3 sprigs of rosemary underneath the roast.

5. Bake for 30 minutes, or until a meat thermometer inserted into the thickest part registers 130°F for medium-rare, 140°F for medium, or 150°F for well-done.

6. Discard rosemary sprigs, and let rest for 10 minutes before slicing and serving drizzled with juices from the roasting pan.

HELPFUL TIP:

For easy 100 calorie portions, slice the roast into 12 thick (and equal) slices before cutting each of these slices in half vertically to make 24 halved slices.

PREP TIME: 2 HOURS • BAKE TIME: 20 MINUTES

100 CALORIE DINNER ROLLS

MAKES 18 DINNER ROLLS

Most of us would love to have a warm, crusty roll with dinner, and now you don't have to think twice about it. We combined a modest amount of melted butter and oil with reduced-fat milk to yield a golden roll that's so light and fluffy it nearly lifts of the table, and did we mention it's only 100 calories?

Recommended Serving:
SIDE DISH – 100 Calories = 1 Dinner Roll

Ingredients:

1 (0.25-ounce) packet active dry yeast

3 ½ teaspoons sugar

¼ cup warm water

2 ½ cups all-purpose flour

1 teaspoon salt

¾ cup 2% milk, warmed

3 tablespoons butter, melted

1 tablespoon canola oil

1 large egg white

1 teaspoon water

Directions:

1 In a mixing bowl, stir the yeast and sugar into the warm water, and let stand for 15 minutes.

2 In a large mixing bowl or stand mixer with dough hook attached, combine the flour and salt.

3 Stir the milk and butter into the yeast mixture before adding to the flour in the large mixing bowl.

4 Knead the wet ingredients into the flour until a firm dough forms, about 5 minutes. Add additional water by the teaspoon if the dough is too thick to knead, or additional flour by the teaspoon if the dough is too sticky.

5 Form the dough into a large ball and coat with 1 tablespoon of canola oil. Place in a clean bowl, cover loosely, and put in a warm spot to rise until it has doubled in size, about 1 hour.

6 Line a sheet pan with parchment paper. With floured hands, break the dough into 18 equal pieces and form into balls, placing them 2 inches apart on the prepared sheet pan.

7 Whisk the egg white with 1 teaspoon of water to create an egg wash, and brush a thin layer over the top of each ball of dough. Cover the sheet pan, and let rise for an additional 30 minutes.

8 Preheat oven to 375°F. Bake for 20 minutes, or until golden brown.

PREP TIME: 5 MINUTES • COOK TIME: 15 MINUTES

REAL CRANBERRY SAUCE

MAKES 9 SIDE DISH PORTIONS

Making homemade cranberry sauce from fresh berries is just about the easiest dish you can prepare for the holidays and a far better choice than grabbing a can of jellied high-fructose "sauce." Not only does the real deal taste better, but the healthy fiber in the berries is still intact. The natural pectin in the cranberries thickens the sauce like gelatin, so for a thicker consistency, refrigerate for at least 2 hours before serving.

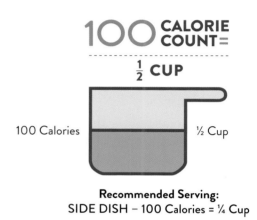

100 **CALORIE COUNT=**

½ **CUP**

100 Calories ½ Cup

Recommended Serving:
SIDE DISH – 100 Calories = ¼ Cup

Ingredients:

1 cup orange juice

¾ cup sugar

1 (12-ounce) bag fresh cranberries

2 tablespoons fresh orange zest, divided

Directions:

1. In a medium-size sauce pot over medium-high heat, bring orange juice and sugar to a boil, stirring occasionally, until sugar is dissolved.

2. Add cranberries and 1 tablespoon of the orange zest to the pot. Bring to a simmer, and reduce heat to medium.

3. Let simmer for 12–15 minutes, stirring occasionally, until cranberries have split and begin to cook into the sauce. For a smoother sauce, use a heavy spoon or potato masher to lightly mash most of the softened berries into the sauce.

4. Remove from heat, and let cool at least 10 minutes, to thicken. Serve warm or chilled, garnished with the remaining orange zest.

HELPFUL TIP:

Though it is most cost-effective to buy fresh oranges and use both the zest and juice for this recipe, zesting fresh tangerines makes this even better by adding a zing that you can't quite get from an orange. Adding a whole cinnamon stick in step 2 (and removing before mashing the berries) will add great holiday spice.

PREP TIME: 25 MINUTES • BAKE TIME: 35 MINUTES

CANDIED SWEET POTATOES

MAKES 6 SIDE DISH PORTIONS

Since sweet potatoes are already, well, sweet, we were able to reduce the brown sugar to just ¼ cup. We added a small amount of maple syrup and butter for richness and were left with a fantastic side dish. It should certainly be on your holiday spread.

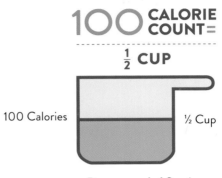

100 **CALORIE COUNT =**

½ **CUP**

100 Calories   ½ Cup

Recommended Serving:
SIDE DISH – 200 Calories = 1 Cup

Ingredients:

2 pounds sweet potatoes, peeled

2 tablespoons butter, melted

¼ cup light brown sugar

1 tablespoon pure maple syrup

¼ teaspoon ground cinnamon

¼ teaspoon salt

1 pinch nutmeg

Directions:

1. Preheat oven to 350°F. Place a large pot of water over high heat to boil.

2. Chop the peeled sweet potatoes into 1½-inch chunks.

3. Boil the sweet potato chunks for 10 minutes, just until fork-tender. Drain and transfer to a 2-quart baking dish.

4. Whisk together all the remaining ingredients, and pour over the potatoes, tossing to coat.

5. Bake for 35 minutes, gently stirring halfway through. Let cool for 5 minutes before serving.

HELPFUL TIP:

If you are a marshmallow casserole kind of person, topping the casserole with 1 ½ cups of miniature marshmallows will add 20 calories per 100 calorie portion. Simply top after baking, and place under the broiler until the marshmallows are golden brown.

PREP TIME: 15 MINUTES • BAKE TIME: 40 MINUTES

SPINACH PIE

MAKES 6 SIDE DISH PORTIONS

This crust-less "Spinach Pie" is actually closer to a soufflé or quiche than a pie. With eggs, ricotta, and Parmesan cheese, it makes a great dish for a holiday brunch, but it's also packed with enough nutrient-rich spinach to serve as a dinner side dish in place of creamed spinach.

100 CALORIE COUNT =

$\frac{1}{12}$ **SPINACH PIE**

Recommended Serving:
SIDE DISH – 200 Calories = 2 Sections

Ingredients:

Nonstick cooking spray

1 teaspoon olive oil

1 cup diced yellow onion

2 teaspoons minced garlic

1 (16-ounce) package frozen chopped spinach, thawed

3 large eggs

4 large egg whites

1 cup part-skim ricotta cheese

⅔ cup grated Parmesan cheese

2 tablespoons diced pimentos

½ teaspoon salt

¼ teaspoon pepper

Directions:

1. Preheat oven to 350°F. Spray a 9 x 9-inch baking dish with nonstick cooking spray.

2. Heat olive oil, onion, and garlic in a skillet over medium-high heat. Sauté for 5 minutes, just until onions are lightly caramelized.

3. In a fine mesh strainer, squeeze as much water from the thawed spinach as possible.

4. In a large mixing bowl, whisk the eggs, egg whites, and ricotta cheese until fully combined. Stir the Parmesan cheese, diced pimentos, salt, pepper, drained spinach, and cooked onion mixture into eggs, and mix well.

5. Pour the spinach and egg mixture into the prepared baking dish, and bake for 40 minutes, or until the center is springy to the touch. Let cool 10 minutes before slicing. For 100 calorie portions, slice into 12 sections by cutting 3 rows by 4 rows.

HELPFUL TIP:

While jarred pimentos add a nice roasted flavor, finely diced fresh bell pepper (cooked in the skillet in step 2) can be used in place of the pimentos (if you already have bell pepper on hand).

PREP TIME: 10 MINUTES • COOK TIME: 45 MINUTES

GREEN BEAN CASSEROLE

MAKES 9 SIDE DISH PORTIONS

Bob's Farm to Table: Most of us have made a green bean casserole from canned cream of mushroom soup and packaged French-fried onions, but making this casserole from scratch, truly from scratch, is well worth the effort. Tender green beans are coated with a rich mushroom gravy and topped with onion-laced crisp bread crumbs. This is a holiday classic you'll want every week!

100 CALORIE COUNT =

$\frac{1}{18}$ **GREEN BEAN CASSEROLE**

Recommended Serving:
SIDE DISH – 200 Calories = 2 Sections

Ingredients:

2 pounds green beans, cut into 1½-inch lengths

4 tablespoons butter, divided

1 red onion, thinly sliced

1½ cups panko bread crumbs

½ teaspoon onion powder

12 ounces baby bella mushrooms, chopped

2 teaspoons minced garlic

1 cup beef broth

1 teaspoon Worcestershire sauce

¾ teaspoon salt

½ teaspoon pepper

⅓ cup all-purpose flour

2⅔ cups 2% milk

Directions:

1. Preheat the oven to 350°F. Place a pot of water over high heat, and bring to a boil. Boil the green beans for 3 minutes, just until bright green. Drain and rinse under cold water. Transfer the drained beans to a 13 x 9-inch baking dish.

2. Melt 1 tablespoon of the butter in a large skillet over medium heat. Add the sliced onion, and sauté for 15 minutes, or until onions have caramelized well.

3. Remove the onions from the heat, and stir in 2 tablespoons of butter, the panko bread crumbs, and onion powder. Transfer to a bowl and set aside. Wipe skillet clean.

4. Melt the last tablespoon of butter in the clean skillet over medium-high heat. Add the mushrooms and minced garlic, and sauté for 5 minutes, or until mushrooms begin to brown.

5. Add the beef broth, Worcestershire sauce, salt, and pepper to the skillet, and let simmer until the liquid has reduced by half.

6. In a small bowl, whisk the flour into the milk. Whisk this flour and milk mixture into the mushroom sauce in the skillet. Bring to a simmer, and cook, stirring constantly, for 2 minutes.

7. Pour the mushroom sauce over the green beans in the baking dish, and stir to combine. Top the casserole with the caramelized onions and bread crumb mixture.

8. Bake for 20 minutes, just until the bread crumbs have lightly browned. Let cool for 5 minutes before serving. For 100 calorie portions, cut into 3 rows by 6 rows.

PREP TIME: 10 MINUTES • BAKE TIME: 30 MINUTES

ROASTED BUTTERNUT SQUASH

MAKES 4 SIDE DISH PORTIONS

Mona's Family Favorites: Butternut squash was the first veggie that I could get both of my children to eat. Roasting it makes it so sweet that they thought I was giving them candy and, for a mother, that is a WIN. Now that my kids are older, I love mixing up roasted squash with spices. The combination of cinnamon and cumin in this recipe gives the squash a true Mediterranean flair to perfectly play off its natural sweetness. Plus, you've got to stay hip with the times, right?

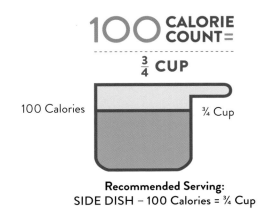

100 **CALORIE COUNT =**

¾ **CUP**

100 Calories   ¾ Cup

Recommended Serving:
SIDE DISH – 100 Calories = ¾ Cup

Ingredients:

4 cups cubed butternut squash (see tip)

1 tablespoon extra virgin olive oil

½ teaspoon ground cinnamon

¼ teaspoon ground cumin

¼ teaspoon salt

¼ teaspoon pepper

Directions:

1 Preheat the oven to 450°F.

2 In a large mixing bowl, toss the cubed squash in all the remaining ingredients until well coated.

3 Spread the coated squash on a sheet pan in a single layer, and bake for 25–30 minutes, stirring halfway through. Squash is done when well caramelized and fork-tender.

HELPFUL TIP:

You can get about 4 cups of cubed butternut squash from 1 (2-pound) squash. Use a heavy vegetable peeler to peel the squash and then remove the pulp and seeds before chopping into cubes. Some stores sell bags of already cubed butternut squash in the refrigerated produce section, making this recipe as easy as it gets!

PREP TIME: 10 MINUTES • COOK TIME: 20 MINUTES

CRANBERRY POACHED PEARS

MAKES 4 DESSERT PORTIONS

Halved pears poach their way to creamy and tender bliss in this amazing holiday dessert. We poach our pears in an orange- and cinnamon-scented cranberry juice to infuse delicious, layered flavor. Top with a dollop of cool whipped cream for a simple, yet beautiful, presentation.

100 CALORIE COUNT =

$\frac{1}{2}$ **PEAR**

Recommended Serving:
DESSERT –200 Calories = 1 Pear

Ingredients:

4 medium pears

2 cups cranberry juice cocktail

2 tablespoons light brown sugar

1 teaspoon orange zest

1 cinnamon stick

4 teaspoons cornstarch

½ cup whipped cream

Directions:

1. Peel, halve, and core the pears.

2. Add the cranberry juice, brown sugar, orange zest, and cinnamon stick to a wide nonstick skillet over medium-high heat, and stir to dissolve sugar.

3. Place the halved pears in the skillet, and bring to a boil.

4. Reduce heat to medium-low, and let simmer, turning pears occasionally, for 15 minutes, or until they are fork-tender. Transfer pears to serving plates. Remove ¼ cup of the liquid, place into a small bowl, and let cool. Whisk cornstarch into the cooled liquid to make a slurry.

5. Raise heat to medium high, and bring mixture to a boil. Add the slurry, and cook for 1 minute, or until thickened.

6. Serve each half of poached pear warm, drizzled with sauce from the pan, and topped with a tablespoon of the whipped cream.

HELPFUL TIP:

A melon baller or serrated grapefruit spoon can make coring the pears a breeze. If the pears have their stems intact, it makes for the best presentation to leave those in place.

PREP TIME: 20 MINUTES • BAKE TIME: 15 MINUTES PER BATCH

PUMPKIN PIE COOKIES

MAKES 36 COOKIES OR 18 DESSERT PORTIONS

These cookies pack all the flavors of a holiday pumpkin pie, with only 100 calories per cookie. They are crispy on the outside, tender on the inside, and are studded with chopped pecans for great texture and flavor. Just be sure to buy 100% pure canned pumpkin and not "pumpkin pie filling," which is already sweetened and seasoned.

100 CALORIE COUNT =

1 COOKIE

Recommended Serving:
DESSERT – 200 Calories = 2 Cookies

Ingredients:

Nonstick cooking spray

2 ½ cups all-purpose flour

2 teaspoons pumpkin pie spice

1 teaspoon baking soda

¼ teaspoon salt

1 ½ cups sugar

½ cup (1 stick) butter, softened

1 cup pure canned pumpkin

1 ¼ teaspoons vanilla extract

½ cup chopped pecans

Directions:

1. Preheat oven to 350°F, and spray 3 cookie sheets with nonstick cooking spray.

2. In a mixing bowl, stir together flour, pumpkin pie spice, baking soda, and salt.

3. In a separate mixing bowl or electric mixer, cream together the sugar and butter. Stir in pumpkin and vanilla extract.

4. Add the dry ingredients into the wet ingredients, folding until all is combined into dough. Fold the chopped pecans into the dough.

5. Drop tablespoons of the dough onto the prepared cookie sheets, at least 2 ½ inches apart, and press down to flatten. You should have enough dough to make 3 dozen cookies.

6. Bake each sheet of cookies for 15 minutes, or until edges are golden brown and firm to the touch. Let cool at least 10 minutes before serving.

HELPFUL TIP:

For the most even cooking, it is best to bake these in 3 batches, rather than filling your oven racks all at once, as that limits the flow of hot air.

8 DRESSINGS, SAUCES & JAMS

PREP TIME: 10 MINUTES

CHUNKY BLUE CHEESE DRESSING

MAKES 8 DRESSING PORTIONS OR 4 DIP PORTIONS

We found the secret to a flavor-packed Blue Cheese Dressing was the cheese itself. Gorgonzola is not only potent, but it's creamy texture allowed us to dial back the mayonnaise while still producing a thick and creamy consistency. Plus, with less mayonnaise, the Gorgonzola can really shine. Perfect for dressing on salads, as a dip, and alongside our Buffalo Wings (see page 185).

3 TABLESPOONS

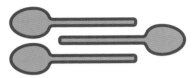

Recommended Serving:
DRESSING – 100 Calories = 3 Tablespoons
DIP – 200 Calories = 6 Tablespoons

Ingredients:

⅔ cup crumbled Gorgonzola cheese

½ cup buttermilk

¼ cup mayonnaise

¼ teaspoon salt

¼ teaspoon pepper

⅛ teaspoon Worcestershire sauce

⅛ teaspoon hot pepper sauce (Tabasco)

⅛ teaspoon garlic powder

Directions:

1 In a mixing bowl, use a heavy spoon to mash ½ of the crumbled Gorgonzola cheese into a thick paste.

2 Add all the remaining ingredients, including the remaining Gorgonzola cheese, and stir until well combined. Serve immediately, or refrigerate overnight for best flavor. Store refrigerated for up to 1 week.

HELPFUL TIP:

Any type of blue cheese will work in this recipe, though Gorgonzola is the creamiest cheese available in most supermarkets.

PREP TIME: 15 MINUTES • CHILL TIME: 1 HOUR

AVOCADO CAESAR DRESSING

MAKES 6 DRESSING PORTIONS

Mona's Family Favorites: I LOVE avocado. It's one of those healthy ingredients that creates creaminess with less fat than mayonnaise. In this recipe, we used puréed fresh avocado instead of the egg yolk and Parmesan cheese. Not only does the avocado make this dressing thick and creamy, it also adds nutrients, great flavor, and only unsaturated fat! This delicious Avocado Caesar Dressing knocks it out of the park.

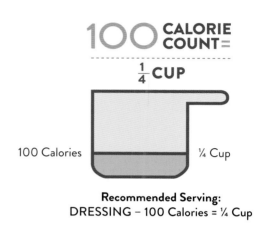

100 CALORIE COUNT =
¼ CUP

100 Calories   ¼ Cup

Recommended Serving:
DRESSING – 100 Calories = ¼ Cup

Ingredients:

1 medium Haas avocado, halved, peeled, pitted, and chopped

½ cup 2% milk

2 teaspoons anchovy paste

1½ teaspoons lemon juice

1 teaspoon minced garlic

1 teaspoon Dijon mustard

½ teaspoon Worcestershire sauce

¼ teaspoon salt

¼ teaspoon pepper

¼ cup grated Parmesan cheese

Directions:

1 Place the avocado in a food processor, and process until mostly smooth.

2 Add all the remaining ingredients, except the Parmesan cheese, and process until smooth and combined.

3 Fold the Parmesan cheese into the dressing, cover, and refrigerate for 1 hour before serving. Store refrigerated for up to 1 week.

HELPFUL TIP:

Anchovy paste can often be found in the Italian food aisle, although 2 whole canned anchovies can be used in its place.

PREP TIME: 10 MINUTES

BUTTERMILK RANCH DRESSING

MAKES 6 DRESSING PORTIONS OR 3 DIP PORTIONS

Why opt for store-bought when homemade ranch dressing simply tastes better and you know exactly what's in it? We combine a sensible mixture of tangy buttermilk and sour cream with a small amount of mayonnaise and herbs and spices for a silky smooth ranch that's off the charts.

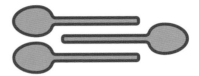

100 CALORIE COUNT =

3 TABLESPOONS

Recommended Serving:
DRESSING – 100 Calories = 3 Tablespoons
DIP – 200 Calories = 6 Tablespoons

Ingredients:

½ cup buttermilk

⅓ cup sour cream

¼ cup mayonnaise

2 tablespoons chopped fresh chives

1 teaspoon sugar

1 teaspoon parsley flakes

½ teaspoon dried dill

¼ teaspoon onion powder

¼ teaspoon garlic powder

¼ teaspoon salt

¼ teaspoon pepper

Directions:

1. In a mixing bowl, add all the ingredients, and whisk well to combine.

2. Add any additional salt and pepper to taste. Serve immediately, or refrigerate overnight for best flavor. Store refrigerated for up to 1 week.

HELPFUL TIP:

This dressing will thicken up nicely in the fridge, making for a great dip. For a thinner consistency you can replace the sour cream with an additional ⅓ cup of buttermilk. This will also lower the calories to 80 calories per 3 tablespoons.

PREP TIME: 15 MINUTES

RASPBERRY VINAIGRETTE

MAKES 6 DRESSING PORTIONS

Mona's Family Favorites: I love making fresh homemade salad dressings. They really add extra flavor, and everyone always notices and wants the recipe. So, here it is! My vinaigrette of fresh raspberries, honey, rosemary, and a hint of Dijon mustard is a refreshing way to dress up a spinach or mixed greens salad. A great vinaigrette is all about balancing the rich oil with the tangy vinegar. Red wine vinegar enhances the fruity and sweet notes of the raspberries. Plus, puréeing raspberries into the vinaigrette adds just enough sweetness. We hit the nail on the head. You'll be sharing this recipe!

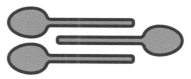

Recommended Serving:
DRESSING – 100 Calories = 3 Tablespoons

Ingredients:

1 cup fresh raspberries

3 tablespoons red wine vinegar

2 teaspoons honey

1 teaspoon Dijon mustard

¼ teaspoon dried rosemary

¼ teaspoon salt

¼ cup extra virgin olive oil

Directions:

1 Add all the ingredients, except the olive oil, to a food processor, and pulse in short bursts for 2 minutes to fully purée the raspberries and create a thick dressing.

2 Add the olive oil to the food processor, a little at a time, processing on low speed to mix it into the dressing. Serve immediately, or refrigerate until ready to use. Store covered and refrigerated for up to 1 week. Stir or shake before serving.

HELPFUL TIP:

Slowly adding the olive oil helps to "emulsify" the dressing by combining the oil with the other ingredients without the water (from the raspberries) and oil separating. If your food processor does not have an opening to drizzle the oil in as it operates, simply transfer to a mixing bowl and whisk the olive oil in by hand.

PREP TIME: 25 MINUTES • CHILL TIME: 2 HOURS

TZATZIKI SAUCE

MAKES 10 TOPPING PORTIONS OR 5 DIP PORTIONS

Tzatziki is a creamy, tangy Greek sauce and dip made from fresh cucumber, dill, and yogurt. It makes a refreshing topping for meats seasoned with Mediterranean spices like oregano, in the same way that you would top a Mexican dish with sour cream. Beyond that, it's also an incredibly low-calorie dip that is excellent with baked pita chips or fresh-cut vegetables.

100 **CALORIE COUNT=**

$\frac{1}{2}$ **CUP**

100 Calories   ½ Cup

Recommended Serving:
TOPPING – 50 Calories = ¼ Cup
DIP – 100 Calories = ½ Cup

Ingredients:

1 medium cucumber, peeled

½ teaspoon salt, divided

18 ounces nonfat plain Greek yogurt

Juice of ½ lemon

2 tablespoons chopped fresh dill

2 tablespoons minced red onion

1 tablespoon minced garlic

1 tablespoon extra virgin olive oil

⅛ teaspoon pepper

Directions:

1 Slice cucumber in half lengthwise, and use a spoon to scrape out the seeds, making sure to get all of the translucent flesh around the seeds and discarding it.

2 Chop the seeded cucumbers, and place in a colander. Cover with a paper towel, and press down to squeeze as much water as possible from the cucumber.

3 Sprinkle the cucumber with ¼ teaspoon of the salt, and toss in the colander to mix. Let drain in sink for 15 minutes, as the salt brings out the liquid in the cucumbers. Press cucumbers through a paper towel once more before proceeding.

4 Add the drained cucumbers and all the remaining ingredients, including the remaining ¼ teaspoon of salt, to the bowl of a food processor, and pulse in short bursts for 1 minute to finely grate the cucumbers and combine everything into a sauce.

5 For the best flavor, cover, and refrigerate for 2 hours to let the flavors marry before serving.

HELPFUL TIP:

Some brands sell nonfat plain Greek yogurt in 18-ounce tubs (Fage brand is 17.6 ounces, which is close enough), but if you are having any issue finding that size, the easiest thing to do is purchase 3 (6-ounce) cups.

PREP TIME: 15 MINUTES • COOK TIME: 15 MINUTES

BLUE RIBBON BARBECUE SAUCE

MAKES 4 SAUCE PORTIONS

Store-bought barbecue sauces may be convenient, but they are typically loaded with sugar or corn syrup. We season a rich tomato base with a little molasses, vinegar, and liquid smoke for a stand-out sauce in a mere 15 minutes.

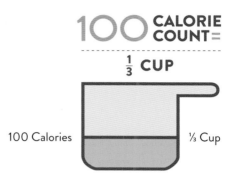

100 **CALORIE COUNT** $=$

$\frac{1}{3}$ **CUP**

100 Calories   ⅓ Cup

Recommended Serving:
SAUCE – 100 Calories = ⅓ Cup

Ingredients:

2 teaspoons olive oil

¼ cup finely diced yellow onion

1 (8-ounce) can tomato sauce

2 ½ tablespoons light brown sugar

2 tablespoons tomato paste

1 tablespoon molasses

1 tablespoon cider vinegar

2 teaspoons Worcestershire sauce

2 teaspoons minced garlic

½ teaspoon liquid smoke (sold near the spices)

1 teaspoon Dijon mustard

½ teaspoon onion powder

½ teaspoon pepper

Salt to taste

Directions:

1 Heat the oil and onions in a saucepot over medium-high heat, and cook until golden brown and softened, about 5 minutes.

2 Reduce heat to medium-low, and stir in all the remaining ingredients, except the salt. Cover, and let simmer for 10 minutes.

3 Remove from heat, and add salt to taste. Store covered and refrigerated for up to 10 days.

HELPFUL TIP:

This recipe makes 1⅓ cups of sauce, about the same amount as a standard bottle of store-bought sauce.

PREP TIME: 5 MINUTES • COOK TIME: 30 MINUTES

TUSCAN TOMATO SAUCE

MAKES 6 SAUCE PORTIONS

Mona's Family Favorites: This past spring, my family and I took a once-in-a-lifetime cooking class in Montepulciano, in the Tuscan region of Italy. Our chefs and hosts, Luca and Stefania of Villa Poggiano, taught us that the simpler the ingredients, the better the tomato sauce. While we only used a handful of ingredients, including fresh basil and spinach, to make this amazing sauce, the flavors melded into something far more than the sum of its parts. Isn't that what great cooking is all about? Today, I use this as my go-to sauce for all of my Italian dishes. Delicioso!

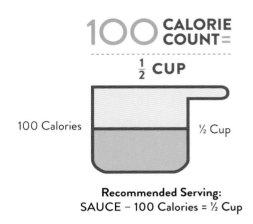

100 CALORIE COUNT =

½ CUP

100 Calories   ½ Cup

Recommended Serving:
SAUCE – 100 Calories = ½ Cup

Ingredients:

2 tablespoons extra virgin olive oil

4 cloves garlic, minced

1 (28-ounce) can puréed tomatoes

¼ cup chopped fresh basil

½ teaspoon salt

½ teaspoon pepper

¼ teaspoon crushed red pepper flakes

2 cups fresh spinach

Directions:

1 Heat the olive oil and garlic in a stockpot over medium heat. Sauté for 2 minutes, just until garlic is fragrant.

2 Add the puréed tomatoes, basil, salt, pepper, and crushed red pepper.

3 Bring the sauce to a simmer, reduce heat to low, and let simmer for 20 minutes, stirring constantly.

4 Add the fresh spinach to the sauce, and let cook for 5 additional minutes before serving.

HELPFUL TIP:

Puréed or crushed San Marzano tomatoes are traditionally used in Italy. You can often find these in cardboard cartons near the canned tomato products in the grocery store. Puréed makes a thick and smooth sauce, while crushed makes a thin and chunky sauce.

PREP TIME: 5 MINUTES • COOK TIME: 10 MINUTES

100 CALORIE ALFREDO SAUCE

MAKES 8 SAUCE PORTIONS

Mona's Family Favorites: My family LOVES Alfredo sauce, but then again, who doesn't? To lighten up the traditional combination of heavy cream and Parmesan cheese, I've made a simple swap from heavy cream to thickened milk to significantly lower the calories without sacrificing any of the rich, nutty Parmesan. This luscious Alfredo is absolutely off the charts!

100 CALORIE COUNT =

¼ CUP

100 Calories   ¼ Cup

Recommended Serving:
SAUCE – 100 Calories = ¼ Cup

Ingredients:

2 tablespoons butter

2 tablespoons flour

1 teaspoon minced garlic

1¾ cups 2% milk

¼ teaspoon salt

¼ teaspoon pepper

⅛ teaspoon ground nutmeg

⅔ cup grated Parmesan cheese

Directions:

1. Heat the butter in a sauce pot over medium-high heat, until it has melted.

2. Whisk the flour and garlic into the butter in the pot, and cook until golden brown, about 2 minutes. Reduce heat to medium.

3. Add the milk, salt, pepper, and nutmeg to the pot, and whisk constantly, until the flour and butter mixture has dissolved and the sauce has slightly thickened, about 5 minutes.

4. Remove from heat, and stir in Parmesan cheese before serving.

HELPFUL TIP:

You want to bring the milk up to a very low simmer without burning or bubbling over, so whisking constantly is extremely important. If the milk begins to bubble up too quickly, temporarily remove the pot from the heat.

PREP TIME: 15 MINUTES

PESTO SAUCE

MAKES 6 SAUCE PORTIONS

Pesto is known for being extremely high in fat and calories thanks to the generous amount of oil it contains. We replicate the same balance of bright basil, toasty pine nuts, sharp garlic, and salty Parmesan with only ⅓ of the olive oil. Now, you can enjoy a full serving of pesto pasta without the guilt!

3 TABLESPOONS

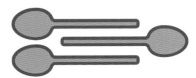

Recommended Serving:
SAUCE – 100 Calories = 3 Tablespoons

Ingredients:

¼ cup pine nuts

2 cups fresh basil leaves

1 tablespoon minced garlic

3 tablespoons water

2 tablespoons extra virgin olive oil

½ teaspoon salt

½ teaspoon pepper

¼ cup grated Parmesan cheese

Directions:

1 Place the pine nuts in a dry skillet over medium heat to toast, shaking the pan to keep them moving, until golden brown and fragrant. Transfer the toasted pine nuts to a food processor.

2 Add all the remaining ingredients, except the Parmesan cheese, to the food processor, and pulse in short bursts for 2 minutes to finely grate the pine nuts and combine everything into a sauce.

3 Add the Parmesan cheese to the food processor, and pulse for 15 more seconds, just to combine. Serve immediately, or refrigerate until ready to use.

HELPFUL TIP:

Pine nuts can usually be found in a small packet in the baking section of your grocery store. Walnuts or blanched almonds can be used in place of the pine nuts (you should still toast them in step 1); however, the pine nuts really give pesto its classic flavor.

PREP TIME: 15 MINUTES • COOK TIME: 15 MINUTES

STRAWBERRY RHUBARB JAM

MAKES 36 TOPPING PORTIONS

Bob's Farm to Table: Rhubarb is sadly underused these days, but it's one of my absolute favorite ingredients for sweet treats like this jam. The rhubarb adds a tart bite that perfectly counters the sweet strawberries and sugar. If you've never cooked with rhubarb before, this quick and easy recipe is a great start!

Recommended Serving:
TOPPING – 100 Calories = 2 ½ Tablespoons

Ingredients:

4 cups trimmed and chopped strawberries

2 cups finely chopped fresh rhubarb

4 ½ cups sugar

2 tablespoons lemon juice

1 (3-ounce) pouch liquid fruit pectin

Directions:

1. Place the strawberries in a food processor, and pulse until mostly smooth.

2. Transfer the puréed strawberries to a sauce pot over medium-high heat. Add the rhubarb, sugar, and lemon juice, and bring to a boil.

3. Reduce heat to low, and let simmer for 10 minutes, stirring constantly.

4. Remove from heat and skim off any foam before transferring to tempered glass jars. Let set, unrefrigerated, for 24–48 hours, or until firm. Once set, store refrigerated for up to 3 weeks.

5. If you would like to preserve this jam for longer-term storage (only recommended for people experienced with canning), you need to work with it while it is still hot. Spoon the hot jam into sterilized jars, leaving ¼ inch of space at the top of each jar. Tap the jars on the counter to remove air bubbles, clean the rims, and secure the lids. Process for 10 minutes in a boiling-water canner.

HELPFUL TIP:

You can find liquid pectin in the baking aisle of most grocery stores and near the empty canning jars in the kitchen supplies of most big-box retailers.

PREP TIME: 15 MINUTES • COOK TIME: 5 MINUTES

BLUEBERRY CINNAMON JAM

MAKES 24 TOPPING PORTIONS

The health benefits from eating blueberries are so great that we decided to preserve them as a jam. Fresh berries spoil, but our fantastic jam is always at the ready. Paired with a bright hit of lemon juice and warm cinnamon, this jam is a keeper.

100 CALORIE COUNT =

3 TABLESPOONS

Recommended Serving:
TOPPING – 100 Calories = 3 Tablespoons

Ingredients:

4 cups fresh blueberries

2¾ cups sugar

2 tablespoons lemon juice

2 teaspoons ground cinnamon

1 (3-ounce) pouch liquid fruit pectin

Directions:

1. Place the blueberries in a food processor, and pulse until mostly smooth.

2. Transfer the puréed blueberries to a sauce pot over medium-high heat. Add the sugar, lemon juice, and ground cinnamon, and bring to a boil.

3. Stir the pectin into the blueberry mixture, and let boil for 1 minute, stirring constantly.

4. Remove from heat, and skim off any foam before transferring to tempered glass jars. Let set, unrefrigerated, for 24–48 hours, or until firm. Once set, store refrigerated for up to 3 weeks.

5. If you would like to preserve this jam for longer-term storage (only recommended for people experienced with canning), you need to work with it while it is still hot. Spoon the hot jam into sterilized jars, leaving a ¼ inch of space at the top of each jar. Tap jars on the counter to remove air bubbles, clean the rims, and secure the lids. Process for 10 minutes in a boiling-water canner.

HELPFUL TIP:

You can find liquid pectin in the baking aisle of most grocery stores and near the empty canning jars in the kitchen supplies of most big-box retailers.

PREP TIME: 40 MINUTES • COOK TIME: 10 HOURS

AMAZING APPLE BUTTER

MAKES 24 SPREAD PORTIONS

We avoid the addition of sweet cider or juice by releasing the apple's natural moisture and sugars in a slow cooker. No constant stirring or scorched pans—just set it and forget it, until the aroma fills your house that is!

100 CALORIE COUNT=

3 TABLESPOONS

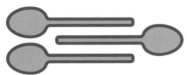

Recommended Serving:
SPREAD – 100 Calories = 3 Tablespoons

Ingredients:

2 ½ pounds Granny Smith apples

2 ½ pounds (any variety) red apples

1 cup light brown sugar

½ cup sugar

2 teaspoons lemon juice

2 teaspoons ground cinnamon

1 ½ teaspoons vanilla extract

1 teaspoon ground allspice

⅛ teaspoon salt

Directions:

1. Peel, core, and roughly chop all apples before placing in a slow cooker.

2. Add all the remaining ingredients to the slow cooker, and toss to evenly coat apples.

3. Set the cooker to low, cover, and let cook for 10 hours, stirring once after 8 hours.

4. Use an immersion (hand) blender to purée the cooked apples until smooth. You can also do this in a traditional blender or food processor, but it may take 2–3 batches.

5. For thicker apple butter, transfer the puréed mixture to a sauce pot over medium heat, and let simmer for 15 minutes, or until your desired consistency. Let cool for at least 30 minutes before serving. Store covered and refrigerated for up to 2 weeks.

HELPFUL TIP:

This makes A LOT of apple butter (about 4 jars), so it is a good idea to freeze ½ of the batch, or give some of the jars as gifts. You could also pressure-seal the jars, but that is only recommended for those who are very familiar with the process.

9 SATISFYING SNACKS

PREP TIME: 20 MINUTES • BAKE TIME: 15 MINUTES

CHEESE CRACKERS

MAKES 72 CRACKERS OR 12 SNACK PORTIONS

These fabulous homemade cheese crackers outshine any store-bought versions we've ever had. We pack an equal amount of Cheddar and flour into our crackers, producing crisp, flaky bites with huge cheese flavor. Not to mention that our quick food processor dough literally comes together in seconds.

100 CALORIE COUNT =

6 CRACKERS

Recommended Serving:
SNACK – 100 Calories = 6 Crackers

Ingredients:

1 cup shredded sharp Cheddar cheese

1 cup all-purpose flour

3 tablespoons butter, softened

½ teaspoon baking soda

½ teaspoon salt

¼ teaspoon onion powder

¼ teaspoon paprika

3 tablespoons water

Directions:

1. Preheat the oven to 350°F. Line a sheet pan with parchment paper.

2. Place the Cheddar cheese, flour, softened butter, baking soda, salt, onion powder, and paprika in a food processor, and process until combined, but crumbly.

3. Add the water to the food processor, and process until a very thick dough forms.

4. On a lightly floured surface, roll the dough out into a large rectangle that is ⅛ inch thick, approximately 9 x 8 inches.

5. Using a knife or pastry cutter, cut the dough into 1-inch squares, and transfer to the prepared sheet pan.

6. Use a toothpick to poke a hole in the center of each cracker.

7. Bake for 15 minutes, or until the edges of the crackers begin to brown. Let cool completely before serving.

HELPFUL TIP:

Any cheese can be used in place of the sharp Cheddar cheese, but the stronger the flavor of the cheese, the better. Aged Swiss cheese works particularly well.

PREP TIME: 20 MINUTES

CAPRESE SALAD STACKS

MAKES 8 SNACK PORTIONS

Cooking doesn't get more simple or satisfying than this. We layer slices of sweet tomatoes, creamy fresh mozzarella, and basil for a fantastic looking and tasting snack or appetizer. Use different colors of heirloom tomatoes for variety.

100 CALORIE COUNT=

1 STACK

Recommended Serving:
SNACK – 100 Calories = 1 Stack

Ingredients:

2 heirloom tomatoes

Salt and pepper

8 (1-ounce) slices fresh mozzarella cheese

16 leaves fresh basil

1½ tablespoons extra virgin olive oil

1½ tablespoons aged balsamic vinegar

Directions:

1. Slice ends off tomatoes, and discard before slicing each into 8 equal slices.

2. Season all sliced tomatoes with a light sprinkling of salt and pepper.

3. Halve each slice of fresh mozzarella cheese to make 16 half-moon-shaped pieces.

4. Assemble the "stacks" by topping a slice of tomato with a piece of mozzarella. Stick the stem of a basil leaf under the mozzarella to hold it in place.

5. Make a second layer of tomato, mozzarella, and basil on top of the first. Repeat to make 8 double-layered stacks.

6. Drizzle all with extra virgin olive oil and balsamic vinegar before serving.

HELPFUL TIP:

This is also great as an appetizer. Lean the second layer of ingredients on a slight bias to create a "leaning tower" of tomato, rather than simply stacking the ingredients straight up.

PREP TIME: 5 MINUTES • COOK TIME: 20 MINUTES

"HOT COCOA" PRETZELS

MAKES 10 SNACK PORTIONS

Anson's American Treasures: You'll be amazed by how much these pretzels taste like a steamy mug of hot cocoa, marshmallows and all! After a quick coating of egg white and vanilla, we toss the pretzels with cocoa and sugar and bake until crisp. It actually tastes like marshmallows! The pretzel, chocolate, and meringue flavors combine as the perfect balance between salty and sweet. This snack is sure to bring back great childhood memories and will definitely satisfy any chocolate craving!

Featured Recipe Story: See next page.

10 PRETZELS

Recommended Serving:
SNACK – 100 Calories = 10 Pretzels

Ingredients:

100 mini pretzels (about 4 packed cups)

1 large egg white, beaten

½ teaspoon vanilla extract

½ cup sugar

3 tablespoons cocoa powder

Directions:

1 Preheat the oven to 275°F, and line a sheet pan with parchment paper.

2 In a large mixing bowl, toss the pretzels in the egg white and vanilla extract until all are evenly coated.

3 In a separate bowl, combine the sugar and cocoa.

4 Add ⅔ of the cocoa and sugar mixture to the pretzels, and toss until well coated.

5 Spread the coated pretzels in a single layer on the paper-lined sheet pan, and sprinkle the remaining ⅓ of the cocoa and sugar mixture over the top.

6 Bake for 20 minutes, flipping pretzels halfway through. Let cool for 10 minutes before serving.

HELPFUL TIP:

You can use either salted or unsalted mini pretzels in this recipe, but salted pretzels add a nice contrast to the sweet cocoa coating.

"HOT COCOA" PRETZELS

Dipped and Delicious —
10 Pretzels for 100 Calories!

OH, THOSE CHILLY WINTER NIGHTS IN NYC.
I have a wonderful childhood memory of going to the
city with my family to hit the local soda shop. I sat,
spinning on the counter stool, dipping crunchy pretzel
rods into rich hot cocoa with marshmallows—my first
taste of sweet and salty delight. I asked Bob and Mona
to figure out a way to re-create that comforting snack.

Marshmallow Meringue! The combination of egg
white, vanilla extract, and a little sugar creates a
meringue that gives these pretzels their wonderful
marshmallow essence.

Cocoa Craving! A dusting of unsweetened cocoa,
combined with a small amount of sugar, truly provides
a chocolate fix.

Sweet 'n Salty! The classic combination of sweet and
salty creates heavenly treats. But, don't worry! You can
eat 10 pretzels for only 100 calories...the PERFECT
portion!

Bob and Mona did it again—they were able to create a
truly satisfying 100 calorie portion! You'll definitely be
sharing this recipe with your friends and family.

1 Once the pretzels are coated in the meringue mixture, toss with part of the cocoa mixture before placing them on a paper-lined cookie sheet. Then add the remaining cocoa.

4 Can you believe you can eat 10 pretzels for 100 calories? Amazing!

2 The best way to evenly coat the pretzels with the remaining cocoa is to use a small strainer to dust them. Anson used some cool music and rhythm moves!

3 After 20 minutes of baking, the aroma of hot cocoa will fill your kitchen!

5 Cheers! For added fun, serve in hot cocoa mugs to get you in the mood for chocolaty fun.

PREP TIME: 5 MINUTES

SKINNY STRAWBERRY MILKSHAKES

MAKES 2 SMALL MILKSHAKES

While this recipe blends into a milkshake that is just as smooth and creamy as you would expect, it has one big secret to keeping the calorie count low. It doesn't actually contain any ice cream! While that may have you turning the page, we promise that blending frozen strawberries into vanilla-scented milk creates the exact texture and flavor you love in a milkshake.

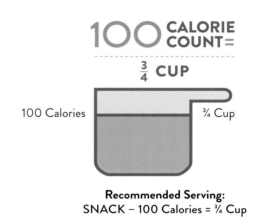

100 CALORIE COUNT =

¾ CUP

100 Calories   ¾ Cup

Recommended Serving:
SNACK – 100 Calories = ¾ Cup

Ingredients:

1 cup frozen whole strawberries

⅔ cup 2% milk

1½ tablespoons sugar

½ teaspoon vanilla extract

Directions:

1 Place all the ingredients in a blender, and pulse 8–10 times to break down the frozen strawberries.

2 Blend for 1 minute, until milkshake is completely smooth. Serve immediately.

HELPFUL TIP:

Top these with 2 tablespoons of canned whipped cream for an additional 15–20 calories, depending on the brand. We prefer Land-O-Lakes brand "whipped heavy cream" that does not contain corn syrup.

PREP TIME: 15 MINUTES • BAKE TIME: 15 MINUTES

CRISPY KALE CHIPS

MAKES 3 SNACK PORTIONS

Mona's Family Favorites: Not only is kale one of the most nutrient-dense vegetables out there, I also have an amazing little secret. When roasted, kale crisps up just like a potato chip! And did we mention that it tastes great as well? These chips truly are a snack you can feel good about eating! You will be amazed!

100 CALORIE COUNT=

1 CUP

100 Calories   1 Cup

Recommended Serving:
SNACK – 100 Calories = 1 Cup

Ingredients:

1 bunch kale, washed and dried

1 tablespoon extra virgin olive oil

¼ teaspoon salt

¼ teaspoon pepper

¼ teaspoon garlic powder

1½ tablespoons grated Parmesan cheese

Directions:

1. Preheat the oven to 350°F.

2. Remove the leaves from the stems of the kale and break into bite-size pieces. Discard stems.

3. In a large mixing bowl, toss the kale pieces in a mixture of the olive oil, salt, pepper, and garlic powder to coat.

4. Spread the coated kale pieces on a sheet pan in a single layer and bake for 15 minutes, or until the edges of the kale have browned.

5. Sprinkle the baked kale with Parmesan cheese, and let cool for 5 minutes before serving.

HELPFUL TIP:

Kitchen scissors make quick (and very precise) work of removing the kale leaves from the stems.

PREP TIME: 15 MINUTES • BAKE TIME: 40 MINUTES

HOMEMADE GRANOLA

MAKES 20 TOPPING PORTIONS OR 10 SNACK PORTIONS

We've packed our granola with whole-grain oats, pecans, raisins, spices, and a small amount of brown sugar and oil for a fortified, absolutely delicious on-the-go snack. Also, thanks to its great crunch, its just as satisfying as a yogurt or even ice cream topping.

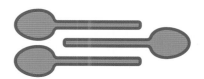

100 CALORIE COUNT=

3 PACKED TABLESPOONS

Recommended Serving:
TOPPING – 100 Calories = 3 Packed Tablespoons
SNACK – 200 Calories = 6 Packed Tablespoons

Ingredients:

2½ cups old-fashioned rolled oats

½ cup chopped pecans

2 tablespoons light brown sugar

1 teaspoon ground cinnamon

¼ teaspoon salt

¼ cup honey

1 tablespoon canola oil

1 cup raisins

Directions:

1. Preheat the oven to 300°F, and line a sheet pan with parchment paper.

2. In a large mixing bowl, toss together the oats, pecans, brown sugar, cinnamon, and salt.

3. In a separate bowl, whisk together the honey and canola oil, and then pour over the oat mixture, tossing to evenly coat.

4. Spread the coated granola on the prepared sheet pan in a thin layer, and bake for 40 minutes, stirring every 10 minutes.

5. Let the granola cool for at least 15 minutes before tossing with raisins to serve. Store in an airtight container for up to 10 days.

HELPFUL TIP:

Any combination of dried fruit can be used in place of the raisins, though nutritional information provided is for 1 cup (unpacked) of raisins.

PREP TIME: 5 MINUTES • COOK TIME: 5 MINUTES

STOVETOP POPCORN

MAKES 8 SNACK PORTIONS

Fresh popcorn is a fantastic snack, because it provides great volume (2 cups for 100 calories!), great crunch, and endless flavors. As a whole grain, popcorn is a wonderful source of dietary fiber, but it's also only as healthy as what you cook it in. We selected fruity, heart-conscious extra virgin olive oil for popping this simple, yet satisfying staple. Try different flavors to spice up your week!

100 CALORIE COUNT =

2 CUPS

Recommended Serving:
SNACK – 100 Calories = 2 Cups

Ingredients:

3 tablespoons extra virgin olive oil

½ cup popcorn kernels

½ teaspoon popcorn salt (see tip)

Spice it Up Blends:

Cracked Pepper and Rosemary:

½ teaspoon cracked black pepper

1 tablespoon finely chopped fresh rosemary

Garlic and Oregano:

¼ teaspoon garlic powder

1½ tablespoons chopped fresh oregano

Tex-Mex Spiced:

½ teaspoon chili powder

¼ teaspoon ground cumin

Directions:

1. Add the oil to a heavy 6-quart pot over medium-high heat.

2. Allow the oil to heat for 1 minute before adding the popcorn kernels and covering immediately.

3. Keep the pot covered, and let sit until you hear the first kernel pop. Once popcorn has begun to pop, shake the pot from side to side while still keeping it over the heat.

4. When popping slows to 3–4 seconds between kernels, remove from heat, and shake for at least 10 more seconds before removing lid.

5. Immediately transfer the popcorn to a large bowl. Season with salt or spice it up with suggested blends (see ingredients).

HELPFUL TIP:

Popcorn salt or "superfine salt" is recommended to better stick to the popcorn, but ordinary table salt can be used if it is the only salt you have on hand. You can also make your own popcorn salt by processing table salt in a spice grinder or small blender/food processor for 1 minute.

PREP TIME: 20 MINUTES • BAKE TIME: 12 MINUTES

OVEN-FRIED POTATO CHIPS

MAKES 8 SNACK PORTIONS

We forego the mess of deep-frying with a tidier and healthier alternative, the oven-fried chip. Rinsing our potato slices washes away sticky surface starch, allowing us to use a mere 2 tablespoons of olive oil and a couple of spritzes of cooking spray to "fry" our chips. Not to mention, they taste fantastic! You can have your chips and eat them too, without any guilt.

100 CALORIE COUNT=

½ CUP

100 Calories   ½ Cup

Recommended Serving:
SNACK – 100 Calories = ½ Cup

Ingredients:

Nonstick cooking spray

1½ pounds Yukon Gold potatoes, scrubbed

½ teaspoon salt

2 tablespoons olive oil

½ teaspoon seasoned salt

¼ teaspoon pepper (optional)

1 tablespoon finely chopped fresh chives (optional)

Directions:

1 Preheat the oven to 475°F. Spray 2 sheet pans with nonstick cooking spray.

2 Slice the potatoes into very thin slices, about ⅛ inch thick. For best results, use a mandolin slicer or the slicing attachment of a food processor.

3 In a large bowl filled with water and the ½ teaspoon of regular salt, soak the sliced potatoes for 10 minutes. Drain well, and pat potatoes dry.

4 In a large mixing bowl, toss the sliced potatoes with the olive oil, separating the slices to ensure that each is evenly coated.

5 Arrange the oiled potatoes in single layers on the prepared sheet pans.

6 Bake for 10–12 minutes, or until the edges of the potatoes are well browned. Season with the seasoned salt, pepper, and chopped chives before letting cool for at least 5 minutes.

HELPFUL TIP:

Soaking the sliced potatoes in salted water helps remove some of their excess starch and liquid content, making for crispier baked chips.

PREP TIME: 5 MINUTES • COOK TIME: 1 HOUR

CINNAMON ROASTED CARNIVAL ALMONDS

MAKES 30 SNACK PORTIONS

Mona's Family Favorites: I make these almonds as a snack for my family and friends, and they always say, "Really, I can have 12 for only 100 calories?" Yessiree! Plus, you can feel good about eating them! Almonds are packed with a slew of nutrients, like fiber, protein, vitamin E, and magnesium, making them one of a handful of "power foods!" Though these are best right out of the oven, they also make a great homemade gift.

100 CALORIE COUNT =

12 ALMONDS

Recommended Serving:
SNACK – 100 Calories = 12 Almonds

Ingredients:

16 ounces raw shelled almonds

1 large egg white, beaten

1 teaspoon vanilla extract

½ cup light brown sugar

1½ teaspoons ground cinnamon

⅛ teaspoon salt

Directions:

1. Preheat oven to 250°F, and line a sheet pan with parchment paper.

2. In a large mixing bowl, toss almonds in the egg white and vanilla extract until all are evenly coated.

3. In a separate bowl, combine brown sugar, cinnamon, and salt.

4. Add ⅓ of the cinnamon-sugar mixture to the almonds, and toss until well coated.

5. Spread the coated almonds in a single layer on the paper-lined sheet pan, and sprinkle the remaining cinnamon-sugar mixture over the top.

6. Bake for 1 hour, shaking the pan to stir halfway through. Let cool for 5 minutes before serving.

HELPFUL TIP:

Using raw or "natural" almonds in this recipe is an absolute must, as pre-roasted almonds will over-roast and get bitter upon baking. If you can't find raw almonds in the baking aisle, check the end caps in the produce section, as they often have fresh seeds and nuts there as well.

PREP TIME: 10 MINUTES

AVOCADO TOAST

MAKES 5 SNACK PORTIONS

Mona's Family Favorites: My daughter Rachel created this recipe, looking for a late breakfast or filling mid-afternoon snack, instead of the traditional bagel and cream cheese. She tops her toast with mashed, flavor-packed avocado for a satisfying and nutritious snack. Enjoy as is or with a topping of fresh tomatoes and basil. Way to go, Rae!

100 **CALORIE COUNT =**

1 SLICE

Recommended Serving:
SNACK – 100 Calories = 1 Slice

Ingredients:

1 medium Haas avocado, pitted

½ teaspoon fresh lemon juice

Salt and pepper

Per Slice:

1 slice light wheat bread

2 slices fresh tomato

Garlic powder

2 basil leaves

Directions:

1. Scoop avocado out of the peel and place in a small mixing bowl. Use a heavy fork to mash the avocado until it is spreadable, but still chunky.

2. Add the lemon juice to the avocado, and season lightly with salt and pepper to taste.

3. Toast the wheat bread to your liking.

4. Spread ⅕ of the mashed avocado onto the toasted wheat bread. Cover, and refrigerate any unused avocado for up to 3 days.

5. Top the avocado toast with 2 slices of fresh tomato, and lightly season the tomato with the salt, pepper, and garlic powder. Place fresh basil leaves over the tomato before serving.

HELPFUL TIP:

This recipe makes enough mashed avocado to prepare 5 slices of avocado toast. If you are preparing all 5 slices at once, you will need about 2 small tomatoes to make the 10 slices of tomato needed.

10 DESSERTS

PREP TIME: 30 MINUTES • BAKE TIME: 14 MINUTES

APPLE PIE TURNOVERS

MAKES 24 MINI TURNOVERS

There's nothing more quintessentially American than Mom's apple pie. Inspired by the iconic cinnamon-scented apples encased in buttery crust, we created "perfectly portioned" turnovers in a quarter of the calories by swapping the traditional double crust for puff pastry sheets.

1 TURNOVER

Recommended Serving:
DESSERT – 100 Calories = 1 Turnover

Ingredients:

1 green apple, peeled, cored, and diced

1 red apple, peeled, cored, and diced

¼ cup sugar

1 teaspoon apple pie spice (may use ground cinnamon)

½ teaspoon lemon juice

⅛ teaspoon salt

2 teaspoons cornstarch

3 tablespoons water

1 (17.3-ounce) package frozen puff pastry sheets, thawed

1 large egg, beaten

2 teaspoons coarse sugar (optional)

Directions:

1. Position the oven racks 3 slots apart, and preheat the oven to 400°F. Line 2 sheet pans with parchment paper.

2. Place apples, sugar, apple pie spice, lemon juice, and salt in a sauce pot over medium-high heat.

3. Whisk the cornstarch into the water, and stir into the pot. Bring up to a simmer, and reduce heat to medium-low. Cover, and let cook for 5 minutes.

4. Remove cover, and simmer for an additional 4 minutes to thicken the apple mixture further. Let cool.

5. Unroll 1 sheet of puff pastry, and use a pastry cutter to cut 3 lines vertically by 4 lines horizontally to create 12 rectangles. Use a floured rolling pin to roll these rectangles about ⅓ larger, pushing the rolling pin away from you to roll the rectangles into more of a square shape. Repeat with the second sheet of puff pastry.

6. Place 1 heaping tablespoon of the apple filling in the center of each pastry square. Brush the edges of the pastry with water, fold over, and press hard to fully seal. Use a pastry cutter to trim any uneven excess to make perfectly folded triangles.

7. Transfer the filled turnovers to the prepared baking sheets, and brush the tops with the beaten egg. Make a ¼-inch-thick cut in the center of each to vent. Sprinkle coarse sugar over each, if desired.

8. Bake for 12–14 minutes, or until golden brown. Let cool for at least 5 minutes before serving.

PREP TIME: 20 MINUTES • BAKE TIME: 45 MINUTES

LEMON BARS

MAKES 20 LEMON BARS

Our Lemon Bars are not only 100 calories each, they also outshine other recipes because of their lemon zing. We top the rich, buttery crust with a very generous amount of custard made from both lemon juice and zest. The perfect marriage of sweetness and citrus tang, we're smitten.

100 CALORIE COUNT =

$\frac{1}{20}$ **LEMON BARS**

Recommended Serving:
DESSERT – 100 Calories = 1 Bar

Ingredients:

Nonstick cooking spray

⅔ cup all-purpose flour

¼ cup butter, softened

1 tablespoon sugar

1 tablespoon cold water

Filling:

3 large eggs

2 large egg whites

1¼ cups sugar

3 tablespoons all-purpose flour

¼ cup fresh lemon juice

2 tablespoons lemon zest

⅛ teaspoon salt

Directions:

1. Preheat the oven to 350°F. Spray an 8 x 8-inch baking dish with nonstick cooking spray.

2. In a mixing bowl, use your hands to combine the ⅔ cup of flour, butter, 1 tablespoon sugar, and water to create a thick dough. Press the dough into the bottom of the prepared baking dish.

3. Bake the crust for 15 minutes, or until the edges begin to brown, and then let cool for 5 minutes.

4. In a large mixing bowl, whisk all the filling ingredients until well combined.

5. Pour the filling over the crust, and bake for 30–35 minutes, or until the top is golden brown and springy to the touch.

6. Let cool for at least 30 minutes before slicing into 4 rows by 5 rows to create 20 bars.

HELPFUL TIP:

Lemon bars are traditionally served garnished with powdered confectioners' sugar sprinkled over the top (as it helps hide any bubbles in the custard). A light sprinkling adds a negligible 1 or 2 calories per serving.

PREP TIME: 20 MINUTES • BAKE TIME: 55 MINUTES

FRESH BERRY COBBLER

MAKES 8 DESSERT PORTIONS

Bob's Farm to Table: I have always grown strawberries and picked someone's raspberry patch. Now that fresh berries are available year-round, I always add them to my favorite cobbler. We offset these bright, lightly sweetened berries with a hearty, oat-studded cake-y topping. The combinations of flavors and textures is out of this world! Serve the cobbler as is or with a scoop of Vanilla Bean Ice Cream (see page 307).

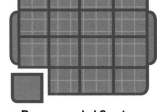

Recommended Serving:
DESSERT – 200 Calories = 2 Sections

Ingredients:

Nonstick cooking spray

2 cups chopped strawberries

1 cup blueberries

1 cup raspberries

⅓ cup sugar

2 teaspoons lemon juice

Topping:

⅔ cup all-purpose flour

½ cup rolled oats

1 large egg, beaten

½ cup sugar

2 tablespoons 2% milk

2 tablespoons butter, melted

1 teaspoon vanilla extract

¼ teaspoon ground cinnamon

¼ teaspoon salt

Directions:

1. Preheat the oven to 375°F. Spray a 9 x 9-inch baking dish with nonstick cooking spray.

2. Add strawberries, blueberries, raspberries, ⅓ cup sugar, and lemon juice to a mixing bowl, and toss until sugar has dissolved and coated the fruit. Transfer fruit mixture to the prepared baking dish.

3. In a clean mixing bowl, use a large fork to whisk all of the topping ingredients together, just until a batter has formed (do not overmix).

4. Drop large dollops of the batter over the berries in the prepared baking dish.

5. Bake for 50–55 minutes, or until the berries are bubbly in the center of the dish and the topping is golden brown. Let cool for 10 minutes before serving. For 100 calorie portions, slice into 16 sections by cutting 4 rows by 4 rows.

HELPFUL TIP:

Four cups of any combination of fresh strawberries, blueberries, raspberries, or blackberries can be used in this recipe.

PREP TIME: 20 MINUTES • BAKE TIME: 10 MINUTES PER BATCH

OATMEAL RAISIN COOKIES

MAKES 36 COOKIES OR 18 DESSERT PORTIONS

These homemade Oatmeal Raisin Cookies are soft, chewy, and bursting with an entire cup of raisins. The secret to making them great is to use real rolled oats, rather than the over-processed quick-cooking oats that turn to mush.

100 **CALORIE COUNT=**

1 COOKIE

Recommended Serving:
DESSERT – 200 Calories = 2 Cookies

Ingredients:

Nonstick cooking spray

2⅔ cups rolled oats

1¼ cups all-purpose flour

1½ teaspoons ground cinnamon

1 teaspoon baking soda

¼ teaspoon salt

½ cup butter, softened

1¼ cups light brown sugar

2 large eggs, beaten

⅓ cup applesauce

1½ teaspoons vanilla extract

1 cup raisins

Directions:

1. Preheat oven to 375°F, and spray 3 cookie sheets with nonstick cooking spray.

2. In a large mixing bowl, stir together oats, flour, cinnamon, baking soda, and salt.

3. In a separate mixing bowl, cream together the butter and brown sugar. Stir in eggs, applesauce, and vanilla extract.

4. Add the wet ingredients into the dry oat mixture, folding until all is combined before folding in raisins.

5. Drop balls of the dough (about 2 tablespoons each) onto the prepared cookie sheets, at least 2½ inches apart. You should have enough dough to make 3 dozen cookies.

6. Bake for 9–11 minutes, just until a light golden brown. Let cool for at least 10 minutes before serving.

HELPFUL TIP:

For the most even cooking, it is best to bake these in three batches rather than filling your oven racks all at once, as that limits the flow of hot air.

PREP TIME: 20 MINUTES • BAKE TIME: 13 MINUTES PER BATCH

CHOCOLATE CHIP COOKIES

MAKES 36 COOKIES OR 18 DESSERT PORTIONS

When it comes to portion control, few recipes are as a famously tempting as Chocolate Chip Cookies. We've slightly adjusted the classic ingredients to give you the the buttery, caramelized, chocolate-flecked cookies you love at only 100 calories a pop.

Recommended Serving:
DESSERT – 200 Calories = 2 Cookies

Ingredients:

Nonstick cooking spray

1¾ cups all-purpose flour

¾ teaspoon baking soda

½ teaspoon salt

¾ cup butter, softened

½ cup sugar

½ cup light brown sugar

1 large egg

1 large egg white

2 teaspoons vanilla extract

1 cup semisweet chocolate chips

Directions:

1. Preheat the oven to 350°F, and spray 3 cookie sheets with nonstick cooking spray.

2. In a mixing bowl, stir together the flour, baking soda, and salt.

3. In a separate mixing bowl or electric mixer, cream together the butter, sugar, and brown sugar. Beat in the egg, egg white, and vanilla extract until well combined.

4. Add the dry ingredients into the wet ingredients, folding until all is combined into a dough. Fold the chocolate chips into the dough.

5. Drop tablespoons of the dough onto the prepared cookie sheets, at least 2½ inches apart, and **press lightly to flatten**. You should have enough dough to make 3 dozen cookies.

6. Bake each sheet of cookies for 13 minutes, or until edges are golden brown. Let cool for at least 10 minutes before serving.

HELPFUL TIP:

For the most even cooking, it is best to bake these in three batches rather than filling your oven racks all at once, as that limits the flow of hot air.

PREP TIME: 30 MINUTES • COOK TIME: 20 MINUTES

KEY LIME PIE TARTS

MAKES 18 MINI TARTS

Anson's American Treasures: When I was directing the Steven Spielberg television series *Seaquest* in Orlando, a few of us decided to take a day trip down to Key West. We spent most of our day trying to hunt down the "best" slice of Key lime pie. This fun memory has made this dessert one of my favorites! By making them into mini pies, my team and I have been able to deliver this tangy treat for only 100 calories.

100 CALORIE COUNT=

1 TART

Recommended Serving:
DESSERT – 100 Calories = 1 Tart

Ingredients:

Nonstick cooking spray

¾ cup graham cracker crumbs

1 large egg white, beaten

1 tablespoon butter, melted

1 tablespoon sugar

2 teaspoons cornstarch

¼ cup fat-free evaporated milk

1 (14-ounce) can fat-free sweetened condensed milk

½ cup Key lime juice

3 large egg whites, beaten

1 teaspoon lime zest

Directions:

1. Preheat the oven to 325°F. Spray standard-size muffin pans (enough to make 18 tarts) with nonstick cooking spray.

2. In a mixing bowl, combine the graham cracker crumbs, 1 egg white, butter, and sugar, folding together to create a crumbly crust.

3. Press 1 rounded tablespoon of the crust into the bottom of each of the 18 muffin cups. Bake for 8 minutes. Let cool completely.

4. Whisk the cornstarch into ¼ cup of evaporated milk, and place in a small sauce pot over medium-high heat. Bring to a simmer, and reduce heat to low. Let simmer for 2 minutes. Let cool completely.

5. In a mixing bowl, whisk together the condensed milk, lime juice, 3 egg whites, lime zest, and the cooled cornstarch mixture to create the filling.

6. Pour 2 tablespoons of the filling over each of the baked crusts.

7. Bake for 10–12 minutes, just until the edges of the tarts come away from the pan and bubbles begin to form at the top.

8. Let cool on a rack for 1 hour. Cover, and refrigerate for at least 1 additional hour before serving.

HELPFUL TIP:

Key lime juice can be purchased in a bottle and is usually found in the baking aisle. Regular lime juice can be substituted in a pinch.

PREP TIME: 45 MINUTES • BAKE TIME: 30 MINUTES

CARROT CAKE BARS

MAKES 36 CARROT CAKE BARS

Bob's Farm to Table: Carrot cake is my perfect comfort food dessert. This delicious dessert bar is ultra moist with a rich presence of comforting, warm spices. Applesauce works as a perfect substitute for a portion of the oil by adding moisture and no grease. Top with a coating of cream cheese frosting.

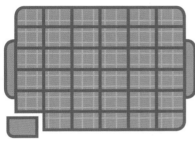

100 CALORIE COUNT =

1/36 CARROT CAKE

Recommended Serving:
DESSERT – 200 Calories = 2 Sections

Ingredients:

Nonstick cooking spray

2 cups all-purpose flour

2 cups shredded carrots

1¼ cups sugar

2 teaspoons baking powder

1¼ teaspoons ground cinnamon

1 teaspoon ground allspice

½ teaspoon baking soda

¼ teaspoon salt

4 large eggs

¾ cup applesauce

¼ cup vegetable oil

1 teaspoon vanilla extract

Frosting:

8 ounces fat-free cream cheese, softened

1¼ cups confectioners' sugar

1 teaspoon vanilla extract

½ teaspoon lemon juice

Directions:

1. Preheat the oven to 350°F, and spray an 11 x 15-inch half-sheet cake or jellyroll pan with nonstick cooking spray. For easier release, line the bottom of the pan with parchment paper sprayed with nonstick cooking spray.

2. In a large mixing bowl, combine the flour, carrots, sugar, baking powder, cinnamon, allspice, baking soda, and salt.

3. In a separate mixing bowl, whisk together the eggs, applesauce, vegetable oil, and vanilla extract.

4. Fold the wet ingredients into the dry ingredients, mixing until well combined.

5. Pour the batter into the prepared pan, and bake for 25–30 minutes, or until a toothpick inserted into the center comes out mostly clean. Let cool completely.

6. Meanwhile, prepare the frosting by putting all the frosting ingredients in an electric mixer and beating until smooth and creamy.

7. For 100 calorie bars, cut the cake into 6 rows by 6 rows to make 36 bars. Spread a thin layer of frosting on each bar before serving (this looks better if done after cutting the cake).

HELPFUL TIP:

For the best presentation, use a pastry bag to pipe a large dot of the frosting in the center of each bar, rather than spreading a thin layer.

PREP TIME: 10 MINUTES • BAKE TIME: 17 MINUTES

CHEESECAKE MINIS

MAKES 18 MINI CHEESECAKES

Mona's Family Favorites: My Aunt Pearl really inspired me to create this wonderful dessert! The cheesecake's ultra creamy texture is out of this world. Forget about leaky springform pans; we use muffin tin liners to make quick work and "perfect portioning." Plus the fresh raspberry topping takes this dessert to the next level of decadence.

Featured Recipe Story: See next page.

Recommended Serving:
DESSERT – 100 Calories = 1 Cheesecake Mini

Ingredients:

Nonstick cooking spray

2 (8-ounce) packages reduced-fat cream cheese, softened

⅔ cup sugar

⅓ cup sour cream

2 large eggs

1 teaspoon lemon juice

¾ teaspoon vanilla extract

⅛ teaspoon salt

Directions:

1. Preheat the oven to 300°F, and line standard muffin tins with 18 paper or aluminum (recommended) liners. Lightly spray the insides of the liners with nonstick cooking spray.

2. In an electric mixer, beat the cream cheese until smooth.

3. Add all the remaining ingredients to the cream cheese in the mixer, and beat until fully combined.

4. Fill each prepared liner with the cheesecake batter until about ½ of the way full.

5. Bake for 15–17 minutes, or until the sides of the cheesecakes are beginning to rise, but center is still soft.

6. Let cool on the counter for 30 minutes. Cover, and refrigerate for an additional 2 hours before removing the paper liners to serve.

HELPFUL TIP:

Make a fresh raspberry sauce topping by lightly mashing 1 cup of raspberries with 1½ tablespoons of honey. Topping each Cheesecake Mini with 2 rounded teaspoons of the sauce will add only 10 calories to the full dessert.

CHEESECAKE MINIS
The Cheesecake Challenge Solved—Make it New York Style!

ANSON REALLY GAVE ME A CHALLENGE: "Mona, can you create a cheesecake for me in 100 calorie portions? It's gotta taste great—like I used to have in New York!" As a native New Yorker (LonGUYland, to be exact!), I'm more than familiar with rich New York-style cheesecake with a buttery, graham cracker crust. How was I going to lose the calories and keep the richness? Then I remembered my Aunt Pearl in Flushing. She used to make the classic New York-style cheesecake without the crust! That would reduce the calories, but probably not enough. I was thrilled when I found her handwritten recipe on her signature blue flower stationery (which, I admit, brought a tear and a smile). Her secret was the combination of sour cream and cream cheese. I had a few other culinary and smart tricks to achieve a delicious goal.

Cake Control! Whenever I am served a piece of cheesecake at a restaurant, I always get a huge portion. I take a few forkfuls and think, "that's enough for now!" But before I know it...uh, oh...I ate the whole thing! How did that happen? *Herein lies my idea—make cheesecake cupcakes with only 100 calories!*

Cool & Creamy! The combination of sour cream and reduced-fat cream cheese doesn't compromise the flavor or creaminess, and provides wonderful texture. The fat content goes down, yet the creaminess goes up. The addition of some lemon creates a delicious piece of heaven!

Fruit Factor! For an additional 10 calories per cheesecake, mash some fresh raspberries with honey for extra indulgence. All fresh ingredients! No fake syrups or sauces!

I'm so happy to share this with you. And Aunt Pearl would be proud, too!

1 The batter is super simple, and the cakes are ready in 17 minutes. Use aluminum foil liners in a cupcake pan for easy release of the cakes.

4 These cheesecake minis are great for entertaining. Add a whole, fresh raspberry to the top to add an extra festive touch.

2 Cool the mini cheesecakes before you remove liners. They should be firm before you fill them. Mash fresh raspberries with some honey for a fresh topping.

3 You can use blueberries or blackberries, too. Two teaspoons of topping adds a ton of flavor and only 10 calories to each cupcake!

5 These cakes are great pick-me-up desserts. Your guests will not believe they have just eaten only 100 (or 110 with the raspberry sauce) calories. So rich and satisfying. Enjoy!

PREP TIME: 22 MINUTES • BAKE TIME: 28 MINUTES

VANILLA CUPCAKES

MAKES 16 CUPCAKES

These moist and fluffy Vanilla Cupcakes are crowned with a luxurious vanilla cream cheese frosting, giving you a double dose of big vanilla flavor you can't resist. Our combination of cake flour and buttermilk is the secret to a light as air cupcake that is sure to be your family's new birthday staple.

Recommended Serving:
DESSERT – 200 Calories = 1 Cupcake

Ingredients:

1 ¼ cups cake flour

1 ¼ teaspoons baking powder

½ teaspoon baking soda

¼ teaspoon salt

¾ cup sugar

2 large eggs

2½ teaspoons vanilla extract

½ cup canola oil

½ cup buttermilk

Frosting:

8 ounces fat-free cream cheese, softened

1 ¼ cups confectioners' sugar

1 teaspoon vanilla extract

Directions:

1. Preheat the oven to 350°F. Line 2 cupcake tins with 16 paper liners.

2. In a large mixing bowl, combine the flour, baking powder, baking soda, and salt. Set aside.

3. Add the sugar and eggs to an electric mixer, and beat until light and pale yellow, about 1½ minutes. Add the vanilla extract and canola oil, and beat for an additional 15 seconds.

4. With the electric mixer on low speed, slowly add the dry flour ingredients, alternating with the buttermilk, in batches, into the egg mixture, and beat just until all is combined into a batter.

5. Pour the batter into the prepared cupcake liners, filling each until about ⅔ full.

6. Bake for 25-28 minutes, or until a toothpick inserted into the center of a cupcake comes out mostly clean. Let cool completely.

7. Prepare the frosting by adding all the frosting ingredients to an electric mixer and beating until smooth and creamy. For the thickest consistency, let chill for at least 1 hour before frosting.

8. Frost each cupcake with a rounded tablespoon of the frosting before serving.

COOK TIME: 10 MINUTES • CHILL TIME: 4 HOURS

CHOCOLATE FUDGE

MAKES 49 FUDGE SQUARES

The beauty of rich, luscious fudge is that a little goes a long way. Just a 1- inch square of our quick and easy Chocolate Fudge is the perfect hit of dessert, whether on the go or at home. For perfect-sized fudge squares, use a straight-sided square baking dish (typically metal), rather than versions with rounded edges.

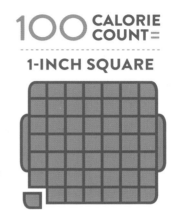

100 **CALORIE COUNT=**

1-INCH SQUARE

Recommended Serving:
INDULGENCE – 100 Calories = 1-Inch Square

Ingredients:

Nonstick cooking spray

3 cups semisweet chocolate chips

1 (14-ounce) can sweetened condensed milk

2 tablespoons butter

¼ cup chopped walnuts

Directions:

1. Spray an 8 x 8-inch baking dish with nonstick cooking spray, then line with parchment paper, and spray again.

2. Create a double boiler by placing a stainless steel or tempered glass bowl over a pot of boiling water.

3. Add chocolate chips, condensed milk, and butter to the bowl of the double boiler, and heat, stirring frequently, until the chocolate has melted and all is combined.

4. Use a rubber spatula to scrape the fudge mixture into the prepared pan. Even out and smooth the top of the fudge before sprinkling with the chopped walnuts.

5. Use another piece of parchment paper to lightly press the chopped walnuts into the top of the fudge.

6. Let cool on counter, uncovered, for 1 hour. Cover, and refrigerate for at least 3 hours before slicing.

7. To slice, use the parchment paper to lift the fudge out of the baking dish, and transfer to a cutting board. Make 6 evenly spaced cuts horizontally and 6 evenly spaced cuts vertically to create a 7 x 7 grid of perfect 1-inch squares. Store refrigerated for up to 2 weeks.

PREP TIME: 20 MINUTES • BAKE TIME: 17 MINUTES

100 CALORIE BROWNIE BITES

MAKES 24 BROWNIE BITES

Mona's Family Favorites: I LOVE chocolate! I found that using semisweet chocolate chips produced knockout fudgy flavor and allowed us to slightly reduce the butter without noticing! Also, I bake the brownies in mini-muffin tins for a PERFECT portion with plenty of the crispy edges that we all crave. Yum, no, super yum!

100 CALORIE COUNT =

1 BROWNIE BITE

Recommended Serving:
DESSERT – 100 Calories = 1 Brownie Bite

Ingredients:

Nonstick cooking spray

3 tablespoons butter

1 tablespoon 2% milk

½ cup sugar

1½ cups semisweet chocolate chips

2 large eggs, beaten

¾ teaspoon vanilla extract

⅔ cup all-purpose flour

¼ teaspoon baking soda

¼ teaspoon salt

Directions:

1. Preheat oven to 350°F, and spray a 24-cup mini-muffin tin with nonstick cooking spray.

2. In a medium sauce pot over medium heat, melt butter into milk, then whisk in sugar until dissolved.

3. Bring mixture to a simmer, remove from heat, and slowly fold in chocolate chips, stirring until melted. Add eggs and vanilla extract, and stir until all is combined.

4. In a separate bowl, combine flour, baking soda, and salt before folding into the chocolate mixture to create a smooth and thick batter.

5. Split the batter evenly amongst the 24 prepared muffin cups, adding 1½ tablespoons of batter to each cup.

6. Bake for 15–17 minutes, or until a toothpick inserted into the center of a brownie comes out mostly clean. Let cool for 10 minutes before serving.

HELPFUL TIP:

You can also prepare this in an 8 x 8-inch baking dish by increasing the baking time to 22–25 minutes. Cut the cake into 4 rows by 3 rows to make 12 delicious brownies with only 200 calories each.

PREP TIME: 30 MINUTES • CHILL TIME: 2½ HOURS

PEANUT BUTTER TRUFFLES

MAKES 24 TRUFFLES

Is there any better pairing than chocolate and peanut butter? These Peanut Butter Truffles make a strong case that there isn't! With only a handful of ingredients, you can easily make your own homemade candies that look and taste as good as the local chocolate shop.

100 CALORIE COUNT =

1 TRUFFLE

Recommended Serving:
DESSERT – 100 Calories = 1 Truffle

Ingredients:

½ cup creamy natural peanut butter

2 tablespoons butter, softened

¼ teaspoon vanilla extract

⅛ teaspoon salt

¾ cup confectioners' sugar

1 cup semisweet chocolate chips

Directions:

1 Line a baking sheet with parchment paper.

2 In a mixing bowl, mix the peanut butter, butter, vanilla extract, and salt until smooth and combined. Fold in the confectioners' sugar to form a peanut butter dough.

3 Roll the peanut butter dough into 24 equal balls (using about 1½ teaspoons of dough each), and place onto the prepared baking sheet. Cover, and refrigerate for 30 minutes.

4 Create a double boiler by placing a stainless steel or tempered glass bowl over a pot of simmering water.

5 Add the chocolate chips to the bowl of the double boiler, and heat, stirring frequently, until the chocolate is melted and smooth. Remove from heat.

6 Using a fork, place one of the chilled peanut butter balls in the melted chocolate, and roll until fully coated. Gently lift the truffle out of the chocolate, and tap the bowl to remove any excess coating. Transfer back to the sheet pan.

7 Repeat this process until all 24 truffles are coated. Cover, and refrigerate for 2 hours before serving.

PREP TIME: 10 MINUTES

FANTASTIC FRUIT PARFAITS

MAKES 2 PARFAITS

Mona's Family Favorites: Easy is often the most delicious! This is my go-to dessert whenever I throw a party for family or friends. The simple combination of fresh berries, cinnamon-scented Greek yogurt, and chocolate makes an elegant, guilt-free finish to any meal. You always have to add a little chocolate, right? While this combination of fruit is our favorite, the variations are nearly endless. Serve in martini glasses for a festive presentation.

100 **CALORIE COUNT=**

1 PARFAIT

Recommended Serving:
DESSERT – 100 Calories = 1 Parfait

Ingredients:

½ cup sliced strawberries

½ cup vanilla nonfat Greek yogurt

Ground cinnamon

½ cup blueberries

2 teaspoons miniature semisweet chocolate chips

Directions:

1. Set out 2 (5-ounce) parfait glasses.

2. Divide the sliced strawberries evenly between the 2 glasses.

3. Place a large dollop of the yogurt into each of the 2 glasses, and sprinkle lightly with ground cinnamon.

4. Top the yogurt in each glass with an equal amount of the blueberries.

5. Top the blueberries in each glass with another large dollop of yogurt, and sprinkle lightly with ground cinnamon. Top each parfait with 1 teaspoon of miniature chocolate chips before serving.

HELPFUL TIP:

Any flavor of nonfat Greek yogurt can be used in place of the vanilla, with berry flavors being obviously good choices. Topping each parfait with 2 rounded tablespoons of Homemade Granola (see page 272) in place of the chocolate chips will make for great 150-calorie breakfast parfaits.

COOK TIME: 10 MINUTES • CHILL TIME: 8+ HOURS

VANILLA BEAN ICE CREAM

MAKES 1 QUART ICE CREAM OR 12 SERVINGS

We gave classic vanilla ice cream a slim-down and a huge boost of flavor. We add a small amount of cornstarch to the ice cream base for ultra creamy texture without the use of heavy cream, and we add both vanilla extract and a freshly scraped vanilla bean for a winning punch of flavor. Divine! Please note that a 1½-quart (or larger) ice cream maker is required for this recipe.

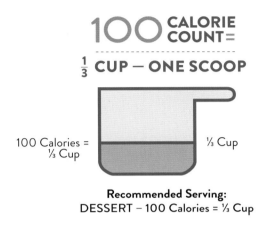

100 CALORIE COUNT =

⅓ CUP — ONE SCOOP

100 Calories = ⅓ Cup

⅓ Cup

Recommended Serving:
DESSERT – 100 Calories = ⅓ Cup

Ingredients:

2¼ cups 2% milk

¾ cup half-and-half

¾ cup sugar

1 tablespoon cornstarch

⅛ teaspoon salt

2 large egg yolks, beaten

1 teaspoon vanilla extract

Seeds scraped from 1 vanilla bean

Directions:

1. Add the milk, half-and-half, sugar, cornstarch, and salt to a sauce pot over medium heat.

2. Cook the ice cream base, whisking constantly, for 10 minutes, or until slightly thickened. Remove from heat.

3. In a mixing bowl, quickly whisk 1 large ladle of the hot ice cream base into the beaten egg yolks, whisking until smooth and combined.

4. Whisk the egg yolk mixture into the pot with the remainder of the ice cream base.

5. Add the vanilla extract and vanilla bean seeds to the ice cream base, and stir until the seeds are incorporated throughout. Let cool to room temperature before refrigerating until ice cold, at least 8 hours.

6. Churn the ice cream base, and chill according to the manufacturer's instructions for your brand of ice cream maker.

BREAKFAST

LUNCH

CALORIE GOAL-PLANNING GUIDE

The first step in deciding how to distribute your calories for the day is knowing how many you should be consuming. This target calorie count varies according to age, gender, and physical activity level. Begin with reviewing the researched-based suggestion from the Institute of Medicine below.

After you've found your recommended daily count, consider if your goal is to lose or gain weight? Or are you simply looking to maintain your weight and eat healthier? In general, if someone consumes the recommended calories for their age, gender, and activity level, they should maintain their current weight. If they consume less than their target calories they should lose weight, while consuming more than their target would result in gaining.

Physical activity also plays a large part in calorie requirements. Active persons require more calories than their sedentary counterparts. Maintaining at least a moderate level of physical activity will contribute greatly to healthy living.

The chart is a terrific general reference, but for a personalized calorie estimate that takes into account individual height and weight, visit: *http://www.globalrph. com/estimated_energy_requirement.htm.*

Number Crunching

Keeping track of your calories and monitoring your weight are keys to learning what works for you. This book makes calorie "counting" a snap, so it's easy to keep track of how many calories you are eating. Weighing yourself once a week is a good rule of thumb, then adjust as needed.

If you do want to lose weight, the *Dietary Guidelines for Americans* recommends slow, steady weight loss by decreasing calorie intake and increasing physical activity. Whether your goal is a small calorie reduction to prevent

DINNER

SNACK

weight "creep" or a larger reduction for greater weight loss, you can generally equate a reduction of 3,500 calories for a pound of weight loss. Therefore to lose one pound in a month you would need a daily reduction of roughly 100 calories, and to lose a pound in a week you'd need a reduction of 500 calories a day. Consult your doctor before making dramatic changes in diet or physical activity.

No matter what your weight loss goal, the *Guidelines* also point out that the healthiest way to cut calories is to reduce empty calories from added sugars, fats, and alcohol AND to pay special attention to portion sizes! Sound familiar?

Gender	Age	Sedentary (Not Active)*	Moderately Active*	Active
MALES	19–30	2,400–2,600	2,600–2,800	3,000
	31–50	2,200–2,400	2,400–2,600	2,600–3,000
	51 years and older	2,000–2,200	2,200–2,400	2,400–2,800
FEMALES	19–30	1.800–2,000	2,000–2,200	2,400
	31–50	1,800	2,000	2,200
	51 years and older	1,600	1,800	2,000–2,200

Based on Estimated Energy Requirement (EER) equations from the Institute of Medicine. Dietary Reference Intakes for Energy, Carbohydrate, Fiber, Fat, Fatty Acids, Cholesterol, Protein, and Amino Acids. Washington (DC): The National Academies Press; 2002.

PERFECT PORTION MEAL PLANNING—DAY 1

In order to guide you in calorie planning, we have created a 7-day perfect-portion planner. Feel free to substitute any of the recipes in the book with the suggested ones, but be mindful of the calorie goals for each meal. Want to create your own plan with other foods you like to eat? No problem. We've included the following charts by food type to show you the 100 calorie portion size. Our commitment to you is to easily help you recognize the perfect portions, and to give you guidance on all the different foods you can eat to be successful. Enjoy!

	1,500 Calories/Day	1,800 Calories/Day	2,000 Calories/Day
BREAKFAST	300 calories	400 calories	400 calories
Buttermilk Pancakes, page 35	1 (100 calories)	2 (200 calories)	2 (200 calories)
Maple syrup	2 Tbsp. (100 calories)	2 Tbsp. (100 calories)	2 Tbsp. (100 calories)
Cut-up cantaloupe	2 cups (100 calories)	2 cups (100 calories)	2 cups (100 calories)
SNACK	100 calories	100 calories	100 calories
Plain nonfat Greek yogurt with honey, blueberries, and Homemade Granola, page 272	⅓ cup yogurt (45), 1 tsp honey (20), 2 Tbsp. blueberries (10), 1 Tbsp. granola (30)	⅓ cup yogurt (45), 1 tsp honey (20), 2 Tbsp. blueberries (10), 1 Tbsp. granola (30)	⅓ cup yogurt (45), 1 tsp honey (20), 2 Tbsp. blueberries (10), 1 Tbsp. granola (30)
LUNCH	400 calories	400 calories	500 calories
Classic Tomato Soup, page 45	¾ cup (100 calories)	¾ cup (100 calories)	1½ cup (200 calories)
Baked Mac & Cheese, page 75	3 sections (300 calories)	3 sections (300 calories)	3 sections (300 calories)
SNACK	100 calories	200 calories	200 calories
Homemade Hummus, page 207	2 Tbsp. (50 calories)	¼ cup (100 calories)	¼ cup (100 calories)
Whole-grain Cracker Thins	5 crackers (50 calories)	10 crackers (100 calories)	10 crackers (100 calories)
DINNER	500 calories	600 calories	700 calories
Parmesan-Crusted Tilapia, page 147	1 fillet (200 calories)	1 fillet (200 calories)	1½ fillet (300 calories)
Brown Rice	½ cup (100 calories)	1 cup (200 calories)	1 cup (200 calories)
Glazed Carrots, page 164	1 cup (200 calories)	1 cup (200 calories)	1 cup (200 calories)
DESSERT	100 calories	100 calories	100 calories
Lemon Bar, page 285	1 bar (100 calories)	1 bar (100 calories)	1 bar (100 calories)

BUTTERMILK PANCAKES, PAGE 35

SAMPLE MENU—DAY 2

	1,500 Calories/Day	1,800 Calories/Day	2,000 Calories/Day
BREAKFAST	300 calories	400 calories	400 calories
The Perfect Omelet, page 18	1 egg white omelet (200 calories)	1 omelet (300 calories)	1 omelet (300 calories)
Orange	1 large (100 calories)	1 large (100 calories)	1 large (100 calories)
SNACK	100 calories	100 calories	100 calories
Skinny Strawberry Milkshake, page 269	¾ cup (100 calories)	¾ cup (100 calories)	¾ cup (100 calories)
LUNCH	400 calories	400 calories	500 calories
Open-Faced Tuna Melt, page 67	1 (200 calories)	1 (200 calories)	2 (400 calories)
Coleslaw, page 157	⅔ cup (100 calories)	⅔ cup (100 calories)	⅔ cup (100 calories)
Apple chips	½ cup (100 calories)	½ cup (100 calories)	
SNACK	100 calories	200 calories	200 calories
Peanuts	2 Tbsp. (100 calories)	¼ cup (200 calories)	¼ cup (200 calories)
DINNER	500 calories	600 calories	700 calories
Mona's Southwestern Chili, page 101	2 cups (400 calories)	2 cups (400 calories)	2 cups (400 calories)
Green Leafy Salad with Buttermilk Ranch dressing, page 245	1 cup (<20 calories) 3 Tbsp. (100 calories)	1 cup (<20 calories) 3 Tbsp. (100 calories)	1 cup (<20 calories) 3 Tbsp. (100 calories)
Savory Southern-Style Cornbread, page 169		1 slice (100 calories)	2 slices (200 calories)
SNACK	100 calories	100 calories	100 calories
Stovetop Popcorn, page 273	2 cups, oil-popped	2 cups, oil-popped	2 cups, oil-popped

OPEN FACED TUNA MELT, PAGE 67

SAMPLE MENU—DAY 3

	1,500 Calories/Day	1,800 Calories/Day	2,000 Calories/Day
BREAKFAST	300 calories	400 calories	400 calories
Banana Bread, page 36	1 slice (200 calories)	1 slice (200 calories)	1 slice (200 calories)
Plain nonfat Greek yogurt	6 ounces (100 calories)	6 ounces (100 calories)	6 ounces (100 calories)
Seedless grapes		1 cup (100 calories)	1 cup (100 calories)
SNACK	100 calories	100 calories	100 calories
Raisins	2 mini-boxes	2 mini-boxes	2 mini-boxes
LUNCH	400 calories	500 calories	600 calories
Hearty Lentil Soup, page 49	1⅓ cups (200 calories)	2 cups (300 calories)	2 cups (300 calories)
Saltine crackers	8 (100 calories)	8 (100 calories)	8 (100 calories)
String cheese	1 (100 calories)	1 (100 calories)	2 (200 calories)
SNACK	100 calories	100 calories	200 calories
Mashed avocado + celery sticks	¼ cup mashed avocado (100 calories)	¼ cup mashed avocado (100 calories)	½ cup mashed avocado (200 calories)
DINNER	500 calories	600 calories	600 calories
Chicken-Fried Steak, page 137	1 steak + 3 Tbsp. gravy (300 calories)	1 steak + 3 Tbsp. gravy (300 calories)	1 steak + 3 Tbsp. gravy (300 calories)
Broccoli rabe	1¾ cup (100 calories)	1¾ cup (100 calories)	1¾ cup (100 calories)
Homestyle Mashed Potatoes, page 221	⅓ cup (100 calories)	⅔ cup (200 calories)	⅔ cup (200 calories)
DESSERT	100 calories	100 calories	100 calories
Fresh Berry Cobbler, page 286	1 piece (100 calories)	1 piece (100 calories)	1 piece (100 calories)

CHICKEN FRIED STEAK, PAGE 137

SAMPLE MENU—DAY 4

	1,500 Calories/Day	1,800 Calories/Day	2,000 Calories/Day
BREAKFAST	300 calories	400 calories	400 calories
Steel-Cut Oatmeal, page 39	1 ½ cups (200 calories)	1 ½ cups (200 calories)	1 ½ cups (200 calories)
Toppings, page 41	2 tsp dark brown sugar (35 calories) + ¼ cup blueberries (20 calories) + 1 Tbsp. chopped walnuts (50 calories)	1 Tbsp. dark brown sugar (50 calories) + ½ cup + 2 Tbsp. blueberries (40 calories) + 2 Tbsp. chopped walnuts (100 calories)	1 Tbsp. dark brown sugar (50 calories) + ½ cup + 2 Tbsp. blueberries (40 calories) + 2 Tbsp. chopped walnuts (100 calories)
SNACK	100 calories	100 calories	100 calories
Granola bar	100 calories	100 calories	100 calories
LUNCH	400 calories	500 calories	600 calories
Mona's Chili (leftover), page 101	1 ½ cups (300 calories)	1 ½ cups (300 calories)	2 cups (400 calories)
Savory Southern-Style Cornbread, page 169		1 piece (100 calories)	1 piece (100 calories)
Raw veggies	10 baby carrots (40 calories); 2 stalks celery (20 calories)	10 baby carrots (40 calories); 2 stalks celery (20 calories)	10 baby carrots (40 calories); 2 stalks celery (20 calories)
French Onion Dip, page 213	2 Tbsp. (40 calories)	2 Tbsp. (40 calories)	2 Tbsp. (40 calories)
SNACK	100 calories	100 calories	200 calories
Apple	1 medium (100 calories)	1 medium (100 calories)	1 medium (100 calories)
"Hot Cocoa" Pretzel Chips, page 265			10 pretzels
DINNER	500 calories	600 calories	600 calories
Shrimp Scampi, page 141	9 shrimp (300 calories)	9 shrimp (300 calories)	9 shrimp (300 calories)
Rice	½ cup (100 calories)	½ cup (100 calories)	½ cup (100 calories)
Lemon & Garlic Broccoli Saute, page 160	⅔ cup (100 calories)	⅔ cup (100 calories)	⅔ cup (100 calories)
Italian bread		1-inch slice (100 calories)	1-inch slice (100 calories)
DESSERT	100 calories	100 calories	100 calories
Carrot Cake Bars, page 293	1 bar (100 calories)	1 bar (100 calories)	1 bar (100 calories)

SOUTHWESTERN CHILI, PAGE 101

SAMPLE MENU—DAY 5

	1,500 Calories/Day	1,800 Calories/Day	2,000 Calories/Day
BREAKFAST	300 calories	400 calories	400 calories
Baked Ham & Egg Cup, page 23	1 cup (100 calories)	2 cups (200 calories)	2 cups (200 calories)
Grapefruit	1 large (100 calories)	1 large (100 calories)	1 large (100 calories)
Light whole-wheat bread, toasted	1 slice (45 calories)	1 slice (45 calories)	1 slice (45 calories)
Whipped butter	2 tsp (60)	2 tsp (60)	2 tsp (60)
SNACK	100 calories	100 calories	200 calories
String cheese	1 (100 calories)	1 (100 calories)	2 (200 calories)
LUNCH	400 calories	400 calories	400 calories
Spinach & Pear Salad, page 57	2½ cups (200 calories)	2½ cups (200 calories)	2½ cups (200 calories)
100 Calorie Dinner Roll, page 227	1 (100 calories)	1 (100 calories)	1 (100 calories)
Raspberry Vinaigrette, page 246	3 Tbsp. (100 calories)	3 Tbsp. (100 calories)	3 Tbsp. (100 calories)
DESSERT		100 calories	100 calories
Brownie Bite, page 301		1 (100 calories)	1 (100 calories)
SNACK	100 calories	100 calories	200 calories
Almonds	13 (100 calories)	13 (100 calories)	26 (200 calories)
DINNER	500 calories	600 calories	600 calories
Eggplant Parmesan Casserole, page 87	3 sections (300 calories)	4 sections (400 calories)	4 sections (400 calories)
Leafy green salad	1 cup (< 20 calories)	1 cup (< 20 calories)	1 cup (< 20 calories)
Raspberry Vinaigrette, page 246	3 Tbsp. (100 calories)	3 Tbsp. (100 calories)	3 Tbsp. (100 calories)
Breadsticks (cracker type)	2 (80 calories)	2 (80 calories)	2 (80 calories)
SNACK	100 calories	100 calories	100 calories
Blueberry Muffin, page 33	½ (100 calories)	½ (100 calories)	½ (100 calories)

EGGPLANT PARMESAN CASSEROLE, PAGE 87

SAMPLE MENU—DAY 6

	1,500 Calories/Day	1,800 Calories/Day	2,000 Calories/Day
BREAKFAST	300 calories	400 calories	400 calories
Light whole-wheat English muffin	1 (100 calories)	1 (100 calories)	1 (100 calories)
Peanut butter	1 Tbsp. (100 calories)	1 Tbsp. (100 calories)	1 Tbsp. (100 calories)
Strawberries	2 cups sliced (100 calories)	2 cups sliced (100 calories)	2 cups sliced (100 calories)
Orange juice		6 ounces (100 calories)	6 ounces (100 calories)
SNACK	100 calories	100 calories	200 calories
Banana	1 small (100 calories)	1 small (100 calories)	1 small (100 calories)
Granola bar			1 (100 calories)
LUNCH	400 calories	500 calories	500 calories
Eggplant Parmesan Casserole (left-over), page 87	2 sections (200 calories)	3 sections (300 calories)	3 sections (300 calories)
Leafy green salad	1 cup (< 20 calories)	1 cup (< 20 calories)	1 cup (< 20 calories)
Raspberry Vinaigrette, page 246	3 Tbsp. (100 calories)	3 Tbsp. (100 calories)	3 Tbsp. (100 calories)
Breadsticks (cracker type)	2 (80 calories)	2 (80 calories)	2 (80 calories)
SNACK	100 calories	100 calories	100 calories
Fantastic Fruit Parfaits, page 305	1 parfait (100 calories)	1 parfait (100 calories)	1 parfait (100 calories)
DINNER	600 calories	600 calories	700 calories
Lemon and Herb Roasted Chicken Thighs, page 117	1½ chicken thighs (300 calories)	1½ chicken thighs (300 calories)	2 chicken thighs (400 calories)
Quinoa	½ cup (100 calories)	½ cup (100 calories)	½ cup (100 calories)
Olive oil for quinoa	1 Tbsp. (100 calories)	1 Tbsp. (100 calories)	1 Tbsp. (100 calories)
Asparagus Gratin, page 163	½ cup (100 calories)	½ cup (100 calories)	½ cup (100 calories)
SNACK		100 calories	100 calories
Oven-Fried Potato Chips, page 275		½ cup	½ cup

FANTASTIC FRUIT PARFAITS, PAGE 305

SAMPLE MENU—DAY 7

	1,500 Calories/Day	**1,800 Calories/Day**	**2,000 Calories/Day**
BREAKFAST	300 calories	400 calories	400 calories
French Toast, page 25	2 pieces (200 calories)	2 pieces (200 calories)	2 pieces (200 calories)
Blueberries	½ cup + 1 tsp (50 calories)	1 cup + 1 Tbsp (100 calories)	1 cup + 1 Tbsp (100 calories)
Maple syrup	1 Tbsp. (50 calories)	2 Tbsp. (100 calories)	2 Tbsp. (100 calories)
LUNCH	400 calories	400 calories	500 calories
Chicken Quesadilla, page 65	1 (300 calories)	1 (300 calories)	1 (300 calories)
Classic Tomato Soup, page 45	¾ cup (100 calories)	¾ cup (100 calories)	1 ½ cups (200 calories)
SNACK	100 calories	200 calories	200 calories
Mango pieces	1 cup (100 calories)	1 cup (100 calories)	1 cup (100 calories)
DINNER	500 calories	600 calories	700 calories
Meatballs Marinara, page 107	6 meatballs + ½ cup sauce (300 calories)	6 meatballs + ½ cup sauce (300 calories)	8 meatballs + ½ cup + 3 Tbsp. sauce (400 calories)
Spaghetti noodles	½ cup (100 calories)	¾ cup (150 calories)	¾ cup (150 calories)
Green Beans Almondine, page 156	½ cup (100 calories)	¾ cup (150 calories)	¾ cup (150 calories)
SNACK	200 calories	200 calories	200 calories
Chocolate Chip Cookie, page 289	1 cookie (100 calories)	1 cookie (100 calories)	1 cookie (100 calories)
1% milk	1 cup (100 calories)	1 cup (100 calories)	1 cup (100 calories)

CLASSIC TOMATO SOUP, PAGE 45

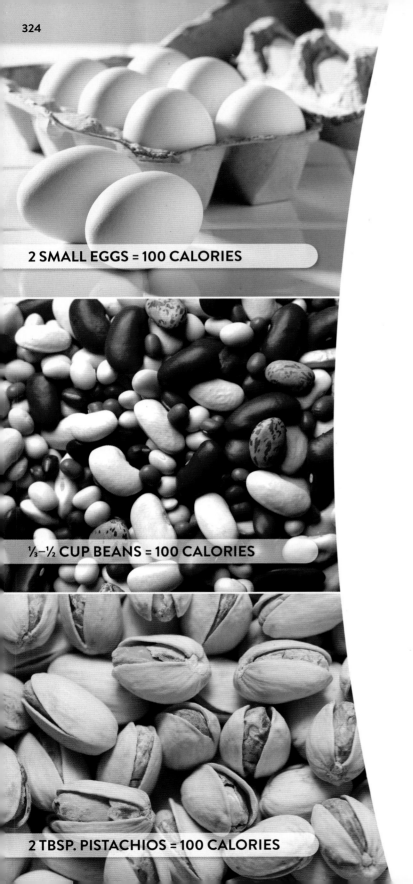

2 SMALL EGGS = 100 CALORIES

⅓–½ CUP BEANS = 100 CALORIES

2 TBSP. PISTACHIOS = 100 CALORIES

Here is a guide to follow if you are looking for simple alternatives to side dishes and snacks. Calorie counts are based on USDA database; packaged foods are an average calorie count of all brands. Always check nutrition labels for actual calorie counts.

PROTEIN
100 Calorie Portions

Almond butter	1 tablespoon
Beans, such as black, kidney, garbanzo, pinto, cooked*	⅓ cup–½ cup
Edamame, cooked and shelled	½ cup
Egg, cooked*	2 small
Egg substitute, cooked*	½ cup
Hummus, commercial	4 tablespoons
Lean deli meat (turkey, ham, chicken, roast beef)	3 ounces
Lentils, cooked*	7 tablespoons
Nuts (almonds, pistachios, or walnuts)	2 tablespoons
Peanut butter	1 tablespoon
Peanuts	2 tablespoons
Seeds, sunflower dry-roasted, with shell	⅓ cup
Soy nut butter	1 tablespoon
Soy nuts	¼ cup
Turkey jerky	1 ounce (varies by brand)

* nal.usda.gov/fnic/foodcomp

CARBOHYDRATES *(cooked product)*
100 Calorie Portions

Bagels, mini	¾
Bread (Italian, French, Sourdough, whole wheat)	1-ounce (1-inch slice)
Bulgur	⅔ cup
Couscous*	½ cup, packed
Crackers, multi-grain thins	11
Crackers, oyster	½ cup
Crackers, saltines	8
Crackers, water	7
Egg noodles	⅓ cup (scant)
Macaroni, small shells*	½ cup, packed
Pasta (elbows, farfalle, penne, ziti,)*	½ cup
Pasta (fusilli, linguine, spaghetti)*	½ cup (scant)
Pasta (whole-wheat, any shape)*	½ cup (packed)
Pitas, minis	1½
Potatoes, boiled*	¾ cup
Potato, baked with skin*	1 small
Quinoa*	½ cup
Rice, brown*	½ cup (scant)
Rice, white*	½ cup (scant)
Sandwich thins	1
Sweet potato, baked*	1 medium
Sweet potato, mashed*	⅓ cup + 1 tbsp.
Tortillas, corn	2 (6-inch round)
Tortillas, flour	1 (6-inch round)

* Amounts listed are for cooked product

½ CUP MACARONI = 100 CALORIES

1 SLICE WHEAT BREAD = 100 CALORIES

½ CUP RICE = 100 CALORIES

31 MEDIUM ASPARAGUS = 100 CALORIES

25 MED. MUSHROOMS = 100 CALORIES

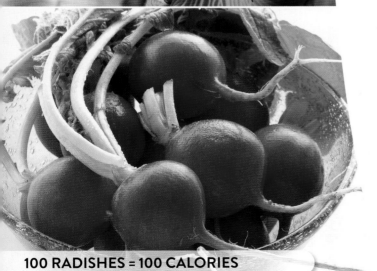

100 RADISHES = 100 CALORIES

RAW VEGETABLES
100 Calorie Portions

Alfalfa sprouts	12 ½ cups
Asparagus	31 medium
Baby carrots	25
Baby corn	17
Broccoli, chopped	5 cups
Carrot slices	3 cups
Cauliflower, chopped	3 ½ cups
Celery	10 large
Cucumber	2 medium
Fennel bulb, chopped	4 cups
Green beans	3 cups
Green onions	25
Kale	13 cups
Jicama	2 cups
Mini bell peppers	12
Mung bean sprouts	3 cups
Mushrooms	25 medium
Peas (sugar snap)	3 cups
Pickles	3 large
Radishes	100 medium
Salad lettuce	20 cups
Spinach	14 cups
Tomatoes, chopped	3 cups
Tomatoes (grape)	25; 3 cups

COOKED VEGETABLES *(no added oil)*
100 Calorie Portions

Asparagus	2½ cups
Broccoli, chopped	2 cups
Broccoli rabe	1¾ cups
Beets	1⅓ cups
Brussels sprouts	1½ cups
Cabbage	2½–3 cups
Carrots, sliced	1¾ cups
Cauliflower, frozen	2¾ cups
Collard Greens	1⅔ cups
Corn, kernels	⅔ cup
Corn, on the cob	1 medium
Edamame, shelled	½ cup
Garbanzo beans	½ cup
Green beans	2¼ cups
Kale	2⅔ cups
Mushroom (button)	3½ cups
Mushroom (portabello)	3 (3-ounce) caps
Peas, (garden), shelled	¾ cup
Peas, (sugar snap)	1½ cups
Rutabaga, cubed	2 cups
Rutabaga, mashed	1½ cups
Sauerkraut, undrained	2 cups
Spinach	2⅓ cups
Squash (spaghetti)	2¼ cups
Squash (summer)	3½ cups
Tomatoes, stewed	1½ cups
Turnips, cubed	3 cups
Turnips, mashed	2 cups
Squash (acorn or butternut)	1¼ cups

2 CUPS BROCCOLI = 100 CALORIES

½ CUP EDAMAME = 100 CALORIES

1 EAR CORN = 100 CALORIES

1 ½ CUPS RASPBERRIES = 100 CALORIES

1 LARGE GRAPEFRUIT = 100 CALORIES

¼–⅓ AVOCADO = 100 CALORIES

FRUIT
100 Calorie Portions

Apples	1 medium
Apricots, fresh	6
Apricots, dried	5 pieces
Avocado	¼–⅓
Banana	1 small/medium
Blackberries	1 ½ cups
Blueberries	1 cup + 2 tbsp.
Cantaloupe	½ medium; 2 cups diced
Cherries	20; 1 cup
Cranberries, dried	3 tablespoons
Figs, dried	5 pieces
Figs, fresh	2 large
Grapefruit	1 large (4 ½ " diameter); 1 ⅓ cups (sections)
Grapes	30 each; 1 cup
Honeydew melon	¼ medium; 1 ½ cups diced
Kiwi	2 ¼ medium
Mango, dried	1 ounce
Mango, fresh	½ medium; 1 cup diced
Nectarine	1 ½ medium
Oranges	1 large
Papaya, dried	1 ½ ounces
Papaya, fresh	1 ½ small; 1 ½ cups diced
Peaches	2 small; 1 ½ cups diced
Pears	1 medium
Pineapple, fresh	1 ¼ cups chunks
Pineapple, dried	1 ounce
Plums, dried	1.4 ounces
Plums, fresh	3 medium; 1 ⅓ cups diced
Pomegranate seeds	¾ cup
Raisins, not packed	65; ¼ cup
Raspberries	1 ½ cups
Strawberries	18 large; 2 cups sliced
Tangerines	2 medium
Watermelon	2 ¼ cups diced

DAIRY
100 Calorie Portions

Milk, fat-free	1 cup + 4 tablespoons (20 tablespoons)
Milk, 1%	1 cup (16 tablespoons)
Milk, 2%	13 tablespoons
Milk, whole	11 tablespoons
Cheese, reduced-fat (1% milk fat)	1.4 ounces
Cheese, reduced-fat (2% milk fat)	1.1 ounce
Cheese, semi-soft (feta, goat, mozzarella)	1.3 ounces
Cheese, hard (Cheddar, Monterey Jack, Gouda, Swiss, Parmesan)	0.9 ounce
Yogurt, Greek, nonfat, plain	12 tablespoons (18g protein)
Yogurt, Greek, 2%, plain	9 tablespoons (13g protein)
Yogurt, traditional, low fat, plain	10 tablespoons
Yogurt, traditional, nonfat, plain	12 tablespoons
Yogurt, traditional, whole, plain	10 tablespoons

TIP: Greek yogurt not only provides almost twice the protein as traditional, non-Greek yogurt, but it also has less carbohydrates (lactose).

12 TBSP NONFAT YOGURT = 100 CAL.

.9 OZ. HARD CHEESE = 100 CALORIES

1 CUP 1% MILK = 100 CALORIES

UP TO ½ CUP HERBS = 0 – 5 CALORIES

1 TBSP SALSA = 10 CALORIES

1 TBSP VINEGAR = 0 CALORIES

SAUCES & CONDIMENTS

Lemon juice	5 calories per tablespoon
Herbs and spices	0–5 calories (up to ½ cup)
Ketchup	20 calories per tablespoon
Mustards	5 calories per teaspoon
Salsa	10 calories per tablespoon
Soy sauce	10 calories per tablespoon
Taco sauce	5 calories per tablespoon
Tomato sauce	15 calories per ¼ cup
Vinegars	0 calories per tablespoon

FATS
100 Calorie Portions

Butter	1 tablespoon
Cream, half-and-half	5 tablespoons
Cream, table (light)	3 ½ tablespoons
Cream, whipping	2 tablespoons
Oil (canola, olive, peanut, or vegetable)	2 ½ teaspoons
Margarine (light or reduced fat)	2 tablespoons
Mayonnaise	1 tablespoon
Mayonnaise, light	2 tablespoons
Salad dressings, regular (will vary with type)	1 ½ tablespoons
Shortening	Scant tablespoon
Sour Cream	4 tablespoons
Sour Cream, light	5 tablespoons

2 ½ TEASPOONS OIL = 100 CALORIES

2 TBSP. WHIPPING CREAM = 100 CAL.

1 TBSP. BUTTER = 100 CALORIES

31 PISTACHIOS = 100 CALORIES

1 OUNCE APPLE CHIPS = 100 CALORIES

⅓ CUP PUMPKIN SEEDS = 100 CALORIES

5 DRIED APRICOTS = 100 CALORIES

25 GRAPE TOMATOES = 100 CALORIES

SMART SNACKING
in 100 Calorie Portions

Surveys show that 90% of adults snack every day, often several times per day in fact. When you are snacking smart, it is actually a very good habit to have. It keeps your body's fire burning while also keeping your blood sugar levels even. The problem is that most Americans snack on processed carbohydrates like chips and candy that are very low in fiber and nutrients.

A better way to snack is to choose those with a combination of food groups or a combination of macronutrients (such as carbohydrates, protein, and fat). An ideal snack would pack both protein and fiber, which will fill you up and boost your energy. As for the portion, a smart snack should fall between 100 and 200 calories for most people. This is just enough to satisfy the between meal hunger pangs without going over your daily caloric needs.

While we have also included an entire section of snack recipes, pages 259–279, here are some quick and easy options that combine necessary protein, carbohydrates, and fat. Not surprisingly, they all contain 100 calories (or even a bit less)!

BALANCED SNACKS

⅓ cup plain nonfat Greek yogurt + 1 tsp honey + 2 Tbsp. blueberries + 1 Tbsp. Homemade Granola (page 272)

5 baked whole-grain cracker thins + 2 Tbsp. Homemade Hummus (page 207)

2 ounces deli turkey + 4 whole-grain cracker thins + 1 tsp Dijon mustard

2 large stalks of celery + 2½ tsp peanut butter

½ ounce baked tortilla chips + ⅓ cup Restaurant-Style Salsa (page 209)

1 rye flatbread crisp + 1 light soft spread cheese wedge + 1 cucumber slice

½ whole-wheat sandwich thin + 2 Tbsp. chunk light tuna + 1 tsp light mayo

½ cup 1% cottage cheese + ½ cup sliced strawberries + minced fresh mint

2 ounces sardines (water-packed) + 1 flatbread crisp

1 cup raw veggies (baby carrots, broccoli florets, sugar snap peas, etc) + 2 Tbsp. Spinach and Artichoke Dip (page 211)

½ English muffin + 1 Tbsp. Apple Butter (page 257)

2 ounces fresh apple slices + 2½ tsp almond butter

1 ounce slice 2% Cheddar cheese + 8 grape tomatoes

1 (6-inch) corn tortilla + 2 Tbsp. bean dip + 1 Tbsp. 2% shredded Cheddar cheese

1 hard-boiled egg + 2 baked snack crackers + minced fresh dill

2 ounces sliced deli ham + 1 Tbsp. light cream cheese + 3 green olives

2 ginger snaps + ½ Tbsp. lemon curd

1½ ounces deli roast beef + ½ Tbsp. horseradish mayonnaise + lettuce cup

¼ cup mashed avocado + ¼ tsp hot sauce + squeeze lime juice + celery sticks

GRAB AND GO SNACKS

1 medium apple

5 dried apricots

1 ounce baked apple chips (about ½ cup)

1 medium banana

13 dry-roasted almonds

40 baked Goldfish crackers

25 grape tomatoes

6 ounces nonfat plain Greek yogurt

16 Hershey's milk chocolate mini kisses

⅓ cup sunflower or pumpkin seeds (with shell on)

17 dry roasted peanuts

31 pistachios

10 "Hot Cocoa" Pretzels, page 265

6–8 braided pretzel sticks

3 cups air-popped Stovetop Popcorn, page 273

2 cups oil-popped Stovetop Popcorn, page 273

2 mini boxes raisins (about 3½ tablespoons)

1 piece string cheese or 2 pieces light string cheese

2 tangerines

2 ounces sliced deli turkey

TIPPING THE SCALES
10 Secrets to Success

1 Make the Meal

Cooking at home not only allows you to control which ingredients you use and in which amounts, it also requires you to literally work for your food, burning calories in the kitchen before you sit down to eat.

2 Bulk Up on Veggies

Most vegetables, especially green vegetables, are so low in calories and high in fiber and nutrients that you should consider them "free" foods. Add them to any dish to create larger, more satisfying portions that keep you feeling full for a longer period of time. To increase the portion size of these recipes, we frequently increased the veggies and reduced the protein with rave results. Bob's Chicken Pot Pie (page 79) is an excellent example.

3 Control the Carbs

Carbohydrates should be a side dish, not the main attraction. When it comes to carbs, especially pasta, we have a tendency to fill the entire surface of our plate before topping with a protein. For a balanced meal, your protein serving should be about the size of a deck of cards, your carbohydrate serving should be slightly smaller, and your vegetable serving should fill the rest of the plate.

4 Cut the Cable

Limiting distractions while eating, such as watching television, will not only allow you to actually enjoy your food, but stop mindless overeating. Just as it's easy to lose track of time while watching television, it's easy to lose track of just how much we are eating.

5 The Perfect Plate

We have a tendency to overload our plates with food and then feel obligated to finish it all, whether we are actually still hungry or not. Choose smaller plates or bowls that allow you to fill them up, but with your perfect satisfying portion.

6 Wet Your Appetite

We should all be drinking eight glasses of water a day, and the best time to drink one is directly before eating a meal. It's also important to drink water throughout meals, as our bodies often confuse thirst for additional hunger while we are eating. Eating soup or broth, especially as a snack prior to lunch or dinner, is another great trick to feeling full.

7 Eat Your Calories

Calories from beverages are almost always empty calories that are best eliminated. Cutting sugary soda and simple fruit juices can greatly reduce your caloric intake alone. Try eating whole fruits or blending fruit and veggies into a hearty smoothie instead!

8 Don't Dress Down

We all like to be comfortable, but wearing loose-fitting clothes at the dinner table can actually affect the amount that you eat! We've all seen the stereotypes in movies that unbutton the top button of their pants after a big meal. If your stomach is expanding to the point that you no longer feel comfortable in your clothes, you probably have had enough.

9 Expect the Snack Attack

It's fine to snack, but be prepared! We tend to make poor snacking choices when we are desperately hungry, so stay ahead of those energy dips by planning out your snacks as part of your daily meal plan. Now that you have a list of great quick snacks and a handful of snack recipes, you'll be prepared!

10 Dial Down Dessert

Dessert is really just a sugary snack that we eat directly after eating an entire meal. Luckily, the protein and fiber from your main meal will slow the digestion of the sugar, and curb the sugar crash that can cause excess hunger, to a point. Large desserts will definitely work against you, so stick to smaller servings of 100–200 calories, and enjoy dessert as what it should be, a treat.

HOW TO BURN 100 CALORIES
Everyday Exercies

When it comes to achieving and maintaining a healthy weight, the calories that go into your body are only half of the equation. Exercise is an essential part of a healthy lifestyle. In fact, studies have shown that.

Now that you have the tools to create your own personal meal plan and a 100 calorie portioning system, here is a list of everyday activities and exercises you can do to burn 100 calories. The times below are based on a 150-pound person performing these activities at a moderate speed.

HOW TO BURN 100 CALORIES

Walking	20 minutes
Jogging	13 minutes
Tennis (doubles)	20 minutes
Stair climbing	11 minutes
Swimming	15 minutes
Yoga	35 minutes
Jumping rope	10 minutes
Jumping jacks	10 minutes
Exercise bike	20 minutes
Elliptical	10 minutes
Supermarket shopping	30 minutes
Cooking	35 minutes
Housework	30 minutes
Vacuuming	20 minutes
Yard work	15 minutes
Car washing	20 minutes
Skiing	9 minutes
Sit-Ups	20 minutes
Golf	15 minutes
Dancing	20 minutes

YOGA: 35 minutes

GOLF: 20 minutes

ELLIPTICAL: 10 minutes

SIT-UPS: 12 minutes

337

WALKING: 20 minutes

JOGGING: 13 minutes

TENNIS: 20 minutes

STAIR CLIMBING: 11 minutes

DANCING: 35 minutes

JUMPING ROPE: 10 minutes

JUMPING JACKS: 10 minutes

EXERCISE BIKE: 20 minutes

SKIING: 9 minutes

SHOPPING: 30 minutes

COOKING: 35 minutes

HOUSEWORK 30 minutes

YARD WORK: 15 minutes

VACUUMING: 20 minutes

CAR WASHING: 20 minutes

SWIMMING: 15 minutes

INDEX

INDEX

INDEX

INDEX

ABOUT THE AUTHORS

Best known for his Golden Globe-nominated role as Warren "Potsie" Weber on the series *Happy Days*, **Anson Williams** is also an award-winning television director, writer, producer, and entrepreneur. He won the Humanitas Award for his writing, has been honored by the United States Patent and Trademark Office, and served on the Board of the USO. Together, with business partner JoAnna Connell, he founded StarMaker Products, a worldwide consumer product company.

Well-known TV personality, **Bob Warden** has proven taste and sizzling passion for great food. In thirty years as a television cooking personality, he has authored over a dozen bestselling cookbooks, including comfort food favorite *Great Food Fast*, the all-time, bestselling pressure cooker book. Bob has also helped develop over 300 kitchen tools, cookware, and appliances for various housewares manufacturers.

Nutritionist and product development expert **Mona Dolgov** lives her lifelong mission of creating healthier food products and inventing simple culinary tricks to create yummy recipes. A graduate of Cornell University in Nutritional Sciences, she has worked in the housewares and food industry for the last 25 years, inventing patented products and launching marketing programs for healthier living. She has authored over 20 cookbooks for housewares manufacturers and grocery retailers, focused on simplicity and using nutritious ingredients.